Human Brain

—and—

Human Learning

Human Brain

Brain

—and—

Human

Learning

Leslie A. Hart

Illustrated by Jacques Ducas

Longman

New York & London

Human Brain and Human Learning

Longman Inc., 1560 Broadway, New York, N.Y. 10036
Associated companies, branches, and representatives
throughout the world.

Developmental Editor: Lane Akers
Editorial and Design Supervisor: Joan Matthews
Production Supervisor: Ferne Y. Kawahara
Manufacturing Supervisor: Marion Hess

Library of Congress Cataloging in Publication Data

Hart, Leslie A.
  Human brain and human learning.

  Includes index.
  1. Learning—Physiological aspects. 2. Brain.
I. Title.
QP408.H37   1983   152.1′5   82-12650
ISBN 0-582-28380-9
ISBN 0-582-28379-5 (pbk.)

Manufactured in the United States of America

*To those many educators, at all levels,
who out of deep concern for children,
students, communities, and nation,
have dared to work and fight for change.*

Contents

Foreword

The future of teaching and learning lies in the study of the brain.

Only in this strange world of nerve cell and synapse will we someday untangle the mysteries of how people learn.

Human Brain and Human Learning makes a major contribution to our grasp of how the brain works. It may well become the basis for important educational reform, and for reexamining all we do in schools, including the organization of curricula and the management of learning. We *must* understand brain functions and operations before schools can be significantly improved.

Leslie Hart's major thesis is that today's educational practice is based on assumptions that relate little to desired student outcomes. He correctly claims that there has been no coherent theory of *human* learning—most of our practices have been based on research conducted with small animals.

In his earlier book, *How the Brain Works*, Hart presented what is known as Proster Theory, dramatically different from conventional theory in that it centers on the brain and explains the learning process in terms of the brain's nature, history, and modes of operation. In the present book, Hart carries his refreshingly new theory forward, relating it specifically to education and particularly to schools. He has also presented Proster Theory in style and language that invites the reader with even minimal technical or scientific background to read with enjoyment and full comprehension. (Those who prefer a moderately technical but still highly lucid substantiation will find it, additionally, in the earlier work.)

Most important to me is that *Human Brain and Human Learning* begins to build a bridge between theory and practice, and offers a broad guide for translating brain research into design and decisions in our schools. On that count it should arouse intense interest among educators, parents, school board members, and educational researchers. With new knowledge of how the brain functions, of what it demands, and of how learning takes place, we can at last create school environments that will far more successfully help all learners to achieve. Teaching can become congruent to learning.

There emerges from this book a whole new way to look at learning, and so a base for a new system of teaching, with the teacher becoming a more dramatic and important "creator" of learning than one who merely instructs. The learning stems from the student's own brain and activities rather than resulting from "being taught." In "brain-compatible" learning—a strikingly new concept—there is a shift "from reliance on raw authority to a far more sophisticated approach of recognizing differences and responding to them in a way that sharply reduces conflict while achieving better outcomes."

While experienced educators will find in the book welcome support for intuitions they have long held (that in fact go far back in the history of education), the reader must be prepared for what can be at first a distressing departure from old and conventional ideas. One must remember that coming at schooling or training from a brain viewpoint is truly new. But Hart draws from a huge amount of present scientific knowledge in a range of relevant disciplines. He builds on the findings and insights of leading brain investigators, including MacLean, whose triune brain concept has vast implications for schools. In addition he uses an intimate familiarity with the realities of schools to relate this large body of new knowledge to one's common experiences and observations. The theory he offers and the suggestions he puts forward rest on a solid foundation.

Read and studied carefully, *Human Brain and Human Learning* can have a tremendous impact on education. It should be read by everyone interested in improving our schools, not in small increments, but in a quantum leap. Hart may have developed what all of us have been looking for: the key to greatly improved learning, the basis and methods of reestablishing public confidence in the schools, and designing human environments for human learners.

What is vital now is that Hart's concepts be tried and explored. This is not a "how to" book, but the brain-compatible approaches he suggests seem thoroughly practical guides to action. Reality testing of the possibilities he presents is urgently needed. If, as appears likely, learning can be dramatically improved when educational practice centers on understanding how the brain works, the sooner that is done the more students will be effectively educated in the schools and other institutions of our nation.

One thing is certain now: this is an enormously stimulating, penetrating, significant book, demanding attention. It may well prove a landmark in educational thought. And while deeply critical, it also offers more hope for major solutions of our problems than most we have seen for a long time.

Dr. M. Donald Thomas
Superintendent of Schools
Salt Lake City, Utah

Preface

The core problem faced by educators today is how to bring about learning. This book is addressed to that question, and is intended for teachers and instructors, administrators, planners, legislators, curriculum developers, and all concerned with effective and humane education and training, including parents. Since failure to learn brings additional problems in discipline, crime, mental health, and social alienation, readers active in these areas may find this discussion of some value.

Because our schools present the most acute needs, and our ideas about schooling color all educational effort, schools are given much attention here. But the brain-based principles of learning put forward, contrasting sharply with conventional views, can be applied at any level and in any learning situation.

We have many brilliant neuroscientists and neuropsychologists at work, and their contributions in recent years have been magnificent. We have, too, many thoughtful, creative educators with intimate knowledge of schools and training—but almost no modern knowledge of the brain. My hope is that this book will help bridge the lamentable gap that exists between these two fields, and bring to educators some sense of the fresh, exciting new vistas that open up when one takes a brain approach to the problem of human learning.

I must stress, however, that this is not an effort to contribute in any way to the neurosciences, except perhaps as it may increase the awareness and interest of some brain researchers with respect to the practical learning problems typical of schools. Also, this book takes a deliberately simplified, holistic approach to the brain, seeking to add to educators' understanding of what the brain is *for*, and of its overall architecture and broad modes of operation. To do so, it attempts to synthesize from many disciplines in addition to the neurosciences. There is no effort made to deal with learning on a molecular, cellular, or synaptic level. This is an area of brain knowledge in which mystery still prevails; and it seems to me most unlikely in any case that breakthroughs on this micro level would importantly affect dealing with the brain on a macro level, as must those who labor to bring about student learning.

Our schools, I believe, are not ineffective because they do not know what happens at synapses or the chemistry of neurotransmitters, but rather because they have yet to address the brain as the organ for learning, and to fit instruction and environment to the "shape" of the brain as it is now increasingly well understood. We know that as the consequence of long evolution, the brain has modes of operation that are natural, effortless, effective in utilizing the tremendous power of this amazing instrument. Coerced to operate in other ways, it functions as a rule reluctantly, slowly, and with abundant error.

As we realize this, we can focus on the problem of matching settings and instruction to the nature of the brain, rather than trying to force it to comply with arrangements established with virtually no concern for what this organ is or how it works best. The term *brain-compatible* seems appropriate for education designed to fit the brain. It seems reasonable to assume that moving from brain-antagonistic settings to brain-compatible schooling and training could produce strikingly better outcomes.

We know amply enough about the human brain as the organ for learning, I submit, to begin making this transition, now. Working out the best detailed methods and related needs will of course require the contributions of a great many creative and knowledgeable people over years to come.

Since my work has heavily involved synthesis, I have drawn from many sources in many fields—too many to attempt to list. I happily express my indebtedness and gratitude, and my appreciation of the many friends who have, often very generously, helped and encouraged.

For some of the quotations that precede chapters I have deliberately reached back many years, to emphasize that there was much "pre-brain" intuition that thrust in the right direction. Now there is scientific support.

I thank the publishers and copyright owners and authors for the many brief quotations that I have used.

LAH
New Rochelle,
New York

Human
Brain
and
Human
Learning

The symptom that a particular branch of science or art is ripe for a change is a feeling of frustration and malaise, not necessarily caused by any acute crisis in that specific branch...but by a feeling that the whole tradition is somehow out of step, cut off from the mainstream, that the traditional criteria have become meaningless, divorced from living reality, isolated from the integral whole.

—ARTHUR KOESTLER[1]

Frustrations: The Need for a New Foundation

"I taught them, but they didn't learn."

That is the classic remark, usually sadly uttered, of the teacher who tried hard but didn't succeed in producing the intended learning by students.

Rare is the classroom teacher who hasn't often felt frustration of this kind, even after presenting an especially well-prepared lesson or unit, with skill and enthusiasm.

"At times," remarks a teacher, "it seems as if an invisible glass wall drops down between me and the students, and nothing gets through."

Teachers may well take such failures personally, wondering what they may be doing wrong. Or, since repeated failure can be hard to bear, they may look for others to blame:

"The parents didn't prepare these children for school. They don't encourage and discipline them."

"You can't really expect youngsters from a neighborhood like this to be interested in learning."

"The teachers in the lower grades passed these students along, without basic skills. What can I do with them now?"

"We don't get the facilities and supplies and support we need."

"Schools reflect society. What can you expect? We have to change society first."

Or teachers may join others in deploring television, electronic games, the breakdown of the family, the weakened influence of religion, too little respect for authority, lower moral standards, government interference and red tape, stingy taxpayers, racial and social tensions, and much more. But we must recognize, when we take a hard look at education, that essentially these "explanations" or excuses serve merely as distractions from the heart of the matter. The schools' first job is within the schools. Under our system, students are compelled to attend. *The schools must receive them as they are, not as one might wish them to be.* No one sensibly minimizes the problems: they are varied, difficult, and often profound. But they are the *schools'* problems; and the schools' ability to cope with them has become more and more the basis of evaluation of how well the schools do, how much public money they should be allotted, and even at extreme whether we should continue to have schools of the kind we have long had.

The resources available to schools, even when restricted, can hardly be called inconsiderable. Typical smaller cities may pay out 10, 25, 50 or more millions of dollars a year—the great bulk of it for salaries and related expenses. About half of local taxes go for education. For many families and individuals, total education expenses are crushing.

Fairly or unfairly, the pressures grow on schools, and most on teachers, to *produce learning results.*

The problem is by no means limited to schools. Great amounts of instruction and training are carried on by colleges, trade schools, profit and nonprofit businesses and organizations, and by various governmental agencies. While they often have the advantage of working with more selected students, their outcomes may leave much to be desired.

Recently, the armed forces have been having extreme difficulties in training recruits, many of whom must be dropped because present training methods fail to work adequately. The armed forces, of course, can blame the schools, but that hardly relieves the problem.

Only adoption of methods and approaches that do, in fact, sharply increase the acquisition of learning will help. The word "sharply" deserves emphasis—a ten percent gain, or even double that, will make scarcely a dent in the need. The programs, sometimes much publicized, that produce what are called "significant" gains must be looked at with a cold eye. The significance is often only in the statistical sense: that a difference probably not due to chance was detected, and the actual improvement turns out to be trivial.

In 1972 The Rand Corporation issued the report on a major study done for the President's Commission on School Finance. Known as the "Averch Report" for its chief investigator, it found, in summary:

> We are saying that research has found nothing that consistently and unambiguously makes a difference in student outcomes.

Further, it observed:

> There is a suggestion that substantial improvement in educational outcomes can be obtained only through a vastly different form of education.[2]

The study recognizes the difficulties it met, including the major question of how to measure learning achieved. Little has appeared since to shake its broad findings.

But I will suggest—as the purpose of this book—that today we do have strong reason to believe that a *"vastly different" approach is now available and practical*, and that it holds the promise of very sharp gains and high reliability, such as we have hardly dared to hope for.

For the first time in human history, I submit, we can give *learning* a firm, clear definition that can be useful in instruction to meet today's needs.

Through many centuries, learning presented less of a riddle because objectives were simpler. Instruction tended to center around a very few books, which represented accepted and lasting authority. Before printing came into common use, books had to be copied by hand, one by one, and were rare and costly. In most cases, the teacher was the one who had the book, or had access to a copy, or more usually had learned the book word for word, and much commentary and interpretation along with it. The teacher's function stood crystal clear: to pass along to students this knowledge of the book. If the student could recite the text, or repeat the official, approved commentary appropriately, learning was judged to have occurred.

But printing made books widely available, and where there had been a few "great" books, thousands appeared. At the same time the duration of authority began to shrink. Knowledge has come to be more and more current, enormously more complex, until our problem has become not obtaining information but coping with the flood that pours out from presses and from the newer media as well. We know this change has occurred—it is close to a cliché to state it—but we have lagged badly in shaping new concepts of what learning is, in modern terms.

The great bulk of this knowledge explosion, and the accompanying decay of "official" authority, has come about in our own century, and indeed most of it in the last half-century. Our class-and-grade school system, however, goes back to Horace Mann's efforts in the 1840s, a time that in our eyes seems remote, bucolic, stable, and simple. *Obviously the system we attempt to use was never designed to deal with present needs.* It is a relic of the distant past.

Teachers, then, are given an unreasonable and all but impossible task: to produce "learning," even though it can't be defined, and to bring it about under the often maddeningly absurd restrictions of working in a graded classroom setting inherited from a very different, bygone age.

As I have suggested earlier,[3] teachers entering on their jobs regularly are pushed into a role that makes no sense when analyzed. It consists of far too many tasks, covering a wide range of difficulty and levels. Seldom has the teacher been adequately prepared for the actual conditions that must be met; and it is hardly a secret that those who have been charged with their preparation may be quite unable to demonstrate that *they* could bring about good learning under the conditions obtaining, or even that anyone working in regular classrooms has been able to, with convincing reliability.

One noted investigator of classroom-learning results, Stephens, concluded after years of research that the same results ensued regardless of the methods used[4]—which agrees with Averch Report findings, and others. Stephens tried to dignify the failure to find differences with a "theory" of "spontaneous schooling"—a fine example, I would suggest, of the common practice of trying to cover large gaps in knowledge and understanding with fancy words. Yet in urging variety rather than a hunt for a single method, Stephens may well have been on the right track—as we shall see.

Tens of millions of dollars have been expended on in-classroom research, with minimal results of practical value. Somehow, the researchers often seem to have missed the key factor operating: that the conventional classroom itself, as a setting, forces teachers into quite similar behaviors as a rule, whether male or female, newcomers or experienced, or teaching lower or higher grades.[5]

John I. Goodlad, Dean of the Graduate School of Education of the University of California at Los Angeles, pinpointed the difficulty this way:

> One of the problems with conventional research on educational effects is that the school settings measured are too much alike ever to produce significant differences. Consequently, the best we are able to get under any circumstances is an increase of 6 percent or 7 percent in achievement scores.... People wrongly conclude, then, that trying to improve educational settings is a waste of time. Nothing could be further from the truth. What we need is actual implementation of far more fundamental ideas.[6]

In short, "the classroom" embraces so many assumptions and relationships—frequently totally unexamined—that it swamps out differences in teaching philosophies, approaches, methods, personality, and attitudes. At the same time it exerts constant pressure on teachers to conform to expected rituals. The beginning teacher is hardly in a position to introduce major breaks with tradition, and the experienced teacher may well become reluctant to depart from well-established ways of handling classes. Some who have tried to break away may have become discouraged by outright opposition, or the wearing-down effect of lack of support from principal, parents, board of education, and others.

"Where do you get," more than one teacher has said to me in substance, "banging your head against a stone wall, trying to change the system? I shut my door and do what I can in my own room."

When teachers seek their individual survival, the school crumbles into a collection of little-related units. Adults build their private fortresses; the need for the children to progress year by year gets short shrift. Under the classroom system, teachers come to be almost exclusively concerned with their own rooms and programs, and may see their job as one of "covering" the syllabus during the school year. If some learning occurs, well and good. If failures and shortcomings abound, the teacher may simply say, "I did what I was supposed to do. I taught, but they didn't learn." The teacher who moves too far from the syllabus, or who commits the crime of not covering the year's work, may be vulnerable to the point of losing employment.

And what of the teacher who lets some able learners run ahead? The wrath of the teacher in the next grade can be expected: "Why did you teach them what is in *my* syllabus?"

It seems largely futile to talk of new, far better learning approaches, if we continue to think in terms of this antique class-and-grade system which expresses the false premise that children are alike, and as students can be processed at the same rate with uniform success. Here again teachers are given an impossible assignment.

The teacher who shuts the door runs into the further difficulty of "lack of feedback," to use that engineering term rather loosely. In most human activities, we end up with some sort of score to tell us how well we did. The profit businessman can see what profit was made, whether sales went up or down, what share of market was obtained, and so forth. The salesman can look at commissions received, the personnel officer at jobs filled, at what cost, and with what success. We enjoy sports and games in part because the score can be seen more sharply than in more complex activities. After golf or bowling, or baseball or tennis, or even fishing or birdwatching, we can look at a quite objective outcome. But in teaching, the score in terms of genuine learning can be hard to obtain. Passing examinations tells us little, because the "right answers" given may be promptly forgotten, and tests can be highly fallible instruments. In any case, the teacher had to begin with the learners put into the class—each one at a different stage of achievement in many learning areas, and those stages largely unknown.

Again the teacher is put in an unfair and intolerable position—on one hand being held accountable for learning achievement, but on the other lacking the means of determining the score.

Even within their own classrooms, it can be difficult for teachers to ascertain what works and what doesn't to produce learning. Teachers being as human as anybody tend to convince themselves that they are doing an effective job. One well-qualified observer, Esther P. Rothman, after long experience states bluntly, "Teaching has become the art of self-deception."[7] In the study *Looking in Classrooms*,[8] the authors remark that teachers are not trained to monitor their own behavior, rarely receive systematic or useful feedback from supervisors, and in general are so busy that they don't have much chance to even observe what is happening. Commonly, they confuse good intentions with actualities. It is hard to find a teacher today who does not profess to give much time and effort to "individualization." When Dean Goodlad and associates visited many classrooms to see how much could be observed in practice, they found almost none.[9]

Many more examples could be offered. Essentially, it is absurd to expect people to give concentrated attention to doing a job, and also to accurately observe themselves doing it. Professional football players spend days after a game viewing and reviewing the movies taken during it, to see what actually happened. Teachers in classrooms, making literally thousands of decisions a day, have neither the equipment nor time.

The graded classroom dominates, and teachers' task of bringing about learning may well be judged hopeless to begin with. There is more than a little evidence (rarely looked at) that at least a considerable share of conventional teaching has *negative* results: it inhibits, prevents, distorts, or holds back learning.

No one has wanted to face this grim possibility, because there did not seem to be available alternatives. The great cry for change that began in the sixties, backed by millions and sometimes even billions of dollars, brought only a pittance of results. In general, the money went down the drain.[10]

The problems of achieving successful change were many, but the fundamental one was that *learning and the process of learning were deep mysteries, far from understood.*

We must face the realities. Despite the myth of local control, schools across the country differ little. Almost all children are in conventional classrooms; only a relative handful are in truly "alternative" programs, and usually even these are limited to a few years, and must comply with larger-system requirements.

The most potent of these seldom get said aloud or published.

Obviously a prime function of schools is custodial, to keep children and youngsters off the street, hopefully out of mischief and worse, and to take them off the hands of parents a good many hours a week. Another is to socialize the children, which translates, I think, as teaching them by coercion to bother adults as little as possible. In older times, writers on education felt less compunction about stating bluntly that children were sent to school to get used to sitting still and doing exactly as they are told, as I believe Emmanuel Kant put it. (If we really wanted to socialize students, about the last way to go at it would be to isolate them in closed classrooms.) Nor can we ignore the bureaucracies' behaviors to get as much funding as possible and to create and maintain jobs, benefits, and emoluments. Educators have no more difficulty than people in other pursuits in seeing their own interests as ranking high. The role of secondary and postsecondary schools of all kinds in delaying the time young people begin to compete for outside jobs has become increasingly evident as students have been persuaded, and their parents as well, that they need more and more credentials. Here educators, unions, and people with jobs that youngsters could do have common interests and tacit understandings.

A good many schools, however, do set down "objectives" in pious, vague language. These are usually and plainly window dressing that has minimum connection with realities.

Administrators and boards have learned that any specific declaration may well produce furious public interest, pro or con, which may be uncomfortable. Fuzzy objectives have their advantages.

These matters bring us into the realm of educational politics and philosophy, fascinating to discuss and examine, but not the province of this book. My effort is to concentrate on *learning*, all too little considered. Perhaps it is possible, and helpful to the reader in disclosing my basic views, to set down some broad objectives that may be largely acceptable to a great majority of citizens and parents who have done some thinking about education.

1.   Schools are necessary, in some organized form, and their success in producing useful learning, and helping young people find their responsible and productive place in society, is critically important to our democracy and well-being as a nation. We have no reason, however, to hold the prevailing form of schooling as sacred, unchangeable, or not potentially subject to great improvement.

2.   Schools cannot effectively operate as an enclave separate and remote from society, but must be integrated with society and especially their communities as they more or less currently and realistically exist. Schools must recognize that learning does not stem only from schooling, nor does in-school learning come only from the official, stated curriculum. The whole school environment has profound effects on students, the more so since the school represents state power, authority, and adult

wisdom. What the school *does*, or fails to do, must be seen as more significant than any declarations. Since almost all young people will be subject to at least a dozen years of schooling, its influence must be considered profound. It should not harm, but importantly benefit, both students and society.

3. The standards that prevail in office, retail store, factory, laboratory or other workplace, or public place should also apply to the school. We expect certain levels of order, courtesy, respect for individuals, management, communications, integrity, and accountability. These should quite naturally apply in schools, as segments of society. There should be neither chaos nor disorder, nor rudeness, disrespect, nor regimentation. Schools should help establish normal values and behaviors by example. It is not a function of schools today to punish the young for being youthful, to "break their spirit," or to make education onerous and distasteful. As we want our homes and workplaces to be reasonably pleasant, positive, and often enjoyable, so we want schools to be on balance joyful, nurturing, and rewarding. Students should leave school with some love for learning, and at least a clear sense of the practical uses and value of learning in dealing with the real world.

4. The day has long passed when a case could be made for preparing students for factory employment by training in punctuality, nominal politeness to superiors, and general docility. We are more aware and acceptant of individual differences and capability. The number of occupations in present society has been estimated as high as 90,000; new ones are added daily. In a world changing at dizzying speed, it is futile to speak of "preparing" students in the old sense; preparation must be in broad terms, with emphasis on flexibility and continuity in learning. (Some definitions of learning will be offered later.) Schools in actual practice, not by lip service, must permit and foster development of *individual* student abilities and talents, rather than inhibit it as inconvenient to the bureaucracy.

5. A basic core of learning can be established, but needs to be realistically related to present-day needs and not simply tradition. Certainly, in my view, it should include ability to read and write for practical purposes with ease; a grasp of mathematics and modest skill in computation; at least some familiarity with the meaning and methods of science; some introduction to the arts, literature, history, and the geography of the world; practical skill in communications; some sense of how families work, child rearing, and marriage; the law, the fundamentals of business, employment, and taxes; and the responsibilities and procedures of citizenship. Others may have different lists, but working agreement seems attainable. Much could be added; but I doubt many today would accept just reading, writing, and arithmetic as adequate.

I hope the reader can accept all or most of these five affirmations. In any case, the discussion of schools, education, and learning that follows reflects these views, where questions of philosophy or politics interface with our main topic.

Today we can tackle the age-old problem of how to bring about effective student learning with grounds for optimism and with some fresh confidence.

We have available new understandings, firmly based on new, scientifically sound knowledge of the human brain. We can stop going around in unproductive circles, and move to approaches never before possible in all the history of education.

The potentials are dazzling. But we cannot expect to fit this new knowledge and its applications into the antique class-and-grade structure that Horace Mann brought back from Prussia almost 140 years ago.

Rather, we must introduce a new concept: *brain-compatible* schools, *brain-compatible* instruction.

NOTES

1. *The Sleepwalkers* (New York: Macmillan, 1959), p. 520.
2. Harvey A. Averch and others, *How Effective Is Schooling?* (Santa Monica, Calif.: The Rand Corporation, 1972), pp. x, xiii. A similar finding appears in Christopher Jencks and others, *Inequality* (New York: Basic Books, 1972): "We can see no evidence that either school administrators or educational experts know how to raise test scores, even when they have vast resources at their disposal" (p. 95).
3. See Leslie A. Hart, *The Classroom Disaster* (New York: Teachers College Press, Columbia University, 1969), particularly Chapter 5. The book remains one of the few detailed analyses of the classroom and its effects as a form of organization.
4. See J. M. Stephens, *The Process of Schooling* (New York: Holt, Rinehart and Winston, 1967).
5. See Raymond S. Adams and Bruce J. Biddle, *Realities of Teaching* (New York: Holt, Rinehart and Winston, 1970). Teachers were videotaped in action to permit repeated study of what they did, analysis, and comparative patterns.
6. Personal letter, January 7, 1974. Used by permission.
7. Esther P. Rothman, *Troubled Teachers* (New York: David McKay, 1977), p. 1.
8. Thomas L. Good and Jere E. Brophy, *Looking in Classrooms* (New York: Harper and Row, 1973). See particularly Chapter 2, "Teacher Awareness."
9. John I. Goodlad, M. Frances Klein, and associates, *Looking Behind the Classroom Door* (Belmont, Calif.: Wadsworth Publishing, 1974). See p. 82. This brief book provides a calm but chilling documentation of the real conditions obtaining in classroom as contrasted with pious talk. Observations were based on visits to over 200 classrooms.
10. Recent change seems to have been more in the other direction, influenced by the budget squeezes and the "back to basics" cry. School boards and legislatures appear to have become more conservative. But schools seldom change substantially, however much there may be talk of change, in whatever direction, so long as they can manage to operate in old ways.

Over the years we have been presented with all kinds of learning principles and theories which were considered basic for understanding human social behavior. In fact, since almost every school teacher has been required in his training to take a course in learning, he was exposed to ideas based almost exclusively on the learning of individual rats. Nobody has ever demonstrated in anything resembling a compelling manner that these principles and theories were or are relevant to learning in the social matrix of a classroom.

—SEYMOUR B. SARASON[1]

Wrong Paths: Mann's Factory to Behaviorism

The human body contains many organs, each of which has one or more functions.

The brain is the organ for learning.

At the present state of science, this is not a matter in question. For all practical purposes, learning occurs only in the brain, and is stored in the brain.

The brain is also the "executive" organ. It runs the organism. The decisions that underlie purposeful activities are made in the brain; and equally, in health, *emotions* are controlled by this organ.

This being the case, and hardly news, we must at once wonder why study of the brain is not the core of teacher education. In hard fact, teachers and administrators usually emerge from their preparation with little or no knowledge of the brain; and as reference to college catalogs will show, it may be difficult to find courses offered that provide a suitable introduction. (I venture to predict that this will rapidly change in the next five or ten years.)

The reasons for this anomaly seem worth examination. If we are to advance to far more resultful, brain-based approaches, we need not only to adopt new theory and practices, but—much more difficult—to abandon old concepts, beliefs, traditions, assumptions, procedures, and authority that obscure or conflict. We have almost all been brought up with many of these old notions, in private life or in training, or both, and they will often prove hard to let go. They can be discarded at least a little more readily if we have a sound understanding of where they came from.

In my experience, the great majority of people engaged in education or training would in a general way love to see students achieve better learning. Having somebody learn as a consequence of one's instructional effort brings great satisfaction. But we are burdened by our own past. We come to formal education with a store of conceptions on "the way things are" that we began to gather at around age three. As a boy, I knew that our winter heat came from a coal furnace, and in the kitchen our food was preserved by blocks of ice in a wooden icebox. It never entered my head that before many years coal would yield to oil or gas, and that the burly iceman with his leather back-apron and tongs would vanish as white, electrical Frigidaires took over. I feel sure that if I had thought about these matters, I would have assumed that coal and ice had always been the accepted sources of heat and cold. But I had no reason to think about it. Why question what was "normal" and in use all about me?

We began learning about age three that schools were "normal," and began attending them by age six or sooner. It did not occur to us to question why they were as we found them to be, or how else they might be. More urgent questions were how to please the teacher, and how to work the drinking fountains. In time various aspects of school displeased us; but we likely attributed any distress to the powerful individuals in charge. We didn't question the existence of classrooms, fixed groups, grades, periods, subjects, courses, evaluations, junior highs and high schools, and the like any more than lamp posts, fences, green grass, or the warm sun of summer. These things *were*.

Those opting for teaching or related careers came to college with a dozen years of things-as-they-are experience. Most returned to the school milieu at around age 22 (a time when real-world experience may be scant and contact with real children at the lowest point) not as revolutionaries but to make a living, fit in, get along, survive. After 16 or more years of status quo exposure, the great bulk of the arrangements and establishment, and the ideas that supported them, were likely accepted, without much question, as normal. This is powerful indoctrination—unlike accountants, music majors, biologists, engineers, and others who enter their milieu after graduation, educators are "brought up" in their field. Old ideas are hardest to shake. On the job, pressures begin at once, problems are insistent. Looking back, to ask "Why is this as it is?" may seem an unaffordable effort.

Yet we must look back to gain insight into why education seems awash in criticism, acute difficulties, frustrations, conflict, gnawing insecurities. Hindsight shows us that education followed two wrong paths that have taken us deeper and deeper into present troubles. However sensible they may have seemed years ago, they explain why we must break away from believing the coal furnace and icebox to be normal for all time, and with some mental pain, turn to the brain and new paths that promise well.

The first of these paths carries us back 140 years to Horace Mann, who had so profound and lasting an effect on our school system. When Mann was named to his position in Massachusetts—what we would now call Commissioner of Education—in 1837, he was an attorney, with no children of his own (until late in life), no previous experience with children or with schools, and no special preparation for the assignment aside from interest. A look at some of the schools then existing revolted him—they were mostly on the old schoolmaster pattern, the teaching being done by having the students, mostly boys, get their lesson by heart and then come forward one by one to recite it to the master. The content was often totally irrelevant to the times and place and student needs, and the whole business was unbearably dull, pointless, crude and mean, with a large overlay of violence: the teacher beat the students constantly if able to, and frequently was beaten and turned out by the larger students if not able to subdue them. At a primary level, school might be conducted by a woman in her kitchen.

Mann, an earnest, able, tenacious, and devoted person, saw quickly that some new system was needed that would be adequate to the needs of a growing population, and before long went to Europe to find one he could adopt. Probably he saw the Prussian system through the tinted glasses of hope and need—and from that source, almost exclusively, came our class-and-grade system, still in use with its essentials scarcely changed.

Another type of school had arisen and spread widely: the one-room school of legend. It was an American form, suitable to communities where students were few in number and of a wide range of ages, and it survived long into the present century—being done in more by the roads and buses of the automobile age than by anything else. When we look back at the miserably small resources such schools had, and the teachers who often had some education but no formal training, we must marvel that they were as resultful as the record seems to suggest. Lacking training, the teachers did what came naturally, working with their charges as individuals without regard to age, grouping them when possible on the basis of their current levels in each attainment, and encouraging some of the more advanced to help others. They did not have to fight the structure to do this; they had little alternative. In small, raw settlements, their content was of course practical and focused on what are now called "basic skills." In those times, we should remember, "book learning" was low on the scale of priorities. Youngsters attended school when there was nothing more important for them to do.[2]

But in older villages, towns, and cities, population growth and increasing density were creating pressure that invited new, larger structures. The Prussian system seemed to present answers to several needs.

Mann's aims were bold, broad, and well ahead of his day. A good many people then acknowledged the need to pay, through "poor rates," for a minimal education for children whose parents or guardians could not provide for it privately, mainly because it was believed that children not able to read religious literature would be easy prey for the devil. Their enthusiasm for paying these rates was hardly keen, we may well assume. Mann sought a great deal more: a system of publicly supported schools available to all, not as charity to the poor or orphaned, but as an expression of public policy that universal education was essential to a flourishing democracy.

The schools Mann inspected revealed the degree of local commitment to formal schooling that existed. They were tiny, ill-kept, poorly heated, furnished with crude benches, and about the only equipment was the inescapable switch for punishment. Many lacked even an outhouse—the woods nearby served, if there were woods. A common view was that "citizenship came by a process of patriotic osmosis,"[3] the result of exposure to communal activities and means of earning a living; and the few hours children might spend in school hardly seemed much of a factor. A lawyer like Mann or a preacher might require considerable formal education, but they were hardly typical.

As possessor of a well-developed sense of practical politics, Mann needed no one to tell him he faced great odds, even with his high reputation and deserved fame as an orator.[4] If a new system were to be introduced, it would have to be one that would meet the least resistance. While Mann talked eloquently and in the most optimistic terms (education could be expected to cure all social problems), and undoubtedly was sincere, he was also introducing a system with some canny and timely advantages.

By dividing the school into classrooms, a huge amount of population growth could be accommodated. The room that at first contained 15 students could later hold 30, then 60, and ultimately as many as could be squeezed in physically, sometimes more than a hundred. Expense scarcely increased at all.

By grading the classrooms, the labor problem was resolved. Male schoolmasters were hard to find. But "respectable" females, especially maiden ladies and widows, had little choice of employment. They could be hired at far less cost, for only as many weeks as might be planned; and needing their employment, they could be directed and managed with ease by male supervisors. Further, they could serve if they had enough knowledge for any one grade level, without need for a more general education if they followed instructions. Thus began the tradition of the meek, genteel, badly paid schoolteacher.

Added to these critical advantages in economy was the overall *apparent* simplicity and order of the structure. Here again we must recall the temper of the times. The factory system came to America a good half century later than to European countries, and it was taking hold in New England as Mann was struggling with his mighty task. On the whole, the new mills and factories (which might even utilize that amazing invention, the steam engine) were admired—by people in no danger of working in them—for their productivity, which was in fact bringing an unprecedented flood of goods and products at lower prices.

By no accident, this model was applied to education. *The new kind of class-and-grade school was plainly a factory.* The students were the raw material, fed in at one end, batch processed, and turned out at the other. The teachers were the factory hands, the principals and supervisors the foremen and managers, and the board of education (which originally had the responsibility of determining who was destitute enough to need assistance from the poor rates) soon became an imitation of a corporation's board of directors.

The model, understandably, had remarkable appeal to communities which, if forced to expand public education, much preferred the cheapest and presumably simplest means.[5] The steadily growing population could not be ignored—especially since each wave of immigration brought a new variety of poor, "inferior" newcomers, deemed desperately in need of the moral support the new schools were intended to deliver. (It was supposed then as now that the weakness of the home was the primary cause of the lamentable state of morality.) The class-and-grade system and its factory school caught on with remarkable rapidity. Other states soon followed the same path, at least where population was dense enough to warrant larger school units.

Mann wrote to a number of friends extolling his exciting new, broader concepts of education, and asked, "Under the soundest and most vigorous system of education which we can now command, what proportion or percentage of all children who are born, can be made useful and exemplary men—honest dealers, conscientious jurors, true witnesses, incorruptible voters and magistrates, good parents, good neighbors, good members of society?" Some replies suggested a failure rate of below one-half percent, another predicted not a single case of failure.[6] To the best and wisest people, it seemed manifest that the schools would teach and the children would learn. How could there be problems?

Very soon after the new kind of schools came into use, however, the problems showed up. The first basic flaw was that the children were *not* inert raw material. They persisted in being individuals, differing enormously. Many did not "process" well. Schools long followed standard factory procedure: if possible, *make* the material fit the factory machinery. If the material is "defective" or does not process properly, throw it out on the scrap heap.

The second error lay in supposing that the children could be processed successfully at *a uniform rate*. Learning was seen as a function of time: in two years a child should learn twice as much as in one year. When it soon became evident that this did not happen, many plans for modifying the rigid system were experimented with. Some actually helped. But by and large class-and-grade instruction was fundamentally fallacious. The economic advantages won out, and self-deception became a tacitly accepted way of life for school people. One could preserve the system only by ignoring, distorting, or disclaiming responsibility for the results it achieved. For decades huge numbers of students were tossed out on the scrap heap (the term "dropout" is of course one example of deception—"pushout" was often more accurate), the more so as the years of schooling offered increased. So long as there were a variety of jobs for those who did not process well, no crisis arose. The schools served as a sieve that separated "better" and "nicer" people from the contemptuously regarded immigrants and native, long-established Indian, black, and Spanish "minorities." The better and nicer group, which held power, found this an acceptable arrangement.[7]

Enunciating this view of the history of our schools only a few years ago would have made one subject to charges of being a nasty radical, a bitter cynic, or a poor patriot. Mann did his propaganda work so well that, as many have noted, faith in the schools eventually acquired virtually a religious quality, a good deal of which still supports myths, now painfully crumbling. But if we focus on *learning*, we see that the class-and-grade system was adopted on naive assumptions.

Few questioned that if students were educated they would become model citizens and admirable individuals. The teaching would automatically and reliably produce learning. The basic teaching method would derive from the centuries-old "learn the book" approach, a simple transference of knowledge from the teacher's head to the student's. Much learning would be achieved by rote, and enforced by beating children as often and as cruelly as seemed required. (Mann was a kindly person, opposed to this torture, but an exception among the many who approved inflicting pain, or perhaps enjoyed it as an available and even respectable sexual perversion.) The great bulk of instructional effort was directed toward training students to give "right answers" to standard questions. The spelling bee was enormously popular, handwriting had to be executed in a precise, official style, arithmetic was done by unvarying algorithms, geography meant storing facts like atlas or gazetteer.

Although the more modern ideas of Pestalozzi, Froebel, Herbart, and others had won some following in Europe, they had little importance in America until much later. The discipline of psychology was far in the future; such thinking about learning as was done was largely the concern of philosophers, who were not addressing practical applications. Though Mann had insights and intuitions far ahead of his day, and saw the conflict between individuals in a free society and masses of youngsters grouped in schools,[8] he threw his weight to the mass approach. The vision was clear: the schools would teach, the students would learn, the social problems would evaporate.

As for the brain, it was then almost completely a mystery. Not until 1850 would instruments be developed to prove that nerves did indeed carry some kind of electrical pulse. (Mann had encountered *phrenology* on his travels, the notion that the shape and bumps of the head signified possession of various capabilities and aptitudes, and was fascinated by this quite wrong but later popular idea.) *Knowledge of the brain had nothing to offer education for over a century to come.*

The class-and-grade system took hold, a triumph for the concept of free education for democracy—and a wrong path for education that we are still struggling to get off.

The second reason why study of the brain was not a concern to educators lies in the rise of psychology, a science just a century old if we date it from Wundt's pioneer laboratory at Leipzig. In America, behaviorist views gradually became dominant. The behaviorists had a sound aim: to get away from introspection, from dubious ideas such as phrenology and worse, and from the inaccessible, baffling brain in general—to try to make the new science more "scientific." A deliberate course was set to stay outside the brain, and to concentrate on what subjects *did* that could be observed.

Like the class-and-grade system, this sounded sensible at the time; but it too, I suggest, has proved a disaster. Psychology became the study of rats, mice, cats, pigeons, and other creatures convenient to deal with in a laboratory, with primates getting relatively little attention and humans even less. The practice of avoiding the brain continued long after it was justified, and still continues.

Ausubel has pointed out:

> The more scientifically conducted research in learning theory has been undertaken largely by psychologists unconnected with the education enterprise, who have investigated problems quite remote from the type of learning that

goes on in the classroom. The focus has been on animal learning or on short-term and fragmentary rote or nonverbal forms of human learning, rather than on the learning and retention of organized bodies of meaningful material.

He adds:

The extrapolation of rote learning theory and evidence to school learning problems has had many disastrous consequences.[9]

Further, Ausubel notes that *educational* psychologists have long concerned themselves with measurement, group dynamics, counseling, and such, and that despite "the self-evident centrality of classroom learning and cognitive development," these areas were both theoretically and empirically "ignored."

Little has changed to invalidate these observations. In general, psychologists of all persuasions only exceptionally pay attention to schooling applications; educational psychology texts freely confess to understanding little about learning; and psychologists working in schools have tended to busy themselves in other directions, especially testing.

The distaste and dissatisfaction teachers commonly express toward the educational psychology they have been forced to study appears to have sound foundation. Massive as the effort has been, *it has contributed almost nothing observable to useful understanding of learning and its encouragement.*[10] On the contrary, it has inhibited and distorted insights by persistently trying to transfer findings from contrived experiments with rats and other small animals to humans—at times with the caution that this should not be overdone, at times without it. Simultaneously, a vocabulary that is a large part of the problem has become conventional among educators: *stimulus, response, motivation, association, mediation, reinforcement, reward,* and more—terms that embody antique and wrong ideas, as we shall see, yet are so commonly used that they seldom are subjected to scrutiny.[11] In my view they are primitive, ill-defined, obsolete terms that continually tend to throw us off a productive track.

Perhaps the worst outcome of the avoid-the-brain, "pure" behaviorist approach is what has often been called *behavior modification,* a name already so suspect that its advocates adopt aliases. In essence, the effort is to apply exactly the techniques used with captive rats to captive people, to force behavior that suits the modifiers, who often appear perfectly willing to play God, sometimes in appallingly ruthless ways. In schools, prisons, and mental hospitals, the modifiers seek to obtain behavior *convenient to the authorities*—an intent that to some has more than a whiff of fascism about it.

Behavior modification approaches relate somewhat to the work of B. F. Skinner, who takes an extreme avoid-the-brain position. Skinner's ideas have repeatedly been torn apart by reputable critics, and at best are debatable, and efforts to apply his claims, as in programmed learning and the teaching machine, have fallen flat. Yet he is considered the country's best known psychologist.

If this very brief review of a long period has served its purpose, we can see that we are saddled with out-of-date school structures and largely useless, confusing psychological precepts. They do not provide foundations on which we can build, but only a thick overlay of historical debris that we must push aside if we are to make progress.

So blunt and sweeping an evaluation of conventional behaviorist psychology in relation to education will, I well realize, give rise to some cries of outrage. The past—especially its ideas that we have all been brought up with—is not easily or unemotionally cast off. But we do not, I think, wrong the memory of the many outstanding people who labored in this field if we now recognize that their contributions have not panned out, and that the structures they erected are now manifestly in tumbledown condition. New discoveries have been made, new ideas have emerged, and weaknesses in the old have become too evident to gloss over.

In part, perhaps, we are all to blame. We have assumed that if valuable insight into human learning was to come, it would be from conventional psychology. We have paid scant heed to how few psychologists have been deeply interested in school learning, to how carelessly the results of animal studies have been applied to humans, and to the possibility that much more insight might come from other disciplines.

And we continue to use Mann's class-and-grade system, endlessly trying to patch it rather than face up to its inherent, incurable conceptual errors.

NOTES

1. *The Creation of Settings and The Future Societies* (San Francisco: Jossey-Bass, 1972), p. 259.
2. In 1839 Mann persuaded the Massachusetts legislature to establish a minimum school year of six months. Attendance remained far below present standards of regularity, however, for many years, especially in more rural areas. Reasons included weather, lack of suitable clothing, illnesses, family needs and circumstances, and child labor outside the home.
3. Jonathan Messerli, *Horace Mann* (New York: Alfred A. Knopf, 1972), p. 253. This excellent biography of Mann illuminates the period and Mann's remarkable abilities and personality.
4. Though a master of oratory, Mann at times felt discouraged in his prodigious efforts to sell the concept of public education. "I seem to myself as if I were standing, on some wintry day, with the storm beating upon me, ringing the door bell of a house that no one lives in, or perhaps where the dwellers are all sound asleep, or too much absorbed in their own minds to hear the summons of one who comes to tell them that a torrent from the mountains is rushing

down upon them." Quoted from Horace Mann, *On the Crisis in Education*, Louis Fuller, ed. (Yellow Springs, Ohio: Antioch Press, 1965), p. 14.

5. The factory system, then new in America, had at the time few negative connotations. The human suffering it could produce became evident some years later.

6. Jonathan Messerli, *Horace Mann* (New York: Alfred A. Knopf, 1972), p. 444.

7. In general, school boards afforded immigrant and minority groups—including women—little or no representation. The idea that "anyone can go to college" is very recent—it was long assumed that youngsters from poorer homes would seek jobs, at the latest after high school graduation, which most did not achieve. For a challenging view of the role of the schools in serving immigrants, see Colin Greer, *The Great School Legend* (New York: Basic Books, 1972).

8. Historian Lawrence A. Cremin has pointed out Mann's struggle with the conflict between his leaning toward kindly, individualized treatment of young learners, and his drive for a socially effective "common school." He observes: "Mann by no means solves this problem but, to his great credit, he recognizes it. He is one of the first to try to work out the pedagogical implications of a universal education for freedom." See *Horace Mann's Legacy*, in Horace Mann, *The Republic and the School* (New York: Teachers College Press, 1957), p. 17.

9. David P. Ausubel, *Educational Psychology, A Cognitive View* (New York: Holt, Rinehart and Winston, 1968), p. 9.

10. In *The Psychology of Learning Applied to Teaching*, 2d ed. (Indianapolis: Bobbs-Merrill Co., 1971). B. R. Bugelski observes: "The fact that many educational practices lack a scientific foundation is not solely the fault of educators. The very nature of their business, learning or teaching, is not really well understood even by those who have attempted to study it under refined laboratory conditions. The psychology of learning is marked by great gaps and theoretical controversies" (p. 15). Bugelski quotes several sources in agreement. For a more recent evaluation, by a number of distinguished psychologists, see *Psychology and Education, The State of the Union*, edited by Frank H. Farley and Neal J. Gordon (Berkeley: McCutchan Publishing Corp., 1981). Farley suggests that one might conclude from the reports given at research conventions that: "cognition bears no relation to the nervous system; that personality, emotion, and motivation have no major bodily aspects; and that an organism could be effectively studied in complex situations without consideration of its evolutionary and biological structural and functional character, including those processes that might serve or control psychological matters" (p. 10).

11. William S. Sahakian notes: "Psychology of learning has throughout the first half of the twentieth century been dominated by stimulus-response learning to the virtual exclusion of any other orientation." *Introduction to the Psychology of Learning* (Chicago: Rand McNally Co., 1976), p. xvii.

3

If we think that we already know how learning takes place, we are not likely to learn anything new about the process, particularly if the new concepts are contradictory to what we already "know." Therefore popular beliefs about learning have to be unlearned or set aside if we are to gain any new insights. Unfortunately, most of the teaching and educational planning that takes place throughout the world is based on outmoded, ineffective concepts of the teaching/learning process. The fact that students do learn is ordinarily taken as evidence that traditional/conventional theories about learning "really work," but evidence shows that they are highly questionable and that students often learn in spite of teachers' theories, rather than because of them.

—HENRY CLAY LINDGREN[1]

Theory: Seeing with New Understanding

At times I have been introduced to teacher audiences as a theorist. The term causes foreheads to wrinkle: what is a theorist? Who needs theory? What will theory do for me Monday, when there is a large, unruly, or bored class to face, in a school where morale is falling apart day by day? What will theory do for the budget threatened with still further cuts; or to quiet parents who want, or oppose, censorship of books in the library with impolite words in them, the teaching of "creationism," programs for the gifted, more art and music, or strictly basics and no frills?

So-called working educators, meaning those who have direct contact with and responsibilities for students (also often described, revealingly, as "those on the firing line"), tend to take a dim view of theory and may even take a pejorative view of the word itself. Theory may be instantly rejected or ridiculed, brushed aside, or possibly distorted to support, very superficially, the practices the educator had decided to use anyway. Or to impress parents, certain buzzwords in fashion may be tossed into the conversation ("We're applying Piaget").

Here and there, to be sure, charismatic trainers of teachers claim to offer theory that teachers can apply in their regular classrooms "on Monday." The ideas may have value for stimulation in the right direction, but the theoretical foundation may be less than rigorously scientific, and the scope limited to small areas of interest. The claimed successes that application supposedly produces rarely stand up when investigated, and the initial enthusiasm does not survive long. Characteristically, these thrusts do not seek to produce broad basic theory from which applications may *later* develop through the work of many who have learned about it. Rather, the theory ties closely to intended proprietary uses. We could call this *private theory*.

In general, working educators and many at "higher" levels feel uncomfortable with theoretical approaches. Even the great bulk of educational research that absorbs large sums of money and produces avalanches of published reports does not attempt to build theory; as Broudy has put it, "researchers do whatever interests them or whatever project can be funded."[2] Many others have made similar observations. A variety of reasons for the educators' coolness are evident. In their training, most were exposed to weak, fragmentary theory, often derived from animal studies, and found almost useless in classrooms. Few educators have much scientific background (including a good many who teach science), and still fewer have had actual experience in fields—today, virtually all except education—where the primacy of theory has long since been accepted. And rarest of all are those who have been involved in efforts to work from basic theory to practical applications.

Foshay, a prominent educator, has stated bluntly:

> Most school practice arises from tradition, ritual, and the context within which schools are conducted. Only during this century has scientific learning theory had an influence and then only in a fairly minor way. The school is a kind of subculture in which are preserved the relics of former times, with a few practices added or subtracted because of contemporary thought.[3]

These attitudes toward theory, I submit, cannot longer be afforded. Hot spotlights focus on schools today, and if they reveal to a now dubious public a subculture rich in relics, support can be expected to tail off even faster. People assume that within human limits accountants, doctors, plumbers, engineers, tailors, business managers, and others with skills or professions *know what they are doing*, because an established body of "how to do it" exists. To discover that education lacks basic theory and proved expertise, and that few are seeking to build and use such a foundation, will be jolting. Debate and dispute rage in education because everyone has an opinion, and the discussion begins and ends on the level of opinion, without ever getting to any sounder basis or demonstrated results. Aukerman's well-known compendium of reading methods, for example, reviews more than 100 approaches currently in use![4] The confusion, the lack of established theory, could hardly be better illustrated. Small wonder that teachers often respond to a flood of opinion-based advice by withdrawing into their classrooms, closing the door, and implementing their own opinions.

Substantial theory (especially theory of learning) welded to practice stands at the top of schools' most urgent needs. With the tolerance of those readers who may be sophisticated in the concept and usage of theory, let us consider some aspects of theory that relate most directly to education but are rarely discussed.

The prime function of good theory, and the reason for striving to build it, is precisely to cut through a morass of opinion and miscellaneous knowledge, or supposed knowledge, by *organizing* what is firmly known, observed, or with solid reason believed, into a unified structure that is internally coherent and consistent. Essentially a theory presents an explanation of how things work.

Explanations, of course, can be dead wrong, and yet hold sway in their day. Epilepsy, for example, was long thought to result from demons invading the victim's body. (We still say "God bless you" to guard against this when someone's mouth is open during a sneeze—earlier viewed as a great opportunity for an alert demon to hop in.) The treatment favored by the best-educated people was to beat the patient severely, to make the demon so uncomfortable it would leave. Since epileptic seizures usually are of short duration, the treatment at times seemed to work, and the theory endured for centuries. Wrong theory, we should note well, can result in counterproductive efforts and *harm* to those supposedly helped. It may well be that a contemporary example can be found in conventional early reading instruction, based on analytical, "logical" theory that reflects no more understanding of the brain than beating for epilepsy.

Other theories may be called "dead end" in that they do not advance understanding. In past ages, for instance, earthquakes were explained as caused by the anger of various gods. Offerings, ceremonies, and contrition had limited practical value. Our present theory, based on the interactions of tectonic plates, seems to be gradually moving toward ability to predict severe quakes and so lessen disasters. One major evaluation of a theory stems from demanding skeptically, "So what?" A good theory should be intensely useful. It should strongly suggest what to do or at least what directions to investigate.

What may be called *word-theory* plagues education and human relations fields generally, and proves equally impractical. A word-theory is verbal, or "armchair." It never touches ground, so to speak, to become more substantial or real than speaking or writing, and hence can never be subjected to hard-nosed testing. To me and certainly many others, Freudian theory provides a mammoth example [5] While Freud's often fantastic word-explanations proved enormously valuable in opening up new areas of investigation, one may question whether they did not produce more confusion than direction. A good theory should not lead us to expend a lot of energy in wrong directions. Efforts to use Freudian word-theory to treat psychosis or severe anxiety, for example, have produced outcomes as much disputed as the theory itself. To accept Freudian ideas, one must have a deep belief, akin to religious faith, that they have validity.

As scientific method has come to dominate our times, good theory has become more and more not a construct to be believed but one to be challenged—virtually a target put up for others in the field to try to shoot down. That can be done by showing it is not internally consistent, or does not fit well with observations, or by cleverly devised tests that if often fragmentary still indicate some weakness. In education, which deals with highly complex interactions, small-scale trials may show whether outcomes move in the right or wrong directions. Even when a theory stands up well, begins to prove useful, and applications produce impressive outcomes, we scientifically accept a theory only on a tentative basis: as the best working explanation we have for a year or a century, but subject to disproof or replacement by a better explanation at any time.

Today, almost all technology depends on theory. Before such a base existed, craftsmen perforce relied on ritualistic procedures. Splendid Samurai swords, for example, were made by processes handed down generation to generation, executed with prayer or ceremony at each step. Early Egyptian glass makers could produce beautiful objects, but attempts often failed because control of material, temperatures, and air moisture content was weak. Failures were blamed on "unclean" participants, astrological influences, or divine displeasure. With no theoretical insight into what they were doing, reliance had to be on slow emergence of detailed methods that often required centuries of efforts and failures. There was still little ability to explain why the process produced good results. But this kind of "do it without understanding why it works" approach has very little usefulness in modern education, where the "raw materials" vary so enormously, the conditions are always in change, and needs shift rapidly. Most teachers in time acquire a bag of tricks that they believe work in certain circumstances; but in general the set procedures, when looked at closely, prove to be mainly rituals and traditions that fail much more often than they work, so far as observable or measurable learning outcomes are concerned. Many relate only to pupil control.

With over 43 million students in schools, and around two million classrooms operating, we have each year a huge amount of opportunity for superior methods to emerge, but that does not happen. We have a vast store of bits and pieces of knowledge, or supposed knowledge, about teaching and learning, and equally vast room to observe; but out of this has come only the mass of conflicting opinion, and almost no theory, no coherent "why" explanation. Without guiding theory, education flounders, often going round in circles by discovering "new" methods that some historical research may show to have been "new" 20 and 40 and 60 years before.

With the brain as a focus, however, it becomes possible to get onto genuinely new paths, using information never previously available, and to arrive at a kind of theory that does explain what learning is and how it comes about sharply enough to be tested in many ways.

A theory, of course, does not have to be perfect to be very useful. If it brings together the solider knowledge we have, fits pretty well with what we observe actually happens, and introduces good new knowledge—rather than adding fancy words that sound impressive but merely cover up ignorance—a theory can help us in practical ways even though later it may need revisions and improvements. There is a theory, for example, that the folk dances done by people in relatively simple societies reflect the way they make their living, by hunting, herding, or kinds of agriculture. It presents ideas that lead to looking at the dancing with "new eyes," to see whether there are—or aren't—relationships never before thought about.

A good theory of learning will help us look for, and perhaps find, relationships in the processes of education that previously were largely ignored, or not understood, or perhaps not generally noted at all. The theory we will explore in later chapters, for instance, suggests that *input* and *threat* are among highly important factors, until now hardly even observed or considered.

In looking at theory usefulness it may be helpful to consider briefly *levels of expertise* and the concept of *knowledge structure*. The automobile makes a convenient illustrative subject, since most of us have to operate or utilize vehicles.

We can think of the ground floor of our structure of expertise as occupied by those who do not drive, but know what a car is, what it is for, that it has an engine that requires gasoline or other fuel, that it has brakes and lights and so forth. We can call these people *oriented*.

A level higher are the many who can operate a car on a *procedural* basis. They know how to start the motor by turning a key, how to move the gear shift, how to press the throttle to control speed, and so on; but they may have little idea of just what happens when the key is turned or the gearshift lever is moved.

On the third story are those who do have a general grasp of the mechanics of an automobile. They can be said to be on a *comprehension* level. By knowing to a degree "what is going on" they may drive more expertly, detect developing problems, and be able to take some simple remedial actions to deal with difficulties.

A floor higher in our structure would be the mechanics and skilled amateurs whose understanding is deep enough to support testing and repairs. This is the *technical* level.

The fifth floor would be occupied by engineers, who employ far deeper knowledge to evaluate materials and parts, direct production, and use sophisticated instruments to test and measure results. This would be the lower *engineering* level, and on the sixth floor would be various *design* engineers with deep knowledge that permits them to design parts, subsystems, and perhaps an entire vehicle. At this level, more and more of the work is done on paper or on computers, making more and more use of theory.

Still higher would be specialists, scientists, and researchers. These might include, to illustrate, a physicist concerned with the behavior of hot gases in a cylinder, or a chemist involved with antipollution catalysts, or a mathematician who analyzes front-end geometries, all working intensively with theory. These *specialist* levels would occupy several floors at the top.

If your car stopped running on a lonely road late at night, you might be luckier to have your garage mechanic come along rather than one of these higher experts. Yet plainly they have vital roles to play in giving us better performing and more reliable cars to begin with. Though the mechanic must have a good grasp of basic theory to be at all expert on a day-to-day practical level, he would not likely be equipped to perform at these higher levels. The higher the responsibility, the greater the need for sophisticated theory.

This kind of knowledge structure, we should note, is quite new in the world. Just a century ago in the United States there were still many families that were largely self-sufficient. They raised their own food; processed and stored it; cared for their livestock, butchered and skinned them; built houses and barns; made soap and candles; spun, wove, knitted, and tailored garments; and made or repaired tools and weapons. Almost all of this was done at the ground floor or procedural levels.

Today our society has become so complex and reliant on technology that we must go to "museum villages" for a glimpse of those simpler times. Where for millenia we did things procedurally, "the way they were always done," we now are far more dependent on theory. As a boy, like many other inquisitive youngsters, I once took a clock apart and got some idea of the works and how they functioned. A child today who takes apart one of the new digital clocks will find nothing inside but mysterious circuits—not a single moving part other than switches! But a three-year-old can procedurally operate a color television, an incredibly complex, precision apparatus—because somewhere there are people at the various levels who utilize the theories that are the foundation for television.

With perhaps some shock, we must realize that we have not had parallel knowledge structure in education. Those "higher up" do not *necessarily* have more grasp of theory. Viable theory of learning and theory of teaching just hasn't existed to any extent! The procedures that are widely used in schools do *not* rest on sound, substantial theoretical foundations. In that sense, education has never entered the twentieth century. It is still fundamentally back in prescientific times and more and more suffering the consequences.[6]

But now theory is available. With it comes the prospect of making advances we hardly dared dream of when all we had was the procedural level to work on.

The argument that schools deal with people and that therefore we can't apply modern scientific and technical approaches is, I submit, largely an excuse. We make cars and typewriters and frozen foods and synthetic textiles and antibiotics not to lie in warehouses, but to be used *by people*. People staff offices, drive trucks, program computers, operate factory machinery, and conduct experiments in laboratories, just as people work in and attend schools. The technology we have developed *to great extent reflects our current people-needs*. The main complaint about schools is that they don't!

Even if the theory that now exists were perfect, most of us in education would face the problem that *we have never before worked from theory to practice*. We have to learn and acquire expertise in this new way (new in education) of dealing with needs and we cannot expect the theory itself to solve our problems, any more than new understanding of a disease will of itself effect cures. The understanding has to be applied.[7] At the same time, the old ways, based on tradition and ritual and often unsupported opinion, have to be terminated and discarded. And "letting go" can often be harder than "taking hold."[8]

NOTES

1. *Educational Psychology in the Classroom*, 6th ed. (New York: Oxford University Press, 1980), p. 262.
2. Harry S. Broudy, *The Real World of the Public Schools* (New York: Harcourt Brace Jovanovich, 1972), p. 104.
3. Arthur W. Foshay, in *The Elementary School in the United States*, 72d Yearbook of the National Society for the Study of Education (Chicago: University of Chicago Press, 1973.), p. 197.
4. Robert C. Aukerman, *Approaches to Beginning Reading* (New York: John Wiley and Sons, 1971).

5. For a recent, very critical view see Martin L. Gross, *The Psychological Society* (New York: Random House, 1978); also *Mainstream Psychology* (New York: Holt, Rinehart and Winston, 1974) and various articles by Benjamin M. Braginsky and Dorothea D. Braginsky. No amount of criticism, of course, should dim the enormously important contributions of Freud in calling attention to unconscious aspects of the brain, the influence of early childhood experiences, parent-child relationships, and individualism.

6. This view is noted widely throughout the literature, as for example George W. Denemark in *Education for 1984 and After*, report of Study Commission on Undergraduate Eduation and the Education of Teachers (Paul A. Olson, Director, University of Nebraska): "Much of what currently passes for theory is simply outdated specific knowledge—for which there should be little room in the teacher education curriculum" (p. 142). Martin Haberman refers to "a few generalizations that we pass off as theoretic principles..." (p. 223).

7. Perhaps it is not too early in this discussion of learning to caution the reader not to expect here neat recipes, offered for use Monday. The work of application of theory requires the efforts of many, over a considerable period. While the author and his associates have studied at least some applications for years, and investigated some in test and practice, this book seeks to deal with aims and principles that, if substantial and scientifically supported, can guide much wider efforts.

8. Peter F. Drucker, in *The Age of Discontinuity* (New York: Harper and Row, 1969) remarks: "The most difficult and most important decisions in respect to objectives are not what to do. They are, first, what to abandon as no longer worthwhile and, second, what to give priority to and what to concentrate on.... The decisions about what to abandon is by far the most important and the most neglected." Drucker is speaking of organizations in general, including schools (p. 192).

4

Schooling in the United States can and must be revitalized. This cannot be done, however, by adding an innovation here or there. Systematic conceptualizations of what is required followed by systematic, step-by-step reconstruction are called for. The major educational challenge of our time is to reform our existing schools and school systems.

—JOHN I. GOODLAD AND
M. FRANCES KLEIN[1]

Proster Theory: Comprehensive New Synthesis

In this book I present *Proster Theory*, in terms I hope will be readily understandable and illuminating to all who are concerned in any way with teaching and training.

Introducing the theory will require a number of chapters, as the various findings and concepts that form its foundations are dealt with. The neologism "proster," pronounced "pross-ter," will be explained in Chapter 10.

Proster Theory, which I have been developing over the past dozen years, is of course *a* theory of human learning. It appears to be the first comprehensive, brain-based such theory to be published[2] and it has by now won a certain amount of attention and interest. The fact that now one brain-based theory can be constructed implies that others can be, too—the basic information is available to all. It will take a lot of testing and applications experience to move any theory into being, at least temporarily, "the" leading theory. But the practical beauty of a theory, if well and carefully conceived, is that it can be immediately useful in suggesting direction: what to examine and what to test.

Typically, a useful theory does not come from the laboratory type of discovery, or long, original research in a limited area. Rather, it is likely to stem from pulling together knowledge and findings from a wide range of sources and arranging information and ideas into a coherent *system*, so that we get a *whole* rather than a litter and jumble of fragments. We have to be sure, however, not to fall victim to the neat appeals of a *word theory*.

There was long a dominant one in education, for example, that envisioned a "trained mind," so strengthened and sharpened by hard study, instruction in logic, and "exercise" through mastery of Latin and mathematics that there would be "transfer" to all other fields. The system, however, had nothing to it but some impressive-sounding words. When tested, it utterly failed. Evidence was overwhelming that what was learned transferred only to very similar applications.[3] That collapse came half a century ago, yet it is not unusual to hear a school board member, for instance, spouting this doctrine that sounds reasonable but has been proved to be fallacious.

As we shall see, Proster Theory touches earth at many points, in two main ways. First, it fits into place and accounts for a great many frequently repeated observations of how people and learners do behave. Second, it fits with much that we now know about the physical nature of the brain, and about its history and development.

Some assurance may also lie in the many sources of the theory. It was generated by deliberately looking in many disciplines, instead of just one or two, for findings that might apply. The list includes:

- Anthropology and archeology, particularly with reference to the early prehistory of humans and the rise of civilization.
- Evolutionary science and the general principles of the development of species.
- Ethology, the study of creatures in their normal, natural environment rather than in laboratories or in confinement.
- The neurosciences, which variously emphasize the physiology, electrochemistry, pathology, and other aspects of the brain, including neuropsychology.
- Evolution of the human brain, about which a great deal is known.
- Computer science, which has contributed enormously to understanding of the brain, a kind of computer—and to considerable degree has itself benefited by the comparison and contrasts.

- The newer "information processing" or cognitive psychologies and modern communication theory.
- Primate studies, especially those using the larger apes, the closest relatives of the human species.
- Behaviorist psychology, in the sense that findings of experiments in many cases held significance, often distorted or obscured (or ignored) in the effort to build nonbrain systems.
- Educational experience, particularly in the contrast between widespread inadequate outcomes and a few notable successes.

The problem, in short, was not one of having to scratch for useful evidence, but of sorting out the solid materials from a great mass, and synthesizing. As is common knowledge, scientists and researchers in different disciplines all too rarely cross their borders to make common cause. Adding to this fractionation are the jargons that tend to make such mutual efforts more difficult. Translation into something closer to plain English was a large part of the task.

In point of time, progress in the neurosciences plays the crucial role. In the last 25 or 30 years the achievement in these fields has been stupendous, in turn largely reflecting the availability of new means of investigation—new tools that were brilliantly used. Many of these stemmed from progress in electronics: the computer in various forms, which not only served as a model but made possible acquisition of huge amounts of data; the electron microscope and its scanning version that permitted a new range of magnification; and probes so tiny they could be inserted even into single neurons of experimental animals.[4] At the same time, direct information on the human brain could be obtained as a by-product of medical procedures that utilized these and other new resources. Any criticism we may feel inclined to make of earlier investigators must in fairness be modified by realization that they lacked the key tools that more recently have been of such great value—in some cases converting speculations to fact, and in others producing surprises.

Because of these quite recent discoveries, we can feel far more certain that we are indeed entering into never before explored territories, and not just going around a cycle one more time even while we may see fresh merit in some earlier educational ideas.

It is not too much to say that with this body of new information on the human brain we can attain an unprecedented understanding of human nature. A theory of learning overlaps a theory of behavior to large degree, because most human behavior is learned. A theory of instruction obviously must be based on a theory of learning, if there is to be a solid foundation, yet in the entire, vast literature of education there is not enough on instructional theory (as opposed to descriptions of practices) to fill half a section of library shelf! In the absence of learning theory of sufficient substance, effort to develop general instructional theory has had to be speculation or declarations of personal beliefs or philosophies. Even less have psychologists contributed. Gage once noted that: "In comparison with learning, teaching goes almost unmentioned in the theoretical writings of psychologists."[5]

Even those who have written about learning directly for educators, after surveying the whole field, have offered little in terms of theory for teaching—and hardly much more practical advice for instructors. For example, the well known and properly admired *Essentials of Learning* by Travers[6] gives virtually nothing in the course of about 500 pages. Nor does *Theories of Learning* by Ernest J. Hilgard and Gordon H. Bower, a somewhat more detailed survey.[7] In *The Psychology of Learning Applied to Teaching*, Bugelski does end with a brief chapter on "Practical Applications" containing a few paragraphs of theory that he describes as "incomplete" and for which "primitive" might be a fair word.[8] The chapter includes a list of 59 "suggestions" which are provided as a summary and self-test of points made in the text rather than as a coherent structure. The list, in my view, does not contradict the admirably frank declaration in the introduction that "at the present time there is little to offer by way of practical advice to the harrassed teachers."[9]

Essentially, these distinguished authorities further testify to the paucity of useful knowledge and theory that pervades the classroom system. Happily, it is now possible to turn to a wealth of new information and theory, offering striking potentials, and to build on scientific foundations the older material so poorly provides.

The new body of material is not an addition to the old. It must be viewed as *replacement*—something like going to vaccines and antibiotics from old drugs that soothed symptoms. To abandon concepts that one has spent much time, labor, and money to acquire must be painful—but less so than trying to cling to ideas and procedures that agonize both teacher and student, while serving society badly.

The arrival of brain-based learning theory, I suggest, forces a choice on all engaged in instruction or administration, a choice not there before. It is between holding to the past—familiar, however inadequate—or breaking sharply away to enter quite new areas which will inevitably suggest and lead to development of new concepts of instruction and settings for learning.

To get to brain-based theory, we must go by way of the brain.

NOTES

1. *Looking Behind the Classroom Door* (Belmont, Calif.: Wadsworth, 1974), p.v.
2. Proster Theory is presented in considerably more detail than here in Leslie A. Hart, *How The Brain Works* (New York: Basic Books, 1975). Most of the

chapters are not technical; those that are have been kept free of jargon and should not present difficulties to readers with some scientific background or interests.

3. See Robert M. W. Travers, *Essentials of Learning,* 3d ed. (New York: Macmillan, 1972), p. 480: "The studies demonstrated that no particular subject-matter field had special powers to train the mind, as the nineteenth-century educators had believed."

4. For a technical but generally lucid glimpse of many aspects of current brain laboratory investigation, see *Scientific American,* September 1979, a special issue on the topic.

5. N. L. Gage, "Theories of Teaching," in *Theories of Learning and Instruction,* 63d Yearbook of the National Society for the Study of Education (Chicago: University of Chicago Press, 1964), p. 269.

6. See note 3.

7. Hilgard writes: "It has been found enormously difficult to apply laboratory-derived principles of learning to the improvement of efficiency in tasks with clear and relatively simple objectives. We may infer that it will be even more difficult to apply laboratory-derived principles of learning to the improvement of efficient learning in tasks with more complex objectives" (New York: Appleton-Century-Crofts, 3d ed. 1966), p. 542. Teachers, of course, usually must deal with extremely complex as well as usually vaguely stated objectives.

8. B.R. Bugelski, *The Psychology of Learning Applied to Teaching,* 2d ed. (Indianapolis: Bobbs-Merrill, 1971), p. 279.

9. Page vii.

5

The brain is a tissue. It is a complicated, intricately woven tissue, like nothing else we know of in the universe, but it is composed of cells, as any tissue is. They are, to be sure, highly specialized cells, but they function according to the laws that govern any other cells. Their electrical and chemical signals can be detected, recorded and interpreted, and their chemicals can be identified; the connections that constitute the brain's woven feltwork can be mapped. In short, the brain can be studied, just as the kidney can.

—DAVID H. HUBEL[1]

The Brain: Where Learning Happens

"An interest in the brain requires no justification other than a curiosity to know why we are here, what we are doing here, and where we are going."

So writes Dr. Paul D. MacLean, a distinguished brain researcher, chief of the Laboratory of Brain Evolution and Behavior at the National Institute of Mental Health in Bethesda, Maryland, and a writer who can turn a phrase.[2]

With our new knowledge of the brain, we are just dimly beginning to realize that we *can now understand humans, including ourselves, as never before, and that this is the greatest advance of our century, and quite possibly the most significant in all human history.*

In this discussion, we have the additional justification of wanting to see learning and instruction as aspects of brain nature and activity. Fortunately for those whose curiosity does not lead them into scientific matters, we do not need to get into any great technical depth. It is not detail we are concerned with, but the broader picture.

We want to know:

- what the brain is *for*;
- how it functions in health and in ordinary use;
- how we came to acquire what is often considered to be the most complex apparatus we know of in the universe;
- how it learns;
- how best to deal with the brains of others, and to use our own.

We can call this a practical, useful, holistic approach, macro rather than micro, since we will look at the brain as a system, considering its interrelations, rather than trying to isolate and focus on one tiny area or function at a time. We will be concerned with the brain in health, not with neurological symptoms and illnesses. We have only incidental need to consider neurophysiological details or specific electrochemical processes—Proster Theory derives from many additional sources, as we have noted.

We can begin by looking at the human brain as a physical organ.

If asked, people generally can give a quite detailed description of the human hand, or eye. They may have a less sharp concept of stomach or liver. When it comes to the brain, however, a lot will have simply a blank, or be able to say only that it has two sides. We don't ordinarily have much reason to study the brain—as I have pointed out, even education is only now beginning to give much attention to the organ of learning.

The adult human brain weighs a little over three pounds or around 1,500 grams, and in volume is a little more than a quart, close to a liter. Individual brains vary considerably but, within a normal range, variations in size do not directly signify greater or less ability. On a species basis, size does tend to be significant. Among mammals, humans have by far the largest brain, except for porpoises, whales, and some other heavy mammals, which we do not as yet have reason to believe surpass us in mental capacities. The ratio of brain to total body weight appears to be a key factor. Women's brains overall tend to be somewhat smaller than men's, to about the degree that the female body tends to be smaller.

We should be clear on what is meant by *brain*. The term implies an *integration* center for the nervous system. The vast majority of creatures do not have any brains at all in this sense; because their various subsystems are not unified in a "head office." True brains are largely (but not exclusively) associated with mammals. *The size and complexity of an animal's brain tends to be directly related to that species' survival needs: the more behaviors it needs to find food and avoid danger, and the more sensitivity to its surroundings it must have, the more brain it requires.* A grazing, herd animal such as a cow will have less in brain resources, especially in proportion to total weight, than a deer, which must be far more alert; the deer needs less than the dog, which must be far more adaptable; and the dog gets along with less than the large apes such as the chimpanzee, which leads a complex social life. Humans have no "standard" way of living. We are the jack-of-all-trades of mammals, extremely adaptable and dependent on a great number of behaviors—a means of survival and a way of living that demands a stupendously large brain.

In truth, humans may properly be regarded as brain freaks. We can regard a giraffe as a neck freak, and the elephant as even more a nose freak, since its snout measures yards rather than inches. But the human brain is millions, even billions, of times more complex than the organ possessed by most other creatures with brains.

Throughout much of human history the brain was not regarded as of major importance. The liver, much larger, was long thought to be far more significant as well as the seat of the soul; and the heart was quite literally considered the seat of courage and wisdom. Our common speech still reflects this: though we don't talk much any more about "lily-livered" cowards, we do still say "learn by heart," "listen to your heart, not your head," "he hasn't got his heart in his work," and "let's get to the heart of the matter."

Nature, however, has no such illusions, as we can see by the elaborate developments that give the brain better protection than any other portion of the body. The skull provides a chamber of sturdy bone, lined with a special coating, and filled with a fluid that further cushions against shock. The few pounds of pinkish-gray, jelly-like mass in this armored box get royal treatment in other ways. The brain has a rich blood supply that brings nourishment and oxygen; and in severe conditions in which these are in short supply, the brain has first call on what may be available. It routinely consumes a much larger share than its size and weight would warrant, at all times—the brain never "turns off," even in deep sleep. In addition, a *blood barrier* prevents most abnormal substances that may be in the blood stream from getting into the brain, although some, such as opiates, can penetrate.

Realization of the all-dominant role of the brain is bringing about even a new conception of what signals death. The old idea that death comes when the heart stops seems to be yielding, even in law, to considering the degree of brain activity instead. With modern support apparatus, the heart can be kept going in certain types of coma cases after the brain has in effect stopped functioning.

While our bodies of course influence the kind of personality each of us has, by far the greatest part of individuality resides in the brain. If Able were to receive a transplant of Baker's heart, Able would still be Able, with Able's knowledge, behaviors, memory, and affections. But if it were possible—as it is not—for Able to have Baker's brain transplanted, *Able would become Baker in Able's body*, with all Baker's knowledge, behaviors, memory, and affections, and none of his own! The heart is merely a pump; the brain is the core and storehouse of personal existence.

Unlike a bowl of jelly, *the brain has a "design" fully as specific as hand or ear or knee joint, but vastly more complicated*. To make any sense at all out of its many, exceedingly intricate structures, we have to bear in mind that our human brain is the product of hundreds of millions of years of evolution. It is not a logical apparatus, like one a computer engineer might design at a drafting table, so to speak (today teams of specialists use computers to design new computers!), but rather reflects the illogical events and accidents of history. This is a fact, a hard fact, of absolutely fundamental importance to learning. The brain is the organ for learning, and it is an organ—material tissue, not abstract concept. We have to deal with it as it is, not as it might be, or as we might wish it, or suppose it. Since behavioral psychologists have long declined to look at it, and have shown hardly the smallest interest in its evolution, or indeed human evolution in general, we should not be too surprised to find that a brain-based theory brings us to some very different insights.

MacLean has given us a very useful simplification of overall brain structure, based on a great deal of available knowledge of how animal brains have actually developed over the last 250 million years or so.[3] He suggests we think of the present human brain as composed of three brains, of very different ages. The oldest can be identified as *reptilian*. It may be compared to the kind of brain possessed by agile reptiles (*Synapsida*) that became the ancestors of mammals, and may roughly be dated as perhaps 200 million years old.

The second brain, the *old mammalian*, is many tens of millions of years newer, and a far more sensitive and sophisticated brain, common to all mammals as they flourished after most reptiles of the dinosaur age perished and became extinct, about 60 million years ago.

The third brain, the *new mammalian*, relatively speaking came into use only recently—it has been around so few millions of years that in evolutionary terms it may be considered, especially as developed in humans, as brand new. It is enormously more subtle and resourceful than the old mammalian, and many times as large as the other two brains combined. (See Figures 1, 2, and 3.)

It can be helpful, in considering the present roles of these three brains, to be a bit fanciful and view them as so many familiar personalities. The reptilian brain can be related to an elderly person who happens to be very

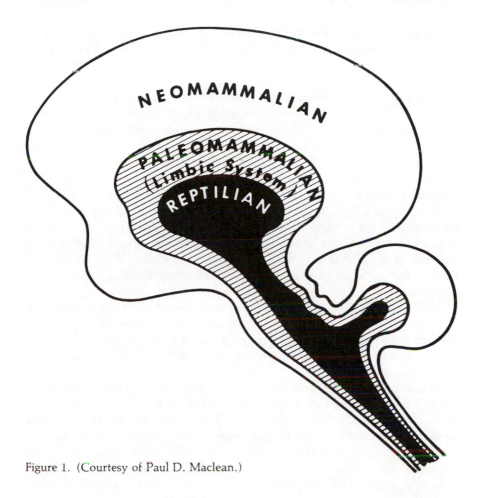

Figure 1. (Courtesy of Paul D. Maclean.)

set in his ways, not too sensitive to what is happening around him, and apt to make oversimplified judgments: absolutely yes or absolutely no, very good or awful, content or terribly unhappy. On the same analogy, we can see the old mammalian section as more alert, much more discriminating as to the details of what is happening—as some middle-aged person might be. While this brain is not nearly as rigid as the older one, the personality is that of a man who has developed accustomed ways of doing things, and departs from them only under some persuasion or pressure. The newest brain compares to an extremely intelligent, highly sensitive young person, quite aggressive in apprehending the situations he is in, and far more open to considering and using new inputs and behaviors—in fact, willing to do things because he *hasn't* done them before, and interested in probing, testing, and experimenting to learn more about his world.

If we visualize a grandfather, father, and son (or equivalent females) with these personalities forced to live and work together—all being partners in a business, let us say—it is obvious there will be constant conflict and contention. This is one of the key aspects of our present day understanding of the human brain that MacLean has brought more clearly into view. *Our brain as a whole is not harmonious, but works through a precarious, constantly changing balance of these three "partners."* This concept throws startling new light on human behavior and makes it far more understandable.

The triune brain results from nature's parsimony. In evolution, old structures are rarely cast off. Rather, they are modified (as seal legs became flippers, or the delicate bones of our inner ear were remodeled from ancient gill structures), improved, or added to. Thus the reptilian brain was retained even as something better evolved, and the newer brain was placed more or less on top of and around the older one. When a still better kind of brain evolved, it again took form over and around the older two.

MacLean uses Figure 1 to diagram this relationship. We should bear in mind that this whole discussion is a simplification to great degree; but for our present lay purposes it can help us get oriented rapidly to major and only recently understood aspects of the fabulous apparatus we are considering.

(The bulge in the diagram, representing the *cerebellum*, or "little brain," is a specialized structure, a tiny but most effective computer that coordinates physical movement. As we learn a new dance, we are at first clumsy, but with some practice the cerebellum gradually smooths out the muscular activity, and then stores the program for future use. If one learned to ride a bicycle as a child, and then got on one after a forty year lapse, the skill would be quickly brought back into use—proof that it has indeed been stored in the brain. See Figure 4.)

The diagram in Figure 2 is one I use to suggest, very roughly, the great differences in size and "power" of these three brains. As we see, the old mammalian has many times the resources of the oldest or reptilian brain; and the newest brain—we loosely use the terms *neocortex* and *cerebrum* in referring to it—dwarfs the others.

In Figure 3, the cerebrum is shown with a gray tone. Here we are looking up from below at the relatively huge neocortical "cap" of newest brain. It accounts for about five-sixths of the entire brain. In all the animal kingdom, there is nothing like this structure. More than any other, it makes us uniquely human.

Virtually all of the learning we are concerned with in formal education must occur in this cerebrum. The two older brains have no speech beyond sounds and cries, and in a sense, some expletives. All the language and symbols that we use, written or oral, and our ability to act

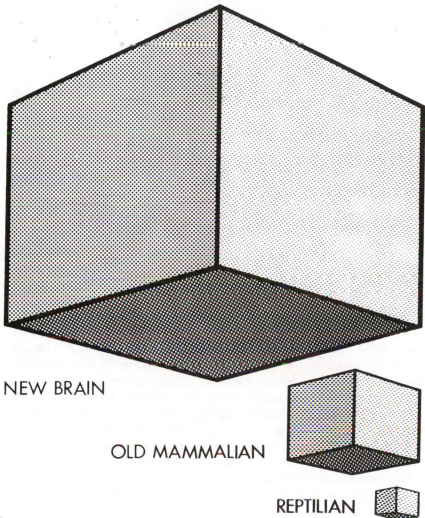

NEW BRAIN

OLD MAMMALIAN

REPTILIAN

Figure 2.

and plan and review abstractly—out of the presence of the people or things or events we are dealing with—stem from this newest brain.

We see then the basic limitation of trying to learn much about higher human capacities and typically human behaviors by studying cats, rats, hamsters, or other small laboratory animals. If we found engineers studying horse-drawn wagons in the hope of coming to know more about automobile engines, we might well think them mad. Yet generations of behaviorist psychologists who have written about humans have based their experimental work very heavily on animals that have only the merest trace, in brains hundreds of times smaller to begin with, of this

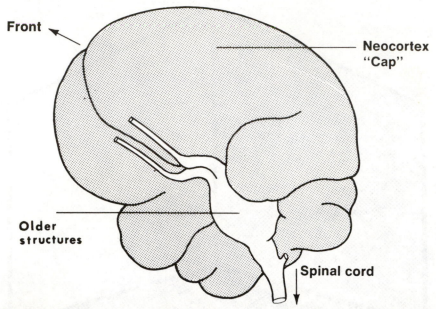

Figure 3.

new kind of brain tissue that dominates the human brain. MacLean has shown that when such animals' neocortex is prevented from developing during gestation, their behavior without it scarcely changes at all![4]

Rat psychology, still taught in the great majority of colleges that give courses in psychology, is often applied to humans, sometimes with and sometimes without apology. It is hardly surprising that it has provided us with a large supply of misleading answers and distortions, and a vocabulary, that now put roadblocks in the way of coming to understand human learning in terms of *human* brains. For example, many uses of "stimulus" suggest a passive person who must be influenced by outside events, rather than an active, goal-oriented person who *selects* inputs to a great extent. "Motivation" suggests the rat in the box which must be starved into action the experimenter wants, rather than inborn and acquired goals that don't have to be externally provided.

The two older brains by no means are unimportant in human affairs—quite the contrary: we are only beginning to grasp their full influence and roles. But enough is known about the human brain to say bluntly that the learning *teachers* are concerned with involves the great cerebrum *that humans have and small animals lack.*

As we shall see, there are other reasons why study of rats can and does grossly mislead us if it is extrapolated to apply to humans. Humans are not rats grown large. Our brains have developed in unique ways and to a unique degree, and we must clear away the mistakes of the past—no matter how brilliant or famous the investigators who made them—if we are to utilize the insights now possible.

The human brain is also remarkable in another way. More than 2,000 years ago Hippocrates, often called the father of medicine, observed that our brain, like that of all mammals, was double. That is, as we see in Figure 4, it quite clearly has two cerebral hemispheres, left and right, which are roughly (but not exactly) mirror images; and the older structures also tend to divide or duplicate left and right.

In animals generally that have backbones, this dual formation reflects symmetrical organization of the body and limbs on either side of the backbone, except that there is a crossover: the left side of the brain, in motor areas, controls the right side of the body, and vice versa. In humans, however, as huge nonmotor areas of the brain have developed, the two sides or hemispheres of the cerebrum have taken on *different* tasks—which suggests a great increase in our brainpower. This division of labor appears to be another exclusively human characteristic, although possibly other large-brained animals may have this arrangement to a much smaller degree. Nothing comparable has been found in small animals.

In the great majority of people, the left hemisphere is concerned with language. The right side is assigned concern with spatial matters, recognition of faces and many visual patterns, and music. But this does not mean the division is complete. The main connection between the two halves of the cerebrum is a bridge called the *corpus callosum*, which consists of 200 million or more nerve fibers. They carry information both ways. (Any time we consider the brain, we must bear in mind that it has no truly separate parts—every part is elaborately interconnected with all other parts, and the brain always operates as an intricate *system*, a whole.)[5]

Some fascinating experiments have been made with small animals, especially cats, which have been operated on to cut connections between the two sides of their brains. Some human studies have also been possible with individuals whose corpus callosum has been severed for medical reasons.[6] The results make dramatic the two-sidedness of the human brain; but it must be noted that the divided brain is very far from normal, and in a real sense maimed.

Work in this field has given rise to some important findings, but also a considerable amount of nonsense and unfounded speculations about "right side" and "left side" aspects of personality.[7] It has been widely suggested that the left side is logical and sequential, because it is usually so involved with language. But a moment's thought should show that language is anything but logical, full of often absurd twists and turns, accidents and usages, and words and phrases that have dozens of different meanings in various uses. Nor is listening to speech more sequential

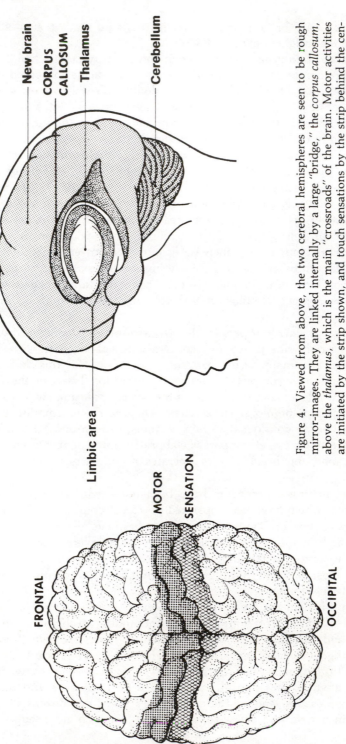

Figure 4. Viewed from above, the two cerebral hemispheres are seen to be rough mirror-images. They are linked internally by a large "bridge," the *corpus callosum*, above the *thalamus*, which is the main "crossroads" of the brain. Motor activities are initiated by the strip shown, and touch sensations by the strip behind the central fissure. Vision is processed mainly by the lobes (occipital) on both sides at the very back of the brain. The neocortex or "bark" of the cerebrum is about 1/8 inch thick. The deep folds of the brain allow more surface for its tens of billions of neurons, but the entire neocortex has only about the area of a large kerchief.

than listening to music. In my view, the two sides of the cerebrum work very much the same way, but have different assignments.

In education, where modern knowledge of the brain tends to be scant, ill-founded notions of left/right functions have had all too hasty and wide circulation, leading to some bizarre activities and enthusiasms. To be sure, the classroom operates in a highly verbal fashion and so gives rise to the objection that it "educates only half of the brain," as some observers put it. But the brain existed long before classrooms, and so can hardly be dependent on what happens in a few hours of school to become "educated." Too simple, too direct conclusions will only compound the error that has long existed.

In still one more way the primacy of the human brain needs to be emphasized, and that is size, or more precisely *number*. The key cell of the brain is the *neuron*. There are a number of types, but they share many characteristics. In essence they are *switches*, and correspond to the diodes and transistors of an electronic computer, but the human switches are enormously more complex. It may be hard at first to view "thinking" as the throwing of great numbers of switches to one position or another, but that is exactly what goes on in a computer and in the brain.

The number of neuron switches intimidates us: the brain has often been said to have 10 or 12 billion neurons; but most researchers today would put the estimate much higher. (For technical reasons, accurate counting is very difficult.) I prefer a compromise figure to use as some sort of guide: 30 billion. The main point is that the numbers we are dealing with are staggeringly large.[8]

Further, some types of neurons may typically be connected to 10 thousand, perhaps even 20 thousand, other neurons. The network that results means that the possible pathways soar up into the trillions and above.

Consider the retina of one eye. It will have more than 100 million receptors for tone (black and white) called *rods*, and roughly another 7 million or more *cones* that enable humans—unlike rats and most other animals—to perceive a wide range of colors.[9] If in daylight we take a quick glance around us, these receptors receive and begin the processing of billions of bits of information in the second or two the glance took. At that point we have not seen anything: we can be said to "see" only when the information has been filtered, reduced, consolidated, transmitted to a way-station midway in the brain, then to areas on both sides of the neocortex in the very back of the brain, where they are interpreted. Only then do we know what we have seen. If we expose a camera, the film records whatever information entered. It does not edit or interpret. But the brain does both. If we are looking on a lawn for a dropped earring, for example, what we see will not be the same as our intake when we are looking at the condition of the grass and its need for cutting.

If this rather discursive chapter has served its purpose, it will have provided some orientation to the brain—as we know it scientifically today—that can serve in concentrating on what new knowledge can be most useful to teachers and instructors in any learning situation. It will help readers push aside, I hope, the grossly wrong and misleading mountain of old psychology that has become a major obstacle, as well as Freudian and other (often superheated) word systems.

To understand and work successfully with humans we must recognize the dominance of brain, and that the human brain is the one that has evolved in our skulls, an apparatus to marvel at and approach in awe.

Suppose I ask you to design a glove, giving you all the resources you may need. You know the shape of the hand, so your glove will emerge, we can feel confident, with provisions for one thumb and four fingers, a palm and wrist, and flexibility to permit finger movement. You will know that the hand's fingers bend forward, but not back, and that the thumb swings in from the side. Because you know the shape of the hand, and its general functions, you can hope to design something that will fit and work on actual human hands.

If next you are asked to design instruction to fit the brain, you see immediately that you cannot hope to do that job unless you know the "shape" of the brain, and its main functions. Without good, hard, realistic knowledge, a design group might labor a thousand years and get nowhere—indeed, in over two thousand years of teaching, a vast amount of effort has produced only fragmentary useful knowledge of how humans learn! We see teachers and instructors failing and frustrated wherever we look—now more than ever, because more is being attempted.

But today we have the knowledge to design brain-fitting, *brain-compatible* instructional settings and procedures. The "compatible" concept may startle us, simply because we are not used to it in education. All around us are hand-compatible tools and machines and keyboards, designed to fit the hand. We are not apt to think of them in that light, because it does not occur to us that anyone would bring out some device to be used by human hands without being sure that the nature of hands was considered. A keyboard machine or musical instrument that called for eight fingers on each hand would draw instant ridicule. Yet we force millions of children into schools that have never seriously studied the nature and shape of the human brain, and which not surprisingly prove actively brain-antagonistic.

We know less than we might and will; but we already know amply enough, I contend, to bring about instructional environments that, being compatible, will produce huge gains in learning.

NOTES

1. *Scientific American*, September 1979, p. 45.
2. *The Science Teacher*, April 1978, p. 32.
3. MacLean's triune brain concept has been presented by him in a number of articles, some not readily accessible. See "The Imitative-Creative Interplay of Our Three Mentalities," in Harold Harris, ed. *Astride The Two Cultures* (New York: Random House, 1975), and "A Mind of Three Minds: Educating the Triune Brain" in *Education and the Brain*, 77th Yearbook of the National Society for the Study of Education (Chicago: University of Chicago Press, 1978). I am here using his concepts freely, based on his writing and conversations with him, and gratefully acknowledge his generous and helpful interest in Proster Theory and my debt to him.
4. See *The Science Teacher*, April 1978, p. 37.
5. For a thorough, up-to-date discussion, see Sally P. Springer and Georg Deutsch, *Left Brain, Right Brain* (San Francisco: W. H. Freeman and Co., 1981). The book can serve as an excellent corrective for many current, over-simplified, speculative, and inaccurate notions. The authors remark: "Our educational system may miss training or developing half of the brain, but it probably does so by missing out on the talents of both hemispheres" (p. 192).
6. For two famous articles on the subject, see Roger W. Sperry, "The Great Cerebral Commissure," *Scientific American*, January 1964, p. 42; and Michael S. Gazzaniga, "The Split Brain in Man," *Scientific American*, August 1967, p. 24.
7. Dr. Robert D. Nebes of Duke University Medical Center has pointed out: "Many people are now attempting to superimpose upon the anatomical and functional duality of the brain many of the philosophical and spiritual dualisms which have fascinated man over the centuries." See *UCLA Educator* (Graduate School of Education), Spring 1975, p. 16.
8. The estimate of neurons keeps rising. Some leading neuroscientists use 100 billion now, and a similar figure may be used for *glial* cells, which likely have some close supporting role for neurons.
9. In his fascinating book, *Eye and Brain*, 2d ed. (New York: McGraw-Hill, 1972), R. L. Gregory says: "If the whole population of the United States of America were made to stand on a postage stamp, they would represent the rods on a single retina." I have used a more conservative estimate. Gregory compares cones to "the population of greater New York."

6

It is the plasticity of the brain which enables learning and
memory to occur, and which impresses upon each individual
a set of unique and characteristic behaviors, thoughts and
emotions . . . allowing essentially the same brain which once
served the cavemen to enable today's men to operate in the
vastly more complex environment that they have themselves
created.

—STEVEN ROSE[1]

Bad Fit: Old Brain in a New Setting

The human brain represents such an incredible achievement of nature that
we can best build comprehension of it, I think, by approaching it from
many directions, trying to grasp some of its main features, rather than
trying to examine it segment by segment under some neat scheme.

Suppose yourself a villager from a remote mountainous region of central Asia. Abruptly, you are transported and set down in the heart of
New York City. You have never seen a city or even a paved street, nor
automobiles, stores, electric lights, elevators, telephones, electronic
devices, railway stations, libraries, business offices, hospitals . . . nor
anything like this crowded, fevered activity, but now you are asked to
make sense of all these strange and often alarming miracles, and to
understand what is meant by the term "modern city."

When one is introduced to the brain as currently understood, after
much brilliant scientific investigation, there can arise a similar sense of
being overwhelmed, and of difficulty in believing. Even as our Asian

villager looks at a 100-story building, it may seem hard to credit. That automobiles are moved by motors which burn a liquid like water and can carry one a mile a minute on thousands of miles of paved highways seems obvious nonsense. Even more so is the information that the picture seen on a television screen is actually of events taking place in another country, and that the voice heard originates not in the box but far away. Most of us, when we come to learn something about the brain, have almost no notion of how it might work; but when we do find out, the answers may strike us as so unexpected and different from all we ever heard before as to strain acceptance.

It may help if we look on the human brain as nature's most fantastic product, and one that took at very least a half-billion years to bring into being. Remarkably much is known about its evolution, and the patient tracing of its development greatly helps understanding (and believing) its present shape and functions.[2] In the same way, some knowledge of early humans and of how they lived and *what they needed to survive* can be extremely helpful.[3]

In a modern industrial society, we take for granted living in a highly structured way. If one is employed, one likely goes to a fixed place of work, on scheduled days, for largely prearranged hours, for example. One's home probably is a permanent address for years at a time. Of necessity, ordinary, routine life requires complying with a great many rules and regulations, from staggeringly complex income tax laws to requirements on how and when the garbage is put out for collection. Lawyers, accountants , surveyors, insurance adjusters, and a host of other specialists pore over fine print to decide fine points that may affect our welfare greatly. All of this may be bothersome, and at times exasperate us beyond easy tolerance, but we are used to such demands as a part of living in communities.

Thus it takes considerable mental effort to move in imagination back in time, to conditions 15,000, or 30,000, or more years ago. Our forebears of those days lived under sharply different conditions. They existed by gathering and hunting—and in the colder, more difficult climates, by gathering and hunting just about anything that might help sustain life. In general, humans developed as *nonspecialists* (in contrast to most animals), able to find and willing to eat almost anything nourishing, and able to survive a great range of climatic conditions in a wide assortment of physical environments.

Study of early humans suggests strongly that in most areas they long lived in bands of around 50 members that had no fixed abode, and that moved around as necessary to find food, water, shelter, and materials. (Not until roughly 10,000 years ago did humans settle down and form cities.) We can see why early humans became better able to survive as they developed bigger, more subtle, more flexible brains, capable of an unprecedented amount of learning. We became "brain freaks" because having a certain type of brain, of enormous capacity, meant continuing to live and breed where less brain, or a different shape of brain, could not cope with the struggle.

How long have humans been on earth? New discoveries of remains keep changing the picture, but some rough approximations can be advanced. It seems probable now that our evolutionary line branched off from that of apes perhaps six million years ago. Good evidence exists, from very recent findings, that creatures that walked fully upright were around about four million years ago (even their well-preserved footprints have been found!)[4] It seems quite clear that evolution gave rise to quite a variety of human or hominid species that found footholds for awhile in many parts of the globe. All humans have died out save *Homo sapiens*, which is to say modern man, which is to say *us*.

Our immediate ancestors, often called Cro-Magnon (and best identified as the creators of the magnificent cave paintings in France, Spain, and elsewhere) seem to have arrived relatively suddenly in Europe, probably having come from the east, although origins are mysterious. These people almost certainly existed a minimum of 50,000 years ago, and in all likelihood much longer than that.

Neanderthal man, often identified with the brutish cave men of popular legend, apparently coexisted with Cro-Magnons, and we must assume lost out in a competitive struggle for living space. They were far from being the hunched-over, apelike creatures they were portrayed to be in the last century—some anthropologists believe that a normally dressed and groomed Neanderthal, alive among us today, would attract no particular notice. Their brain, it is startling to learn, was if anything larger than ours on average—but with a difference. The Neanderthal skull lacked the high, bulging forehead that we typically exhibit. The front of the head was lower and flatter, and relatively more of the brain space was further back.[5] The significance of this difference may well have been critical, as we shall see when we look more closely at the prefrontal lobes of our brain, the portion immediately behind the forehead. It is the part of the brain that directs the rest of the brain—a "top executive office" that handles more intricate and longer-term plans.

Of vital interest to teachers (and parents) is the fact that this prefrontal section does not fully mature until at least the late teen years—for practical purposes, we can say, until adulthood is achieved.

If we think about hunting, an activity that appears to have had a powerful influence on our history as a species, we see quickly that there is a huge gap between happening on an animal and killing it for meat and skin, and hunting in the full sense of a planned, organized, directed mutual activity involving many individuals, using well-developed weapons, equipment, and tactics, and communications. Only an impressively large and sophisticated brain can conceive and carry out so elaborate an enterprise; or build a fishweir to trap that prey; or go through all the steps of finding suitable stone and fashioning it into exquisitely worked tools.

The ability *to make plans and carry them out is the key aspect of human intelligence*—a truth that becomes strikingly evident when we look at our history as humans. Yet as teachers or instructors we commonly do the planning ourselves (or follow those laid down for us by authorities), and the students, told what to do at every turn, get little chance to use their brains in this basic, human way.

If we look at these ancestors during their long gathering-hunting period we also observe—with perhaps more than a little shock—that *they had virtually no need or use for what we now commonly term logic*, meaning a step-by-step, linear, sequential way of thinking. The concept of logic did not appear for tens of thousands of years. These people slowly but steadily made progress in many areas, developing, for example, clothing, tools, weapons, utensils, housing of various sorts, dance, music, painting, sculpture, ever richer language, religion, social customs, mining, uses of fire and the great invention of cooking, and far more. It can be a shock to realize that in none of this huge area of achievement—the broad foundations of society, culture, and technology—did they employ or need what today many commonly tend to esteem as the best, most respectable, most admirable, type of thinking: Greek-type intellectualizing and sequential logic.

We use the term logical very loosely in ordinary speech and writing. Logical thinking can mean sensible, or unemotional, or correct, or resultful mental effort, and one can be complimented on a logical presentation, for instance, when more precisely it has been simply thorough or orderly.

Here I am using the term with a specific meaning: the kind of logic in which there is a deliberate progression from fact or observation or statement A to B and then to C, D, E or more, all connected by "therefore" or "it follows that...." This was the broad method we associate—a bit too simply—with the philosophers of the Golden Age of Greece, and others who for centuries in Western culture held to related approaches. We find similar chains of reasoning in the more familiar areas of mathematics. And we usually use at least the appearance of this format when findings or studies are being reported to others. The businessman who has reached a conclusion after mulling over a complex matter does not tell his board that he woke up one morning feeling convinced that a proposed plant should be delayed. Rather he presents logical arguments to support that position. The scientist who stumbles on a solution to a knotty problem several times and finally realizes that he has something of value often isn't eager to detail what now seems his stupidity in not grasping implications sooner. He writes a formal paper, in the standard format, presenting his findings logically.

There seems nothing wrong with this procedure. It serves usually as a convenience to all. But we are misled if we assume that the decision or discovery was *arrived at* logically.

On the other hand, the rise of modern science after 1500 (to use a loose, general date) depended heavily on *breaking away* from this sequential logic. For example, it was long held that God had personally set the planets in their paths; that what God does must be perfect; that the circle is the perfect form; that the planets must then move in circular orbits. For centuries astronomers strongly influenced by this logical word chain failed to make sense of their observations. When finally Kepler saw that undeniably planets move in ellipses, he was dumbfounded and horrified, and not a little fearful of how his discovery might be received by authorities. Even Newton, often thought of as the embodiment of logic and mathematical thought, has been described by Keynes as a "magician" who looked on the whole universe as a riddle set by the creator. Keynes writes: "By pure thought, by concentration of mind, the riddle, he believed, would be revealed to the initiate."[6] The study of the struggle of early scientists to free themselves of the medieval magic and alchemy traditions as they moved toward natural philosophy or science suggests the difficulties and even guilt many people feel today in escaping this traditional respect for sequential logic.

Even if "pure thought" of this kind were the highest achievement of humans (a proposition I for one would deplore), plainly it is quite a recent activity—let us say developed within the last 2,500 years. And we need only look around us to see how little part it plays in literature, arts, politics, economics, science and technology or our daily life, today. It played *no* part in the lives of our direct ancestors of 10,000, 20,000, 30,000, and more years ago—this kind of logic had not yet been invented.

In mathematics, for example, we have need for precision and ability to deal with complex problems. They did not exist in gathering-hunting societies, where (we can feel fairly sure from ancient evidence and study of now vanishing primitive, essentially Stone Age peoples) they counted only to four or five, then went to a few, many, a lot, a great many, or some similar progression. They owned no land, conducted no business, used no money, had neither lawyers nor engineers, and handled decisions by recourse to traditional ways, permeated by elaborate magic.

These ancestors had, to the best of our knowledge, brains virtually identical to those in our heads today. They had taken their shape over millions of years, and had reached their present level of development at least this long before "civilization" and the rise of kings and increasingly intricate trade, record keeping, laws, and interfaces.[7] The implications of this must be seen as staggering for anyone engaged in instruction: *the brain we are dealing with was not "designed" by evolutionary needs for logic, manipulation of symbols, for dealing with tight, sequential structures or word-systems, which today constitute the main concerns of conventional schooling and much training.* While the flexibility of the brain is so great that it can usually, under duress, accommodate such matters, they go against the grain—*they are superimposed, not natural.*

In *The Universe Within*, Morton Hunt observes:

> For many centuries, philosophers and others who have studied the human mind have believed that reasoning takes place according to the laws governing logic. Or rather, that it should, but regrettably often fails to do so. . . . Such is the tradition that runs unbroken from Aristotle to Piaget. But the findings of cognitive science run counter to it: logical reasoning is not our usual—or natural—practice, and the technically invalid kinds of reasoning we generally employ work rather well in most of everyday situations in which one might suppose rigorous deductive thinking was essential.[8]

Among those who study the human brain and its workings, this view is hardly likely to cause surprise or disagreement, but the growing recognition of the artificiality and limitations of logic, so long enthroned, has still not come to general public awareness. The idea can prove upsetting to those who have never had occasion to question or examine a very old and broad tradition.

Instruction that recognizes and is compatible with the natural (precivilization) brain functions will go far faster and be vastly more successful—much as it is easier to go with the current of a swift river than against it. For example, the human brain typically does a poor job of routine mathematics. Even the astronomical and navigational tables of premachine days were full of errors. We are delighted to turn such chores over to "stupid" computers that can do them a millions times as fast, with very high accuracy. As scientists, engineers, and inventors rid themselves of this symbol-pushing burden, it becomes all the more apparent that large advances in these fields come almost entirely from accidental discoveries, blunders that in effect produced unplanned experiments or observations, transfers of ideas and techniques from one field to another, pure serendipity, chance conversations or shared knowledge, fortuitous incidents, and above all, intuition. Creative people have frequently reported waking up in the night with the solution to a problem suddenly "delivered" by the brain, or having ideas and solutions "pop into the head" while doing chores or relaxing. "Sleep on it" can be productive advice: the morning often produces insights or decisions based on nonlogical, nonconscious brain activity.

The brain our *Homo sapiens* ancestors had 50,000 years ago worked well enough to allow humans to survive and become dominant in all habitable parts of the globe. To expect this successful, established brain to change its natural ways of working to conform to schools—a very recent invention—or to readily accept demands that it work logically seems to me obviously absurd. We have all been brainwashed by the undeserved respect given to Greek-type sequential logic. Almost automatically curriculum builders and teachers try to devise logical methods of instruction, assuming logical planning, ordering, and presentation of the content matter or skills is the plainly correct and only respectable approach to take. They may have trouble conceiving alternative approaches that do not go step-by-step down a linear progression, and not surprisingly little research on these alternatives has been encouraged.

It can be stated flatly, however, that the human brain is not organized or designed for linear, one-path thought. Most electronic computers do work linearly, one step leading to the next (although most recent, sophisticated types give hints of not remaining quite so limited). But the brain operates by *simultaneously going down many paths*. We identify an object, for example, by gathering information—often in less than a second—on size, color, shape, surface texture, weight, smell, movement, any sound it may make, where it is found, what else is with it, any symbolic information with it (such as label or price sign), how other people are responding to it, and so on. All of these investigations by the brain to answer the question "What is this?" go forward along many different paths, and branching paths, among the brain's trillions of connections, at the same time. From the vast information stored, answers or tentative answers get pulled out, then assembled, compared, and interpreted by, if possible, extracting a pattern.[9] The whole miraculous procedure bears no relationship to linear processing; it helps explain the incredible subtlety and sensitivity of the brain—and why, in recognition, a six-year-old child can with ease outperform the costliest electronic computer devised by a small army of able engineers.

To try to demand that this brain meekly put aside its mighty resources and go step-by-step down one path is to cripple and inhibit it. We can all too readily see that fundamental error built into curriculum almost anywhere we look, and observe it in action in any classroom where teaching goes on conventionally, uninformed and unguided by knowledge of the brain's real nature. Experienced teachers widely agree that the more different approaches they use the better the learning is apt to be, yet most yield to pressures for logic.

Once we begin to look critically at this notion of teaching in logical sequence, we can see that usually a further giant—and utterly wrong—assumption has been made: that if a subject is fragmented into little bits, and the student is then presented with the bits in some order that seems logical to somebody, the student will be quite able to assemble the parts and emerge with the whole—even though never given an inkling of the whole! Teachers may or may not have some grasp of the whole; certainly there are many who in mathematics or science simply present the parts by following a text or manual. But even if they do possess the large concept, the synthesis they demand of the student may be extremely difficult. We would hardly expect that if we show a young boy all the parts of a television, he would then be able to assemble the receiver, and also grasp how the interrelated, interdependent components work *as a system*.

The logic that seemed apparent to the curriculum builder, textbook writer, or teacher may be invisible and incomprehensible to the student. The parameters, the structure, are missing. Consider the ordinary jigsaw puzzle given to a child, with a picture of the completed assembly on the box, and rectangular edges that provide helpful clues. Most children soon become quite adept at such puzzles. But now substitute a puzzle that is "blind," with no picture, and an irregular shape. The child has a far harder time—as do most adults. The diagramless type of crossword puzzle provides a similar example. The author knows what the diagram is, but the solver flounders. The brain has a hard time extracting patterns, or making sense, of the effort.

This kind of difficulty, there is much reason to believe, underlies our greatest educational embarrassment, the reading problem. Conventionally students are given a mass of parts, in the form of rules, phonics, and a long list of subskills. Students who have learned to read before school or who have at least grasped what reading is *for* may be able to survive this kind of instruction, but the majority become confused and distracted, make little sense of what is going on, and may never in their lifetimes become able to read with ease, confidence, or enjoyment.[10]

The instruction of older, advanced, sophisticated learners can be "logically" organized with less harm. A group of process chemists, for example, can be taught the functions of a new catalyst this way, because they already have an established, broad understanding to which the new material can be related. (It would still be hasty to conclude that the logical presentation necessarily will work best.)

If we look around us at how most learning occurs, we quickly see that it is not by logical sequence or blind assembly. Watch Little Leaguers play baseball, and you can marvel at their skill and grasp of an intricate game, and related knowledge, picked up over years in random fashion, mostly by participation as opportunity offered. If the game were to be taught logically, there would be a unit on its origins and history, on terminology, on the playing-field geometry, on hitting, on fielding, on baserunning, and so on down a long list. Obviously, none of the players learned this way. They "picked up" the game by exposure over many years, in an utterly random, unplanned way—perhaps with no formal teaching at all. If they do get coaching, it will likely be on a purely individual basis, as the need is seen. For example, the coach, after an infielder misses a stop, shows the player how to handle that situation; or works with the catcher to explain how to throw off the mask to catch a high pop foul.

Or compare how people learn to drive cars, an activity that demands life-and-death knowledge and expertise. Most of us begin learning about steering, braking, obeying traffic signals, parking, and servicing the vehicles from early childhood on, both in the family car and through toys. Even those who at some point take instruction in driving come to it with a great deal of accumulated knowledge of hazards, types of roads, normal driver behaviors, and much more. We acquire our ability to use and manage cars in a dominantly *random* fashion. And we are likely to see clearly, if we will but look, *that the great majority of major abilities we have came about in just this manner.* Once, after presenting these ideas to a school's faculty, one teacher approached me to ask whether I would care to be operated on by a surgeon who had had this random kind of training. I had to point out that there was no other kind: surgeons get their real preparation as interns and residents, dealing with a variety of cases as they happen to come into the hospital!

The incident suggests how blinded we can be by unexamined conventions. Almost anywhere we look in formal schooling and instruction, we see teachers using plans and curricula that have won approval as being logical and well ordered; and often they must submit daily or weekly lesson plans. While many instructors struggle to follow these guides (some resolutely ignoring outcomes that suggest how wrong they are), it is scarcely hard to find many others who cheerfully depart from or ignore the plans about as soon as the ink is dry. But plans are respectable and mandatory.

The "teaching machine" stands as a vivid demonstration of how far off the mark logical presentation can be, even when the most basic tenets of behavioral psychology are applied. Essentially, the teaching machine is any of many devices that present the material, broken down into small bits, in some logical, sequential manner, providing immediate right-answer/wrong-answer feedback and perhaps some kind of quick "reward." For a period of years, mostly during the sixties, millions of dollars were poured into this so-called programmed instruction. (The word *programmed* should not be confused with similar terms I will shortly be using in another connection.) These teaching machines were hailed as the perfect application of behaviorist psychology, and bound to bring striking results.

But the actual outcome was a fiasco. Little gain in learning effectiveness was found, but much in student boredom. Even more devastating was the painful discovery that it seemed to make little difference whether one sequence of presentation was used rather than another, or whether or not reward was given, or whether the machines were used in schools (where they might be resented as a threat to teachers' employment) or in commercial applications. The big companies that had hurried to get in on this bonanza soon hurried to get out and end their large losses, and the teaching machine virtually disappeared from sight and thought. (In my opinion, the machines do have some limited usefulness, if the programs reflect brain-compatible approaches rather than old psychology and somebody's notion of logical sequence.)

Currently, the sharp drop in the cost of small computers has encouraged many schools to put in a few, mostly on a window-dressing basis.[11] What computers can do, of course, depends on the programs or software available, just as the usefulness of a book depends on its contents. In at least some instances, the software seems to be an effort to revive the teaching-machine approach in new guise, a lamentable misuse of a device which has large potentials.

Many adults engaged in planning or carrying on instruction operate from a conviction that certain learning must occur before other learning. It seems obvious, for example, that numbers must be learned before any mathematics can be tackled. But when carefully studied, truly mandatory sequences, even ones as simple as this, become hard to find. Without numbers, using modular blocks or counters (bottle caps will serve nicely) children beginning mathematics can acquire some major, fundamental concepts such as *square, equation, reversibility,* and *conservation* that routine teaching may fail to give them in nine years. In fact, if the numbers are learned in rote fashion as the names of symbols not clearly understood, the numbers can easily get in the way of the more basic concepts! In reading, we see many children who learn a number of words *before* they master the alphabet; and an excellent way to begin mastery of their letters can be to begin with such words, especially their names. And since words in print are neatly spaced apart, unlike spoken language where the pause *within* a word may be greater than between words, grasping the convention of evenly spaced words may be one of the earliest needs for a sound start in reading.

Since the brain is indisputably a multipath, multimodal apparatus, the notion of mandatory sequences, or even of any fixed sequences, is unsupportable. Each of us learns in a personal, highly individual, mainly random way, always adding to, sorting out, and revising all the input — from teachers or elsewhere — that we have had up to that point. That being the case, *any group instruction that has been tightly, logically planned will have been wrongly planned for most of the group,* and will inevitably inhibit, prevent, or distort learning.

Let me hasten to say that this does not imply that instruction should be haphazard and uncontrolled, or that the students should do the planning — which would likely be worse than that of the school's. Rather it suggests that (1) the planning should have broad objectives clearly defined, with specific *learning achievements* listed rather than only teaching lessons or units; (2) planning should be for long periods of time rather than a few hours, days, or weeks; and (3) it should not try to move large groups of students along in lockstep, but instead be highly flexible and designed to accept individual progress over a wide range.

Perhaps there is no idea about human learning harder to accept for people familiar with classroom schools than this: that the ideal of neat, orderly, closely planned, sequentially logical teaching will in practice, with young students, guarantee severe learning failure for most.[12]

The most common, visible experience conventional classroom teachers have is that of presenting lessons this way and finding that extremely little learning results, as revealed by recitation, tests, or homework. Yet teachers cling to this procedure, often feeling inadequate or guilty and suffering what it is now fashionable to call "burnout." Instructors have been led to believe, as they believe day will follow night, that students *should* learn from logical, sequential presentation.

The reason, it seems to me after many discussions with teachers, is simply that *school*, from early childhood, has meant above all an institutional building characterized by *classrooms* in which active, aggressive *teaching* goes on, much as a tennis court is a specialized place where tennis is played. Teachers feel that they have been *hired* to teach, that they must control all that goes on in the room, that it is rather wicked and reprehensible not to "drive" the class, and that their status with coworkers will rest mainly on their aggressive teaching/management effort, as perceived by others. Not to *teach* in a school is seen, or felt, as a breach of behavior, something like going to church in a bathing suit or eating popcorn at a symphony concert. School does not signify a place where continual study goes forward on how best to educate children for the world they are in, but rather a building dedicated to certain old, little-changing activities. One enters the building as an employee to perpetuate these rituals; otherwise one goes elsewhere. As Katz has said,

> Education has not suffered from any freedom granted teachers to run schools as they see fit; it has suffered from the suffocating atmosphere in which teachers have to work.[13]

Slavin maintains:

> The problem is not with teachers, who I find to be overwhelmingly dedicated and hard-working, but with the classroom system they are trained to use that guarantees failure for so many.[14]

A disconnection, indeed a head-on contradiction, exists between the aggressive behavior forced on teachers and what they have observed about learning. They know that students in today's information-rich world learn a great deal, though not necessarily what fits the official curriculum, and that both youngsters and adults "pick up" learning in quite random, happenstance fashion from all sorts of exposure. Such useful competencies as money management, cooking, home maintenance and repair, games and sports, crafts and hobbies, health care, and social skills are plainly acquired this way rather than through course work; and even where courses are taken (Chinese cooking, home electrical wiring, bridge) they often have defined limits and can account for only a fraction of the whole attainment. Again and again teachers find students have specific learning only because of a family trip, the mother's political activities, the father's occupation, what has been seen recently on television or read, or some chance event. A child can spell *Labrador* and locate it on a map because he has been given a Labrador puppy!

Administrators, too, know how ineffective logical instruction can be, but even those who would like to make change may dread the task of challenging the logic myth, either with their public or with their teachers. They too are caught in the system's trap. Few have had the experience of bringing about anything more than marginal student-learning gains, except where exceptional failure has been rectified to usual failure—and even that is rare. But as public pressures for learning increase, the logic myth can become intolerable.

The conventional, outworn system supports the logic myth, and the myth supports the system. The brain approach offers at least the hope of cutting this Gordian knot, by changing the question from "How should schools be run" to "What does the brain, the organ for learning, require for best learning to occur?"

To summarize:

1. The brain, the organ for learning, took its shape tens of thousands of years before Greek-type, sequential logic was invented. *No part of the brain is naturally logical.*

2. While a logical arrangement or presentation may serve the needs of transfer of information between people with good knowledge of the material, this kind of presentation produces consistently very poor learning results with students not already familiar with the material. Students, *prior* to learning, cannot perceive the logic that may seem apparent to the instructor after learning.

3. Since we learn individually in different, multipath sequences, with previous *individual* experience as the foundation to which more learning is added, logical group-instruction inevitably produces a large degree of failure.

4. Examination of the *useful* learning we have acquired as adults shows that the great bulk has been acquired at random, from random experience.

5.   The tremendous acceleration of learning and human capabilities attributable to science resulted from breaking away from old-style logic, especially word-theories. The great bulk of scientific and technical discovery has occurred fortuitously, in the course of persistent effort and high input.

6.   We can point to little in our world that has been accomplished by old-style, sequential logic, especially *word* logic.

7.   Our view of logic as respectable, high achievement rests on a surviving tradition that has been little examined.

8.   Sequential logic plays a large part in the building of curriculum, and the conventional classroom school system has become a specialized place where this kind of aggressive teaching is done. Alternatives are little considered. Both teachers and administrators are caught in the trap. Considering the requirements of "the organ for learning" may suggest a new and fruitful path.

NOTES

1. *The Conscious Brain* (New York: Alfred A. Knopf, 1973), p. 173.
2. For a fairly technical, brief discussion, see C. U. M. Smith, *The Brain* (New York: G. P. Putnam, 1970), Chapter 10. This excellent book by an English neuroscientist is a standard work, and gives a very complete overview of recent knowledge of the brain.
3. See John E. Pfeiffer, *The Emergence of Man* (New York: Harper & Row, 1969) for an outstanding and readable as well as broad-ranging discussion. The same author's *The Emergence of Society* (New York: McGraw-Hill, 1977) deals with prehistory in remarkable detail.
4. See *Science News*, March 31, 1979, p. 196, for pictures of the "Leakey footprints" found in northern Tanzania.
5. For a comparison of brain sizes, see Richard E. Leakey and Roger Lewin, *Origins* (New York: E. P. Dutton, 1977) pp. 198–199 and accompanying text.
6. See Hugh Kearney, *Science and Change 1500–1700* (New York: McGraw-Hill, 1971). John Maynard Keynes, the economist and student of Newton, is quoted on p. 190.
7. "There is no sign of further brain development...if changes have occurred they have been very small." Steven Rose, *The Conscious Brain*, (New York: Knopf, 1973), pp. 139–140.
8. Morton Hunt, *The Universe Within* (New York: Simon and Schuster, 1982), p. 121.
9. "The initial stages of processing are largely parallel rather than serial, and feature analysis results from patterns matching rather than from feature detection." See Karl H. Pribram, in *Cognition and Brain Theory*, Spring 1981, p. 110.
10. Recently, the listing of reading subskills appears to have exploded, in some quarters, climbing into the hundreds—in one large city school system reportedly over 800, until the teachers rebelled! A list of 250–300 is fairly typical of this approach.

11. In factories, offices, laboratories, warehouses, etc., equipment is justified on a "trade-off" basis: the saving in labor will offset the expense of the machines (or they will permit doing what labor alone cannot do). In schools, as a rule, any equipment for instruction becomes a cost to be *added* to that of the teacher's salary, if classroom structure prevails. If machines get put in as more than window dressing, we can expect to hear loud protests from teachers' unions.

12. Benjamin S. Bloom has stated explicitly: "Group instruction, as presently used in most countries of the world, may approach optimal qualities of instruction for only a small proportion of students in a given class. Even when this is the case, it is likely that the majority of students in the class are paying a heavy price for the ways in which the different qualities of instruction serve the special needs of a few members of the class." *Human Characteristics and School Learning* (New York: McGraw-Hill, 1976), p. 136. Bloom echoes a complaint common ever since there were classrooms, but perhaps too seldom made today.

13. Michael B. Katz, *Class, Bureaucracy, and Schools* (New York: Praeger, 1971), p. 131.

14. Robert Slavin, in *Character*, March 1981, p. 12. Dr. Slavin, a professor at Johns Hopkins University, is widely known as a leader in cooperative learning approaches which permit students to aid one another, rather than always compete.

7

Pattern-matching is inherently pleasing because that is what
our minds are designed (or programmed) for.... Quite apart
from anything the teacher does...the student, being human,
is a pattern-finder and a pattern maker. Possibly the greatest
obstacle to our making use of this not very startling principle
is our ingrained notion that education is the acquisition and
mastery of new material. What we "teach" and they do not
"learn" is the "material."

—DAVID B. BRONSON[1]

First Fundamental:
The Detection
of Patterns

Let me suggest that there is no concept, no fact in education, more directly important than this: the brain is, by nature's design, an amazingly
subtle and sensitive *pattern-detecting* apparatus.

The brain detects, constructs, and elaborates patterns as a basic,
built-in, natural function. It does not have to be taught or motivated to
do so, any more than the heart needs to be instructed or coaxed to pump
blood. In fact, efforts to teach or motivate the pattern detection, however
well meant, may have inhibiting and negative effects.

This key aspect of learning—patterns, and the related concept of
modelling—has scarcely penetrated education at all, as a glance at the index of almost any major work on learning will show. Yet it can hardly be
called a new idea in psychological, ethological, or behavioral contexts.

Over 20 years ago, for example, Aldous Huxley remarked:

> What emerges most strikingly from recent scientific developments is that perception is not a passive reception of material from the outside world, it is an active process of selection and imposing of patterns.[2]

The findings Huxley was referring to were well known then in fields of effort more scientifically oriented than education, and are thoroughly established now. We do not have to look far for confirmation—our own daily experience tells us most convincingly that the brain has this ability, to astounding degree.

Imagine that you are attending a sporting event. People by the thousands stream by you as you find your seats. The merest glance tells you they are all strangers. But now you see two figures that immediately seem familiar, and in a moment more you have identified them as former neighbors, Francine and Peter. Somehow, your brain has picked them out of this vast crowd, and somehow it has separated them from all the other people you know, so that you can identify them, greet them warmly by name. There is no question that our human brain can do this—usually effortlessly. (If we simply look at what we all can *do*, we begin to glimpse the enormous powers of the brain.)

The feat is even more impressive when we note that you haven't seen these friends for three years, had no expectation of running into them here, both are wearing clothes you have never seen them in previously, Francine has a new hair style, Peter has sunglasses that partly hide his features, and you first saw them as familiar while they were still 50 feet distant.

Clearly the recognition does not stem from any logical process. You did not rely on checking Francine's height in inches or Peter's weight in kilos. You put no measure to their middle finger bones, Bertillon fashion,[3] nor used a color-comparison guide to determine the shade of skin and hair. While Peter has a distinctive walking movement, and Francine an animated manner, trying to measure or describe these exactly would be a giant and perhaps impossible task. Let us grasp firmly the clear fact that your brain does not work that way, but that it did quickly, accurately accomplish recognition and identification by some other means.

Nor was this an isolated, unusual phenomenon. If I were to display before you a teakettle, a paint brush, a handsaw, a necklace, a bunch of carrots, a pencil sharpener, a violin, a telephone, a sweater, a microscope, a toothbrush, a slice of Swiss cheese . . . you would recognize and name each in the same effortless way. You were plainly not born knowing these objects, so all this recognition has been *learned* at some time between birth and the present.

We are so used to looking at something and knowing at once what it is that we come to think of the process as automatic. Comparisons of eye and camera may also mislead us. A camera can't recognize anything; our brain can, using not only vision but also hearing, smell, touch, and other aspects of senses. When we are exposed to something quite unfamiliar we simply do not see it in any meaningful way. To look into the inside of some complex machine, for example, may be to see nothing but a confusion of forms. Or, in a museum, observe some fossilized remains of various ancient animals—you see only a vague shape, in contrast to what the curator sees. I often dramatize this in workshops by showing participants a newspaper in Arabic or Chinese. They see only squiggles that a moment later they are hopelessly unable to reproduce—although a person knowing the language would see headlines, news, information at a glance.

If we take a teakettle and place it before a month-old infant, the baby will regard it with momentary interest, but plainly can have no notion of what it is. As adults we can see a vessel, a handle, and a spout; the baby can see none of this arrangement, but only edges, shapes, and surfaces.

The teakettle we so easily recognized as a teakettle, we find, is not exactly like any we have seen before: it has a different design, and is made of unfamiliar materials. The paintbrush, too, can be of size and construction that is new, and the necklace or telephone unlike styles familiar to us, but unless the new design is bizarre to an extreme, our recognition of the object remains quick and easy. Moderate differences do not bother us a bit.

Consider, for instance, the 20 different forms of the letter *a* that appear in Figure 5. Despite the range of shapes they cover, we have not the slightest difficulty seeing any one as *a*. We could, of course, carry this recognition much further, to letters of many larger sizes, in different colors, formed of lights or dots, put into three-dimensional materials, tilted, laid on the floor, or seen on the side of a moving vehicle. Even holding just to typefaces available for printing, there are literally thousands of alphabets; and handwritten, drawn, or printed forms add thousands more. There is no *letter a*, only a pattern we conventionally call *a*.

In the same sense, teakettle, paint brush, carrots, violin, and the rest are patterns. Our knowledge of the pattern is what enables us to say what

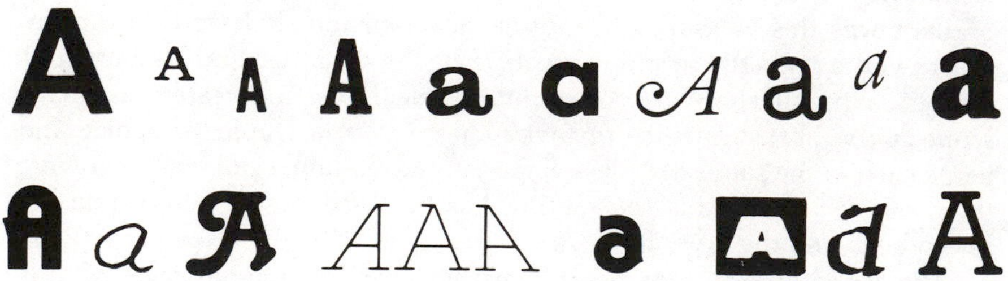

Figure 5.

object is what. But we are by no means limited to hard, visual patterns—we can detect and learn those far more subtle or complex. In time adults normally become quite familiar with such patterns as pet, park, affection, boss, fraction, racial bigotry, jealousy, or adventurousness.

Just how the brain detects and recognizes patterns cannot be explained easily or quickly, except to observe in general that it is an astoundingly powerful, subtle kind of computer with billions of neurons at its command. We do know in a general way that *the brain detects characteristics or features, and also relationships among these features.*

The lower-case letter *a*, for example, may consist of a hook facing left which may take a variety of forms,

connected to a more or less round enclosure form.

The relationship between these shapes has a key role. If the hook were 20 centimeters tall and the enclosure only a millimeter high, one might have much difficulty seeing it as an *a*. On the other hand, there is a different pattern for small *a* that lacks the hook altogether,

that we can readily learn to accept as an alternate. It is illogical to have two forms, but as we have seen, logic is the least of the human brain's concerns.

Our brain's ability to detect and identify patterns is not least impressive for its flexibility. We can feel quite certain about an identification without any need to have perceived most or even many of the features and relationships. With experience, in fact, we normally become extremely expert in using *clues* (sometimes the term *cues* is used in the same sense) to make very rapid judgments. We would not be able to read at all if we had to study all the features of letters. The capable reader goes much further, and uses clues for whole words and even phrases.[4]

A variety of studies seem to make clear that the brain naturally works on a *probabilistic* basis. We do not have a kind of adding machine that must reach a correct total. Seeing a creature that has four legs, a tail, fur, and barks as we enter a friend's home, we jump to the conclusion that the pattern "dog" applies. Why is it not "cat"? Because we pick up *negative* clues: cats do not bark, and ordinarily do not come aggressively to the door when a stranger enters. Why is it not a monkey? Because the relationship of limbs is different. Situation also gives clues: we expect to find a dog in a home often. If we visited a zoo and found this same animal exhibited in a cage, we would assume it was not a dog, but some similar creature—dogs are not displayed this way, we know.

In practice our pattern-detecting ability depends on clues from vision, hearing, touch, or other senses, on the behavior and relationships, on the situation. In short, *the ability depends heavily on our experience, on what we bring to the act of pattern detection and recognition.* The more experience tells us what we are likely to be looking at, or dealing with, the less detailed, feature-type of information we need to jump to a probably correct conclusion.

One reason we can rely on little information is the sensitivity of the brain to negative clues. When they do not fit together rapidly within a pattern, or when one or more are jarringly strange or contradictory, our pattern-detecting apparatus quickly senses something wrong. Suppose that I am going to the house of people I have visited a couple of times before, on a dark suburban street where house numbers are hard to find. As I walk toward what seems to be the house, I come to a flagstone walk. It "doesn't feel right," and prompts me to retreat and try the house next door. Or perhaps one day I am looking at what I identify as a grackle, an all-black bird, when I see a flash of color on the wing, and must revise my identification to "red-wing blackbird."

In the instance of recognizing friends Francine and Peter, only a yes/no kind of decision was involved—they were those individuals, or they were not. But more common is the detection and recognition of patterns *within* patterns, which leads to finer and finer discriminations, or what can be called *categorizing down*, a most important aspect of learning. Thus one can detect the pattern "animal," then categorize it down to "dog," and then to "Afghan hound." Or observing a number of people at a gathering, it may be categorized further by noting that the people are festive to "party," and then on seeing a cake with candles to "birthday party." But we must note that a person coming from a country where birthday cakes are not a custom would not be prepared to interpret that clue the way we so easily do. Again, what the observer *brings* to the recognition act in experience, in previously acquired knowledge, plays a critical part.

In small children, the process of enlarging pattern detection and extending and refining categorizing-down chains often may be clearly observable. A girl just starting to talk may say "Daddy!" while pointing to any man who comes into sight—we gather she is using *daddy* in the sense of *man*. A little later, guided by such feedback as "No, that is not daddy—daddy is at work," the child may point to only men who come into the home, whether young cousin or elderly grandfather, as *daddy*. With further feedback, categories gradually get straightened out, and daddy is used to mean only one person. It may take much longer for the child to become clear on the fact that her friend also has a daddy, and some years to grasp the relationship; and still more to be able to categorize surely from people to males, to relatives and friends, neighbors, policeman, mailman, Mr. Jackson (who lives next door), as well as boys, girls, and many subtle relationships.

This is the process of learning that Frank Smith and others call aptly "making sense of the world."[5] The ability that even infants have to gradually sort out an extremely complex, changing world must be considered astounding, as well as evidence that this is the natural way learning advances. But more surprising still is the clear fact that the learner manages to learn *from input presented in a completely random, fortuitous fashion*—unplanned, accidental, unordered, uncontrolled.

Consider, for example, the sorting-out problem a child has to grasp such patterns as *dessert*, *pie*, and *cake*. Since a great variety of dishes may constitute dessert, the child must extract the idea that meals have a sequence (programs) and dessert is the last course. It must also learn that *dessert* does *not* mean a particular dish, or even a tight group or class of dishes. *Pie* presents few problems to an adult with years of experience to draw on, but to a toddler an open pumpkin pie, a crusted blueberry pie, and a lemon pie heaped with meringue topping present little in common. Or does *pie* mean *round*, the most obvious feature? Unfortunately many desserts are round, particularly cakes—which vary from pie-like cheesecake, to coffee cake, to layered birthday cake elaborately iced and decorated.

While adults and older siblings may provide gentle, casual, and almost incidental corrective feedback when the child calls a pie a cake or does not regard a fruit dish as dessert and cries in frustration, it would be most unusual for anything much resembling teaching or instruction to deal with dessert, pie, and cake as subjects. Yet in a few years, from this confused, random exposure and experience, the child has extracted the patterns, gradually coming to see which features and relationships have significance in which settings, and which can be ignored. Frequently, however, the child extracts a pattern that sooner or later has to be revised in the light of new information. For example, everything if let go falls—until someone presents a gas-filled balloon. Children often find the need for revision disturbing. The world keeps proving more complicated, with more exceptions, than they previously thought. Adults have a similar problem, we may note; in time they may become less flexible, cling to old ideas, refuse to revise, and even try to avoid the input that forces the contradiction. "Nonsense...that's crazy...I won't listen... don't bother me!"

Perhaps even more amazing is the obvious ability of children in the preschool years to extract rules about language from the quite random speech they hear about them and engage in. We hear such expressions as *sheeps* and *deers*, plurals plainly not picked up from adults or older children. The added *s* makes unmistakably clear that the small child has extracted a general rule for plurals—end with the *s* sound—and is applying it even to what will later be learned as special exceptions. In the same way, most youngsters will use such constructions as "Tommy hitted me," or "I falled down," showing that they have extracted the pattern of past tense and the use of the *-ed* sound, again even where there are common exceptions. Yet it would be absurd to expect a three- or four-year-old to explain *plural* or *past tense*.[6]

The familiar experiences I have recited are so prevalent that we cannot reasonably doubt that all of us, at whatever age, do extract patterns from the quite random, confused mass of input we are exposed to in the course of normal living. Nor can it be easily denied that the great bulk of practical knowledge we have and use to get along in the world is acquired this way.

My experience in presenting these ideas to educators has shown that they are likely to meet heavy resistance. That is understandable: from earliest exposure to school, as we noted in the last chapter, just the opposite approach has been relied on. The notion has been drummed into our heads that we learn by being *taught*, and conversely that if we aren't taught we won't learn. The teaching, educators in particular are endlessly told, must be planned, tightly organized, sequential, logical. Much of the skill of instructors, in fact, is taken to lie in exactly this area, and they may even be hired on the partial basis of "competency" tests which are intended to demonstrate ability to perform in this manner, and partially on having completed courses addressed to this behavior.

There enters also the concept of discipline, the old notion that the child is inherently evil, lazy, disinclined to learn, and incompetent, and therefore must constantly be pushed ("motivated"), threatened, held in check, and often reprimanded or punished. In most conventional school systems, for example, the most admired teachers are those who most effectively *control* their charges, quite regardless of how much learning results, or how much the students acquire a lifelong distaste for schooling and the subjects involved. And as I think anyone who has dealt with many parents of school children will attest, not a few of them *want* the school or institution to punish and discipline their offspring and make them "toe the line." Today's parent is often frustrated by efforts to exercise control from the home, and the task may be wishfully turned over to the school.[7] Pressures, stated or unstated, may be put on those in instructional roles to apply a repressive approach.

Nevertheless, the observations we have examined here cannot be wished away, any more than can the learning failure that brings our schools and colleges, and much other training, into increasing disrepute. The real nature of natural learning may be startling and disturbing; but once it is seen it is hard to deny.

It leads to a Proster Theory definition of the *process of learning: the extraction from confusion of meaningful patterns.*

In my view, the great bulk of general learning occurs in this way. The only other important method is via rote. But while "pure" rote learning—straight memorization—appears quite possible, as in the case of learning the alphabet in sequence, it seems apparent that even rote learning is greatly helped by detecting the patterns involved where patterns clearly exist, as in the multiplication tables. Or consider the marching band, very much a rote activity. If the patterns in the music and in the maneuvers are apprehended, learning can be far faster and surer.

If my acquaintance with the educational literature serves, attempts to define the process of learning have been rare, indeed. The one that emerges from Proster Theory, I submit, can be immediately useful in guiding educators to effective, brain-compatible approaches.

Pressures of tradition have blinded education to what, once seen, stands obvious:

1. The brain is by nature a magnificent pattern-detecting apparatus, even in the early years.
2. Pattern detection and identification involves both features and relationships, and is greatly speeded up by the use of clues, and categorizing down procedure.
3. Negative clues play an essential role.
4. The brain uses clues in a probabilistic fashion, not by digital "adding up."
5. Pattern recognition depends heavily on what experience one *brings* to a situation.
6. Children and youngsters must often revise the patterns they have extracted, to fit new experience.

This learning process, being natural, appears effortless, but (as we are about to examine) it requires much random, fortuitous exposure and experience—*input.*

We need only look around us to see people learning well and easily this brain-compatible way: preschool children rapidly making sense of their home world; middle-school youngsters racing ahead as they follow enthusiasms for electronics, animal care, music, some form of collecting, a science or some aspect of history; teenagers successful in an apprentice situation, or adults in on-the-job training; middle-aged and older people evolving a specialization. In contrast we see formal, classroom-type, aggressive teaching producing boredom, conflict, misbehavior, apathy, cheating, confrontations, acceptance of minimal standards, and every variety of learning inadequacy.

NOTES

1. "Towards a Communication Theory," *Teachers College Record*, May 1977, p. 453.
2. See *The Human Situation* (Lectures at Santa Barbara, 1959), Pierro Ferrucci, ed. (New York: Harper & Row), p. 173. Also compare George A. Kelley, *A Theory of Personality* (New York: W. W. Norton, 1963): "Man looks at his world through transparent patterns or templates which he creates and then attempts to fit over the realities of which the world is composed" (p. 17).
3. Alphonse Bertillon (1853–1914) devised an elaborate system for positively identifying individuals in spite of their variety, intended primarily for criminal justice purposes. In due course fingerprinting proved far simpler, but the system is still made use of in part by physical anthropologists.
4. John B. Carroll, speaking of the mature reader, suggests that it may be true, "astounding as it may seem, that reading is based upon a capability of instantly recognizing thousands or even tens of thousands of individual word patterns, almost as if words were Chinese characters not structured by an alphabetic principle." See *Theories of Learning and Instruction*, 63d Yearbook of the National Society for the Study of Education (Chicago: University of Chicago Press, 1964), p. 341. For actual use of Chinese, see "American Children with Reading Problems Can Easily Learn to Read English Represented by Chinese Characters," by Paul Rozin and others, in *Psycholinguistics and Reading*, Frank Smith, ed. (New York: Holt, Rinehart and Winston, 1973), Chapter 9.
5. See Frank Smith, *Comprehension and Learning* (New York: Holt, Rinehart and Winston, 1975), p. 1. The "make sense" concept has been widely expressed by brain researchers. Harry J. Jerison, for example, suggests that reality is "a creation of the brain, a model of a possible world that makes sense of the mass of information that reaches us through our various sensory (including motor feedback) systems." See *The Human Brain* (Englewood Cliffs, N. J.: Prentice-Hall, 1977), p. 54.
6. This stage of language acquisition is familiar to many parents, teachers, and others who have contact with children, and has been discussed by many psycholinguists. See, for example, James Britton in *The Teaching of English*, 76th Yearbook of the National Society for the Study of Education (Chicago: University of Chicago Press, 1977), p. 11.
7. The George H. Gallup poll of public attitudes toward public schools has persistently shown "lack of discipline" as the number one problem, though this view is not shared by teachers or administrators. Just what is meant is not too

clear, and possibly some racism could play a part. The last poll suggests, however, that schools are seen as lax, not demanding homework or themes, or high standards of performance and behavior. Perhaps a general uneasiness finds expression this way. It should be noted, however, that the discipline figure has never risen above 30 percent, until the 1982 poll, published in September, amplified the question; then 70 percent expressed concern as "very serious" or "fairly serious." The annual polls are reported in *Phi Delta Kappan* each fall.

8

Man is no longer viewed as a passive sponge soaking up a flood of information. Instead, he is seen as an active seeker of information which he then filters, processes, encodes, and organizes into complex hierarchical schemes.

—DAVID L. HORTON
AND THOMAS W. TURNAGE[1]

Input: Essential for Pattern Development

Again, let me introduce an idea that has had little attention in education, at least in the special sense that it is used within this discussion.

The concept of *input* is a key factor in Proster Theory, and like some other aspects of natural, brain-compatible learning, becomes obvious enough once one has had a good look at it. I suggest that input has critical importance in any kind of learning situation, whoever the learner and whatever is to be learned.

The process of learning has been defined in the preceeding chapter as the extraction from confusion of meaningful patterns; input can be thought of as *the raw material* of that confusion: what is perceived by the individual that bears on that particular pattern in any way.

Think of a suburban boy of around 13 who has as yet still no clear concept of what is meant by *city*, although his teachers, his texts, and others have often presented that term. It often can seem incredible to adults that children or adults less experienced in some specific area do not grasp a pattern idea already familiar to those who have had occasion to understand it. Once we have done the pattern extraction—a gradual process—and melded the concept into our collection of patterns, it seems so *obvious* that we have trouble putting ourselves into the brain of someone who has not acquired the pattern!

But how will our youth come to understand the main connotations of *city*? If he is told in school that a city is a place where many people live close together, he may fail to see why his suburb is not a city, or at least those poorer or denser parts of it. If he has contact with commuters, he may very well come to assume that city means Boston or St. Louis or Los Angeles, or whatever city his community is a suburb of. If he visits that city occasionally, he may be impressed by traffic, noise, many stores, busy sidewalks, bridges, tall buildings, apartment houses, or development houses—yet a visit to another city may bring quite different features to his attention, such as zoo, museum, or historic places. A trip to a downtown part of a nearby suburb may impress him as being to a city, since he experiences crowded sidewalks, many stores, movie houses, considerable dirt, and apparent crowding—yet if he refers to this place, technically a village, as *city* he may be corrected or receive some kind of negative feedback, such as being tolerantly laughed at.

It seems simple enough to *tell* him what city means. But it isn't simple, when we get down to trying it. A dictionary may say something like "a closely settled place of significant size," or "a chartered, incorporated municipality," but such definitions simply introduce new questions. With little effort, the boy can learn by rote a "right answer" to give in school, but that hardly amounts to pattern extraction. It may function more as a cover-up answer to conceal uncertainty or lack of insight. (The distress of teachers who by accident discover that students able to give right answers actually don't understand at all has long been familiar. Most adults, too, experience chastening moments when by some circumstance they discover that conventional right answers are like thin ice over a deep lake of ignorance or misconception.) Educators have long been aware that "telling" methods can prove extremely ineffective in instruction—though one can find them in heavy use almost anywhere teaching is going on.

One difficulty with telling arises from the failure of words to convey much meaning except as the hearer already has experience and extracted patterns to relate the words to. Consider a stockbroker saying: "If you sell a security to establish a loss, you must wait 30 days to buy it back or it will be viewed as a wash sale, but the waiting period does not apply to gains." Or an engineer: "If you put the recorder in the record mode, the erase head will wipe the tape before the new signal is encoded." Or a musician: "Since the B-flat clarinet is a transposing instrument, the note you play from the written music will actually sound a full tone lower." All of these serve as perfectly clear, simple statements provided one brings to them understanding of what is being talked about, but otherwise they can be quite baffling. Telling and lecturing works somewhat better with *older* students and adults as noted earlier, simply because with age the chances increase of having the experience necessary to comprehend what is said. The inexpert or insensitive lecturer assumes that if the language used is correct the meaning will be conveyed, and may be astonished to find the audience grasped very little, or got even that twisted.[2]

Verbal communication, we must remember, also depends heavily on *nonverbal* aspects. The speaker's tone of voice, gestures, expression, and muscular tensions add a great deal to properly receiving what is intended. In most instances, the *setting* also contributes heavily. If two cars collide, the conversation that follows between the drivers is likely to illustrate both points. Inquire in a kitchen, "How do I light the oven?" and the query will probably be heard and understood. Ask the same question in the same way while strolling through a meadow, and the response will likely be some form of "Hunh?" A question or remark out of context often will not be heard correctly, because *even hearing speech intelligibly demands bringing information to the situation.*[3]

While the telling kind of input may be the commonest and usually the easiest to provide, it can prove ludicrously ineffective even in supposedly simple situations. For example, a primary-grade teacher tells the students to "leave an inch margin at the top, put your name at the left and the date on the right." The instructions are full of booby traps. How much is an inch? Adults know fairly well, young children may not. What does *margin* mean? One does not automatically know—it calls for extracting a pattern of blank space around written matter, a sort of frame. To some children, leaving space may seem rather wicked, especially if they have been urged not to waste paper. In any case, does the inch refer to space above name and date, or only to space above the main text or answers? What is the date, and how does one write it—is the first figure the month, or day? Since the name of the day seems most familiar and impor- tant to the child, should *Tuesday* be put down? Which was to go left and which right? What does *name* mean—first name or full name? (I have seen a child baffled by the term *first name* and insistent that her name was the only name she ever had!) A child's given name is intimately important, and so may be put first, in great capital letters.

I discovered how hard it can be even for perfectly competent adults to follow simple but unfamiliar directions when for a period my wife and I instructed in folk dancing. "Start with your left foot," would appear clear enough, yet normally solid citizens would stand immobile, leap forward madly, or start with the right. As we shall discuss shortly, people may lack the *program* necessary for doing what somebody asks, directs, or recommends, and purely verbal input may prove at best only slightly helpful and at worst devastatingly confusing.

What may be called the *reality principle* (with no reference to uses of that term in other fields) seems to be a neglected but critically important aspect of input. Shooting at a basketball hoop offers a sharp example. One shoots; the ball either goes in or it does not. If it misses, the shooter does not need anyone—a second party—to say whether or not the shot was successful. That information, which we can loosely call *feedback*, comes *directly and usually instantly from the reality*. In a playground, one can see some children climb to the top of a pipe structure or fort, and others who stop sooner out of caution or difficulty. None need to be told whether they went all the way or not—they clearly see for themselves. If an adult making a repair tries to remove a stubborn screw, it comes out or it does not, or it may stick halfway. The real outcome is apparent.

In a teaching situation, however, the second party often plays a dominant role. The student performs a task, but the degree of success may not be evident from outcome, from reality. Rather, the student must wait for the teacher or instructor to evaluate and provide verbal feedback. A letter to the mayor (not to be sent) is written as an exercise; it is not a real letter, a communication intended to produce some outcome. It is essentially a fake, though it may more kindly be called simulation, or practice—the great bulk of what students write throughout the 12 grades usually has this fake quality, and most of what is given verbally, too, is not communication in the sense of producing real outcome. The student who writes an essay or report or answers a verbal question on science or civics or history *becomes dependent on a teacher telling whether it is right*, and normally right will mean *comforming to authority*—that of the teacher or some more distant decider—rather than resulting from any feedback from reality.

Under these conditions, a new, distorted form of reality enters: pleasing the teacher, getting a good mark, passing an exam all affect the outcome, and the material or skills supposedly being learned become simply a means to that end. Clever students figure out what kind of response the teacher or instructor is looking for, and try to provide it. Even very young students expertly read the nonverbal signals a teacher may emit as to what answer or behavior is wanted.

With younger children especially, a further problem arises: it can be hard to separate what the authority, the teacher, feeds back about the quality of the answer from how the authority views the *person* who gives it. The student whose efforts frequently produce negative or put-down evaluations may soon conclude that these reflect personal dislike or disapproval. We can hardly pretend that the child may not have good reason for such feelings where social class or minority factors enter in, or when the student is perceived as smart-aleck, contrary, annoying, or withdrawn because of superior ability or background. Teachers, being human, tend to view *their* personal standards and values as, in broad, those to which students should aspire. And since teachers usually work under stressful conditions within an antique and brain-antagonistic structure that creates constant difficulties, *they quite naturally seek the right answer that fits most neatly into their plans and rituals for conducting the class.*

The *feedback from authority* in classrooms also suffers from the widespread belief among teachers and instructors that praise is helpful to learners. The rationale for it probably most used stems directly from behaviorist psychology: the praise is intended as a reward, and the giving of rewards is supposed to be motivating—two ideas that could hardly be more obviously wrong, yet persist. We need merely watch the youth endlessly shooting baskets; or the girl who pursues anything to do with horses beyond her parents' patience; or the high school student (of my acquaintance) who became an expert on snakes despite the opposition and revulsion of family and friends. Strongly "motivated" people seem largely disinterested in casual, superficial praise. Teacher praise often takes the form of "Very good," or "Fine, Thomas, you are really trying!"—remarks that appear to applaud effort and behavior rather than outcomes. As schoolteachers have become more conscious of criticism of racial, class, and ethnic prejudice or bias, the use of praise with such students appears to have increased. In at least some cases, the consequence has been serious: students have been led to believe they were doing well when actually their progress was very poor.

The input of the classroom—almost any kind of classroom—thus proves on examination to bring a largely undesirable feedback from authority rather than feedback from reality; and it is further overladen with the problems of personal relationships we have noted. But in addition, *the overall, gross input tends to be extremely low.* As many observers have found,[4] the conventional classroom characteristically has low input, incessant interruptions for control, discipline, announcements, etc., and a great deal of time allotted to noninstructional activities (settling down, distributing materials, record keeping, changing classes, organizing, and the like). A good part of the time nothing that an observer could call input even by the most generous definition is being presented.

But we are still not at the end of the classroom's input deficiencies. From a Proster Theory viewpoint, the worst aspect of classroom input is oversimplification. By tradition and logic, teachers try hard to organize their presentation and reduce its apparent difficulty, in the firm belief that the simpler, more restricted, and clearer the input, the more easily and certainly it will be grasped. Such is the power of logic and common sense that the constant failure of this belief to produce the hoped-for results may be given little heed; and when I show educators, from their own familiar experience, that the *process of learning is the extraction of patterns from confusion—not from clarity and simplicity*—they usually find that view at first hard to credit, and a distressing turning upside-down of previous assumptions. (At one session, an experienced teacher was moved to burst out, "That's *crazy!*" —a thought I'm sure others were able to suppress. The history of science, of course, is one of "crazy" ideas: Gallileo maintaining that light objects would fall as fast as heavy ones of the same shape; Pasteur insisting that microbes could cause many diseases; Einstein submitting that atoms could be converted into an enormous amount of energy. Good scientific ideas are not correct because they sound crazy, but they often do until they become familiar.) To clarify the process of extracting from input let us return to our youth and his problems in grasping the pattern of *city*. Over a period of time, let us say, he receives these inputs:

- Driving into the nearby city, he observes a sign, "City Limits." He also notices that the pavement changes at that point from concrete to blacktop.
- Looking at a road map before a trip to the circus he notices "City Limits" borders for the first time.
- He hears in a news broadcast that the city population has fallen, and exact figures are given. He has never had a clear idea of what population meant, but gets a hint that a city has a finite number of inhabitants.
- A family friend, in the city fire department, talks about fearing for his job because the city is short of money. The boy gathers that the city must be an entity, if it can be short of funds like a person.
- He sees a documentary on television about the excavation of an ancient city.
- His mother asks a friend who has returned from a European trip what cities she visited.
- After a heavy snow storm, the news on television shows several views of residential streets and reports that citizens are angrily complaining to city hall about delay in plowing.
- His brother, attending college in a distant city, mentions on a visit that it is holding a celebration, having become a city 150 years before.
- His father remarks that a local milk strike will not stop supplies "in the city," and if necessary he will bring some milk home.
- He hears a remark that only a few American cities are large enough to support a symphony orchestra.

From such bits of input, random and unorganized, over a long time period, our youth gradually extracts a fairly accurate and complete pattern of *city*. The concept may continue to sharpen and deepen. He may come to understand why early cities fostered craftsmen and specialists, and were essential to bring about various cultural gains; that there can be "twin cities" such as Minneapolis and St. Paul; and that the word city is related to the ideas in *citizen* and *civilization*. The features and clues in time add up to permit recognition and discrimination.

This is the process of learning that leads to an individual possessing an inventory or collection of patterns, eventually in great number—possible in humans because of the huge size of the brain and its more than 100 billion specialized cells.[5] To repeat, the brain was designed by evolution to deal with *natural complexity*, not neat, "logical" simplicities, not lesson plans. Should that surprise us?

In educational institutions of almost any kind we find virtually an obsession with *levels*: the curriculum and the work must be exactly tailored to the age and supposed competence of the students. But let us shift once more to what we can commonly see children achieving, and be guided by realities, not word-systems.

In the typical home, young children will have some toys and playthings, and perhaps a few pieces of furniture such as crib, highchair, low tables, or scaled-down chairs. *But by and large our children grow up in adult homes.* The great bulk of the furnishings, the bathrooms, the kitchen, the stairs, the windows, the light switches, the utensils, plates and cutlery, the car, the appliances, the tools, and much more are all on adult scale. The conversation that goes on, most of the programs on television and radio, the newspapers and magazines, the entertainment, the sports, games, and fitness activities will normally be heavily adult dominated. In short, while the presence of children certainly will be evident in a house and will markedly affect family lifestyle, there still can be little question that children are brought up in adult environments. Even the more fortunate child who has a good supply of children's books, records, and playthings will still be overwhelmingly exposed to adult input. And as we have noted, learning in this environment—language, daily activities, operation and use of physical facilities, extraction of interpersonal relationship patterns, acquisition of traditions and development of many skills—usually proceeds so rapidly and well we scarcely give heed to how successful it is.

But the moment the astonishingly competent five-year-old enters the environment of formal education, he or she will likely be treated as idiot and incompetent. The child who has explored the neighborhood must now get into a line to move to another room. The girl who has acquired a vocabulary of thousands of words, covering a great range of length and complexity, must now work with a basal reader that uses 300 selected, short, "regular" words. The real world outside is banished in favor of whimsy and talking animals. The boy who has learned to ride his bike around his home, with frequent spills and minor injuries, must now use blunt-end scissors; the girl who is a daring, confident, aggressive athlete must now be protected (the school might be sued.) At every turn, the rich, random input of the real world is choked off, and the sparse, anemic, filtered, highly contrived input of the school is substituted.

When I visit classrooms, I make a habit of observing the entire room to see what I can find that is real world, rather than "school stuff." In many cases, I have found almost nothing in the room that could be put under the first heading. The world of reality, the world of rich, random input, has been totally shut out.

Does my stress on random input suggest that instruction must be muddled, unplanned, even unfocused? I am of course not putting forward that view at all. The key thoughts are these:

1.   The extraction of patterns in real life is from confusion, because real life input is fortuitous and random. The brain copes readily with such input. Broadly planned instructional input can well be random, covering an area but not with effort to be logically sequential, over an extended period of time.

2.   The learning process, by which patterns are sorted out so that increasingly more sense is made of a complex world, goes on incessantly, and each individual, in a purely individual way, gathers features and clues that gradually mount up. Progressively, the pattern is grasped more sharply and greater discrimination becomes possible.

3.   Direct, orderly, lesson-plan verbal presentation may ignore the fact that the learner must bring information *to* the words to understand what is being said.

4.   Feedback is essential to the learner to verify that learning has occurred. Feedback from reality will usually be clearer and more acceptable than second-person feedback from authority, which introduces complicating, distorting aspects.

5.   Schools and schooling tend to put strong emphasis on trying to adjust the level of input to the supposed students' level, ignoring the excellent learning children plainly do accomplish in the home and other adult settings. To achieve low enough level, the real world is excluded.

6.   The classroom tends to seriously reduce the amount of input that students get, and thus the amount of raw material from which patterns may be extracted. The variety of activities permitted may be severely restricted.

If now we turn from criticism to construction, we can see that brain-compatible instruction calls for a greatly increased amount of input—I believe, from observation and some experimenting, a feasible goal would be around ten times as much as the typical classroom provides. Further, the input should be random rather than orderly—youngsters simply do not learn from a logical presentation, first because what is logical to one person often makes little sense to another, and second because they need to come at a pattern—as in the city instance—many ways, from many directions, in many contexts to flesh it out. *Repetition* within the input can be valuable, however, because what a particular brain is not ready for at one time will be welcomed and utilized at another.

Suppose we give 25 jigsaw puzzles, all the same, to 25 students, whether children or adults. Each will put the pieces together in a different sequence and at varying speeds; but given time, all will likely complete it. Any learning of patterns, as we have seen, involves just this kind of jigsaw assembly—but more complex, because the pieces to be used have to be separated from many other pieces present which are not part of this particular puzzle, and different learners will have different assortments of pieces. Once we grasp the individual way that human brains extract patterns, we can begin to see the futility of offering a standardized, limited input.

Among those investigating and substantiating this approach M. C. Wittrock, a professor of educational psychology in the Graduate School of Education at the University of California, Los Angeles, ranks as a highly influential pioneer and leader—the more so for present purposes since he works on the learning and instruction of school-age children. He writes:

> The brain does not usually learn in the sense of accepting or recording information from teachers. The brain is not a passive consumer of information. Instead, it actively constructs its own interpretations of information and draws inferences from it. The brain ignores some information and selectively attends to other information.

In short, a teacher aggressively instructing a class of 25 is actually not addressing a group at all, but rather 25 individual brains each of which will attend to what *it* chooses, then process that input in an individual way, relating it (if at all) only to previous individual input, or experience. "The basic implication for teaching," Wittrock adds, is that teachers need "to understand and to facilitate the constructive processes of the learner," who is given "a new, more important active role and responsibility in learning from instruction and teaching."[6]

NOTES

1. *Human Learning*: (Englewood Cliffs, N.J.: Prentice-Hall, 1976), p. 223.
2. The point has been made by many writers on instruction. For instance, see David R. Olson and Jerome S. Bruner in *Media and Symbols*, 73d Yearbook of the National Society for the Study of Education (Chicago: University of Chicago Press, 1974), p. 141: "If the information intended by the speaker falls outside the listener's 'competence,' the listener will interpret that sentence in terms of the knowledge he already possesses."

3. Scientific investigation of speech and hearing language has created an impressive body of knowledge, much of it long established, but apparently all but unknown to most educators, who commonly refer to "auditory" and "listening" skills and similar ideas far off the mark. For an excellent, up-to-date discussion, see George A. Miller, *Language and Speech* (San Francisco: W. H. Freeman and Co., 1981), especially Chapter 6.

4. See Philip W. Jackson, *Life in Classrooms* (New York: Holt, Rinehart and Winston, 1968) for a well-known and colorful account. He notes, "it is surprising to see how much of the students' time is spent in waiting" (p. 14). Since the concept of input has not engaged researchers, to my knowledge, there is no direct measure. There seems little doubt, from observation alone, that input typically is low, often nearing the zero point. Time on task does not equate input; input involves raw material from which patterns can be extracted— amount and nature, not time.

5. The figure is far understated. In addition to neurons themselves, the glial cells, which appear to nourish and assist neurons, by themselves number near this total, as we have noted.

6. See *Education and the Brain*, 77th Yearbook of the National Society for the Study of Education, Part II, Jeanne S. Chall and Allan F. Mirsky, eds. (Chicago: University of Chicago Press, 1978) p. 101.

9

[Man] creates *intentions*, forms *plans* and *programs* of his actions, inspects their performance, and *regulates* his behavior so that it conforms to these plans and programs; finally he *verifies* his conscious activity, comparing the effects of his actions with the original intentions and correcting any mistakes he has made.

—A. R. LURIA[1]

Second Fundamental: We Live by Programs

Our discussion of extraction of patterns has shown the outcome of that process of learning as being recognition of patterns, to various degrees of discrimination. But plainly we do not live by sitting in an armchair and detecting patterns. We live by doing, by action.

For centuries, back to the dim origins of humans, behavior has seemed largely a mystery. What people did seemed utterly haphazard, unpredictable, unexplainable. Teachers have long struggled with the behavior of their charges, to the degree that class management threatens often to push instruction into a secondary function. But even corporate personnel specialists confess to being frequently surprised and baffled by the behavior of workers, for all the "motivation" that pay and prospects of some form of advancement would seem to offer. As more than half of marriages go astray, the inability of spouses to understand each other, even after years of intimacy, stands out. And any gathering of parents may bring up the difficulties of comprehending the strange worlds children inhabit.

But in the last three decades or so, researchers in brain areas and several other disciplines have made progress on many fronts. When their findings are brought together and unified, our understanding of human behavior can take a great leap. This opens the door to revolutionary advances in education, and gives us the chance to catch up, at least some, with the dazzling and often upsetting advances in technology.

In studying the way creatures behave, two approaches represent opposite poles. One way, the stock-in-trade of the behaviorist psychologists, is to put an isolated creature in captivity, do things to it, and try to make sense of what the animal does as a consequence. The subject animal is regarded as passive, inert, a "sample" that must be stimulated from without to take any action.

The opposite approach is that of ethologists, who primarily observe creatures who are as far as possible free and in their natural setting, to see what they do on their own. There is recognition from the outset that these are not sample, but individual, social, living animals, far from passive, in no need of contrived outside stimuli to be active.

It can hardly be surprising that the manipulators have, after a century, produced little that illuminates human (or even rat) behavior. They have not really sought to observe the natural way various creatures behave in their natural environment.

If a teacher takes some students to an old-fashioned zoo with cages, and subsequently has some of them report that "tigers are large, striped animals that pace back and forth all the time," he or she might feel constrained to point out that that is what tigers may do *in a cage*. Captivity has a profound effect on most animals. We can suspect that for millions of years loss of freedom to move was a prelude to early death, probably by being eaten. Humans, too, are put in captivity, commonly in three settings: prisons, mental hospitals, and schools—and it seems unreasonable to expect behavior more normal than that of the caged tiger in any of those places. We are used to the classroom; as I have on frequent occasions pointed out,[2] it seems to become invisible to those who work in it or deal with it. Though manifestly the classroom is a grossly arbitrary, artificial setting and form of captivity, the behavior of inmates is somehow expected to be normal and compliant. Such is the power of wishful thinking that resistance, rebellion, and withdrawal are regarded officially as misbehavior rather than as perfectly natural, to-be-expected consequences. Elaborate studies are conducted of "how students learn" in this oppressive setting—the exact equivalent of observing "how tigers behave" in a zoo cage.

If, following the lead of ethologists, we begin to observe humans in ordinary, free settings, and apply modern understandings of the brain, much of the old mystery surrounding behavior evaporates.

The key is the realization that we act very largely by *programs*. The word need not alarm us with visions of robots. It means simply a fixed sequence for accomplishing some intended objective. In other words, we act to carry out some purpose, some personal, individual, and usually self-selected purpose—the exact opposite of robot behavior.

Suppose, for example, that I wish to telephone my brother. I pick up the phone, push the buttons in a certain order, and put the receiver to my ear to wait for the call to go through. I have executed a program for making a phone call. Should I call him again tomorrow, I will go through just about the same procedure.

Should I wish to phone a local store, I may have to use an additional program to find the number. I get the phone book, look up the listing, then dial—a variation of the program I used to call my brother.

If now I want to visit the store, I must implement a longer program. I go to my car, take out my keys, find the right one, unlock the door, open it, get in, put the key in the ignition switch, fasten the seat belt, turn the switch and start the engine, release the parking brake, put the car in gear, press the accelerator pedal—just to start on my trip. To get there in my accustomed way I go through a series of dozens of steps, including the right choices of turns at street intersections. Yet I can "reel off" this program with the greatest of ease, hardly giving any attention to what comes next, much as I can put a cassette in a player and have the tape reel off a musical or other program.

Clearly one of the reasons for our huge brain is that as humans we need and use a great number of programs to carry on our complex activities—thousands of times as many as the most intelligent of other animals. The programs we learn are stored in the brain. Exactly how that is achieved remains unknown, although the progress of researchers in the neurosciences suggests that we may have a good start toward understanding the neuronal, chemical, and molecular mechanisms involved within another 10 to 20 years.

Present knowledge makes clear that programs can be acquired two distinct ways: *by being transmitted with the genes, or by being learned after birth*. As a general rule, the more brainpower an animal has, the more it learns after birth, and particularly the more neocortex or new brain it possesses, the greater the relative reliance on after-birth learning. We see once more why the laboratory rat and other small experimental animals can throw so little light on human learning: their programs are largely *species wisdom*, transmitted genetically, while humans use the splendid new brain to do most learning after birth, over many years.

No aspect of being human appears more dominant than this incessant accumulation of programs. The process of course is most rapid in the earlier years, and gradually tapers off. But since we live in a world that changes constantly, we are under far greater pressure than our forebears to continue to learn, to keep acquiring new programs. The man of 75 who is given a video tape recorder to honor that birthday must master some new programs if he wishes to operate his new machine. A few centuries ago the programs acquired by age 25 would pretty well see one through a long life; today much of what is learned by age 25 will become obsolete, and failure to keep on learning can prove restrictive, costly, or embarrassing.

As we become more familiar and at ease with the concept of *programs as the building-blocks or units of behavior*, we must wonder why many brilliant pyschologists and other investigators did not long ago see this rather simple explanation. A partial answer, I think, is that the present knowledge of DNA molecules and their ability to hold an enormous amount of information—the instructions for building the next generation—lets us readily believe that the storage of elaborate programs is biologically possible. We have also the advantage of being familiar with phonograph records, magnetic tape, photographic film, holograms, and other means of storing information. Each of these was a miraculous innovation in its day. The earlier investigators did see programs in action, as their writing reveals, but did not know how directly to make sense of them as we so easily can now. They turned to far more complicated and unsatisfactory explanations, such as stimulus-response sequences, habit chains, "superstitious" behaviors, and the like. Today, leading brain researchers accept the concept of stored programs as a basic of brain function.[3]

To carry on activities, one must constantly *select* a program from those that are stored in the brain, and *implement* it—put it into use. Even to walk across the room, one must use an extremely complex program involving many of the body's 600-plus muscles and the shifting of weight from one side to the other as the feet alternate in moving forward. The program has to be repeated every two paces, with continual fine adjustments to change direction, or to pick up and carry articles. To walk, one program is used; to go up stairs, another; to go down stairs, a third. To take a stroll outside one may have to use programs for going uphill, downhill, crossing rough ground, jumping over a puddle, or running a few steps to avoid traffic. *Each time, the program in use has to be switched off, and another selected and switched on*. The brain does this so smoothly that we ordinarily are not aware of the switches being thrown.

But if I am getting dressed in the morning, and open a drawer full of shirts, I must make an aware or conscious selection of which I will put on, as a rule. After I have made that choice, opening up the shirt, putting it on, and buttoning it up "runs off" as a kind of automatic program, to which I don't have to give any conscious attention, unless something goes wrong—I find a button missing—and interferes.

Which shirt will I select? It depends on a perception of the *pattern* I will be dealing with. If I am going to a business meeting, I will select a dress shirt; if I plan to make some repairs, I choose a work shirt; if tennis is a prospect, another type of shirt is called for. Even subtler patterns may influence me: I may want a conservative dress shirt for the meeting or a brighter one if the meeting will become a celebration with old friends. Though the decision may be trivial, I cannot *act* until some decision is made.

In much the same way, we select the *most appropriate program* from those stored in the brain to deal with what is seen as the pattern in effect. Seeing stairs ahead, I select a going-up-stairs program. Having accidentally jostled somebody, I choose an offering-apology program. Facing an arithmetical problem, I see division as the kind of program called for. Meeting a neighbor I know, I select a greeting program, with smile, nod, and suitable words.[4] A basic cycle is plainly in use. One must:

1. *Evaluate* the situation or need (detect and identify the pattern or patterns.)
2. *Select* the most appropriate program from those stored.
3. *Implement* the program.

As human behavior is looked at in these terms, it may hardly become simple, but insight into what is happening can become a great deal more penetrating. For educators, some key relationships immediately become evident:

1. Unless the learner can reasonably accurately evaluate the need or problem the situation presents (that is, detect and identify the patterns involved) the cycle goes astray at the outset. The student simply does not know *what* to do.

A familiar example is the student trying to cope with an arithmetic problem couched in words. The pattern is not detected, and the student flounders, wondering whether to add certain numbers, or divide others, or gives up entirely. The same failure may be seen in the spelling of longer words: the student lacks any sense of the structure or pattern of the word, and tries to simply remember the order of the letters—perhaps producing some weird versions.[5]

2. Individuals can use only those programs they already possess. However much one may be coerced or urged, or motivated or rewarded,

there is no way to perform the program unless it has already been stored by that individual. He or she does not know *how* to do it.

There is no way to force a person to ride a bicycle, or play Chopin on the piano, or write a scientific paper, if those programs have not previously been acquired. That some or many other persons can do these things has no bearing. Yet in almost any classroom, at any level, one can see this principle being ignored. On the playground, one can hear a child being called "clumsy" or "poorly coordinated" when the real difficulty is that certain programs have not yet been learned. In homes parents scold children; in business bosses scold employees, in the same futile way. *If the program has not been acquired, the solution lies in having it acquired*, not in criticizing, labeling, or giving a poor mark, practices that prove devastating to learners when long continued.

3.   A student cannot implement a program unless given the chance to do so.

On a test, the question might be asked, "How can the correct spelling of a word be verified?" The answer intended is, "Look it up in a dictionary." A student who gives that answer, we must note, is not using that program. Rather, he or she is using a program *for answering a question on a test*. So commonly are tests used in instruction that this all-important difference may be overlooked, and students who have passed tests prove unable to carry out the programs themselves—a complaint loudly uttered today. Similarly, if students are always *directed* to use certain programs, there is no way of knowing whether they grasp pattern detection, selection of program, and implementation. Rather, they are implementing programs *for following directions*. The learning apparently achieved may prove fictitious.

I have indicated earlier that a program always has a goal, an objective—it is an activity to achieve some intended outcome. What happens if the program selected and implemented does not work?

Let us say that I have taken out my keys to open the car door. I insert the key, but it will not turn—the program *aborts*. I must now go through the three-step cycle again: reevaluate the situation, select another program that seems appropriate, and implement that. Perhaps I have the wrong key, in which case I recycle to find the right one and try again. Perhaps the lock has jammed, so I recycle to the unusual program of going around to the opposite door. In some cases of abortion, of course, no workable alternative program can be found, and that can abort other programs. If in this instance I can't get into the car, I have to abort larger programs for using it.

Abortion of a program always causes some degree of emotional shift, because the failure of a program to work is in general disturbing and threatening. The degree to which programs usually work when implemented to achieve the intended goal serves as a direct, continuous measure of how well one has "made sense of the world," learned to detect specific patterns, and stored and selected appropriate programs. Programs *should* work. When they do, confidence in oneself increases; when too often they don't, confidence diminishes.

While instructors have long sensed that self-image and belief that successful learning is possible play a large role, this concept of programs working or not working may sharpen that perception, as well as help clarify why an individual's confidence rises or falls. We can see, too, that children whose parents or teachers have overdirected their activities, and overstressed second-person estimates of achievement, may mistrust their own ability to evaluate situations and select appropriate programs.

This program view of behavior, I submit, is consistent both with present scientific understandings of the brain, and with what we can clearly see—once we know where to look—in the normal functioning of children, other adults, and ourselves. True, we cannot see into another person's brain to observe what pattern-detecting abilities and programs have been established there; but we can see with new insights what happens when that person is allowed to use what he or she considers the most appropriate program—or when the individual has none to apply.

From this approach, too, we can draw a new and much sharper definition of learning (as distinct from the *process* of learning, the abstracting of pattern from confusion) than the unsatisfactoy old "change of behavior" kind,[6] long all that educators have had. *Learning is the acquisition of useful programs.*

Educators are accustomed to thinking in terms of knowledge. But we can see that certainly the great bulk of knowledge, if not all, takes the form of stored programs.[7] One learns a mathematical, mechanical, artistic, or horticultural *procedure*; or how to answer a question. It has long been observed by philosophers as well as those in behavioral fields that however splendid or intense our private thoughts may be, they do not have an impact or effect until we act in some way. While we commonly tend to think of motor and intellectual activity as in different categories, observation shows quickly that mental activity involves motor activity: speaking, writing, operating machines or equipment, doing something with the hands, performing in some fashion. Even to accept input demands acting—to see, we use elaborate muscle control to orient body, head, and eyes, which move millions of times an hour. To feel, we extend arms and fingers; to listen, we orient the ears; to smell, we sniff.[8]

We also talk to ourselves, or within our heads, sometimes aloud and more often subvocalizing, a process that appears often to involve very small muscular movements. The distinction between motor and intellectual programs does not seem to have much practical value, I suggest. Arguments about whether action is externalized thought, or thought internalized action, seem to demonstrate only that the two are tightly linked.

When we define learning as the acquisition of useful programs, we plainly move in the directions of "behavioral objectives," a much-abused term in schooling. Its main idea is to focus, at the outset of instruction, on what the student will be able to do after instruction. In practice, however, teachers may simply continue their old approach, "covering the material," merely giving lip-service to behavioral objectives. Or the objectives are seen in *test* terms—students will be able to pass some kind of examination, as directed, when directed. I suggest this supports a narrow concept of behavior, telling us little about what the student can and will do when not ordered to perform in a prescribed way. Will the student detect the key *patterns* involved, without help? Will he or she select an appropriate *program* from those stored in that individual's brain? Will it prove, in use, an adequate program that achieves the intended *goal* and does not abort?

When behavioral objectives become interpreted in these sharp Proster Theory terms, it can be practical to pinpoint, and list, what goals are sought over a flexible period of time: several weeks, or months, or perhaps a year or two in some cases. Equally, individual learning achievement can be precisely noted by seeing what programs a student has and when appropriate *uses* that were not evident previously. It will rarely matter much in what order these programs are acquired.

A caution should be given here again on the "subskills" approach, which in at least some instances seems to have gone wild. Reading, for example, has been broken down into literally many hundreds of subskills, with the poor teacher supposed to keep full records of which each student has mastered, on the dubious assumption that this is how one learns to read. Program, as defined, is a sequence *for attaining a goal preselected by the individual*; we may doubt that subskills often represent such a goal for the learner. Subskills and programs are emphatically not identical, and may have little in common.

One does not learn to ride a bicycle by separately learning (1) steering, (2) pedalling, (3) balancing, (4) leaning into a turn. The *coordination* of these makes easy riding possible, and that is the essential learning.

The Proster Theory version of behavioral objectives also leads to scrapping, to great extent, the use of tests, quizzes, and examinations that call for "right answers," and so direct the student's behavior. *We almost never can find out from directed behavior what a student would do if not directed.* This might seem apparent, yet billions of man-hours and huge amounts of money are expended on testing futilities. Most testing, in all forms down to recitation questioning by the teacher, directs the student what to do, usually in explicit detail. (That, in fact, is a common criterion of test making!) In many years of schooling, students perforce acquire examination-answering programs that have little relation to real skills and real-life situations, where we don't (apart from bureaucracies) give people a paper-and-pencil questioning-answering test, but instead try to find out what they can do. In schools, contrived, simplistic testing is an ingrained bad habit that tends to distort learning. It is axiomatic that as testing is emphasized, "teaching to the test" increases; and testing may become a regressive screen behind which administrators seek shelter from criticism. Standardized testing can also represent a large vested interest, well removed from students, with ample funds to sell and lobby for products and services. Because formats that can be scored by machine cost far less to process, the multiple-choice type has largely driven out what little nondirective testing used to be done by teachers, and only the scantiest attention now goes to this far more informative technique.

The word *useful* in "acquisition of useful programs" deserves attention. Primarily, it means useful to the individual who will possess the program, in that person's view, rather than in some other person's view or by some supposed social or other standard. While it is true that one can be coerced into acquiring a program, and may use it under duress, such programs are likely to become unused as soon as the duress ceases, if good mental health prevails. If use of the forced program continues, it usually will signify either superstitious ritual, with anxiety that something dreadful will occur if it is not used, or the inappropriate behavior that goes under the common name of neurosis. *Inherently, the use of a freely learned program satisfies, while that of a coerced program brings back the old fears under which it was built.* We see this in mildest form when people do arithmetic with obvious pain and reluctance, and in more serious degree when individuals who have been forced to learn a musical instrument well cannot bear in later life to play before an audience.

But in a far wider sense, useful conveys the possibilities of *transfer of learning*, which can greatly increase the speed of new learning. To give simple examples, a program for roller skating can readily transfer to ice skating; one for using a typewriter keyboard can easily be extended to using a computer keyboard. The ability to transfer some of these behavioral building blocks, adapting and adjusting them to new needs, explains why some individuals can master a new task far more rapidly than others who lack the programs to transfer, or who in some cases may not yet have recognized the similarity of pattern involved which leads to and permits transfer.

The capacity to use old programs in fresh combinations seems to underlie what we call creativity. Greater sensitivity to pattern similarities facilitates the transfer. While I would doubt that sensitivity can be directly taught, it seems probable that it can be facilitated.

The implications for education of the program concept of behavior, and of the *evaluate, select, implement* program cycle, appear to be stupendous, bringing not only fresh insights into human behavior, but also some major guidelines for improving learning achievement. To summarize:

1. We live by programs, switching on one after another, selecting from those that have been acquired and stored in the brain.

2. As humans, we are far more dependent on programs acquired by the tens of thousands after birth, in contrast to animals that rely more on programs genetically transmitted.

3. A program is a fixed sequence for accomplishing some end—a goal, objective, or outcome. Our human nature makes the working of a program pleasurable; the concept of some after-the-event reward is neither necessary or valid. But feedback is essential to establish that the program did work more or less as intended.

4. We can use only those programs that have already been built and stored. What programs another person has, or many people have, has no bearing. If a person does not possess a program, efforts to force its use are absurd.

5. We routinely use a three-step cycle: evaluate the situation (involving pattern detection and recognition), select the program that seems most appropriate from our store, and implement it.

6. The abortion of a program—its failure to work—calls for recycling. When a high proportion of self-selected programs work well, confidence rises; when too many abortions occur, confidence is reduced and the individual may become poorly able to self-select programs.

7. Fully acquired programs, though laboriously built, have an automatic quality that can easily lead one to forget that other individuals may not have acquired these programs.

8. Learning can be defined as the acquisition of useful programs.

9. Learning progress can be properly evaluated only by observing *undirected* behavior.[9]

10. Effective transfer of learning depends on using established programs in new applications and combinations. (Skill in effecting new combinations may equal creativity.) The learner who can adapt established programs to new tasks, by seeing similarities of patterns involved, learns much more rapidly than one who cannot.

11. In general, if we regard human learning and behavior in terms of continually asking "What program is being used?" sharp new insights can be gained, and many confusions avoided.

NOTES

1. *The Working Brain* (New York: Basic Books, 1975), pp. 79–80.

2. See for instance Leslie A. Hart, "Is the Classroom Door Your Enemy?", *K-Eight*, September–October 1972, and "The Case Against Organizing Schools into Classrooms," *The American School Board Journal*, June 1974.

3. For example, see such dominant books as A. R. Luria, *The Working Brain* (New York: Basic Books, 1975), and Karl H. Pribram, *Languages of the Brain* (Monterey, Calif.: Brooks/Cole, 1971). A famous and influential presentation of the program concept appeared in 1960, *Plans and the Structure of Behavior*, by George A. Miller, Eugene Galanter, and Karl H. Pribram (New York: Holt, Rinehart and Winston.) *Plans* here is interchangeable with *programs*. For a recent discussion, see J. Z. Young, *Programs of the Brain* (Oxford: Oxford University Press, 1978.)

4. Dr. José M. R. Delgado has stated this as: "To act is to choose one motor pattern from among the many available possibilities, and inhibitions are continually acting to suppress inappropriate or socially unacceptable activities." See "Intracerebral Mechanisms and Future Education," *New York State Education*, February 1968, p. 17.

5. James Doran, director of Algonquin Reading Camp, Rhinelander, Wisconsin, has demonstrated to me a simple, quick technique for giving students a sense of pattern that produces startling gains in their competency in spelling. His brain-compatible methods also produce large, rapid gains in reading.

6. Millions of teachers and other instructors have been taught that learning is something that causes a change in student behavior—unless, of course, that change is due to something else. Hilgard has offered a well-known version: "Learning is the process by which an activity originates or is changed through reacting to an encountered situation, provided that the characteristics of the change in activity cannot be explained on the basis of native response tendencies, maturation, or temporary states of the organism (e.g., fatigue, drugs, etc)." This effort, while perhaps better than some, seems manifestly useless, and almost doubletalk. In using the terms *reacting* and *response* Hilgard clearly suggests that learners are passive, rather than the active, aggressive creatures humans obviously are. Hilgard adds: "The definition is not formally satisfactory because of the many undefined terms in it, but it will do to call attention to the problems involved in any definition of learning." With that estimate few will disagree. The problems, of course, arise from trying to use bits of rat-based theory rather than comprehensive, human, brain-based theory. Ernest R. Hilgard and Gordon H. Bower, *Theories of Learning*, 3d ed. (New York: Appleton-Century-Crofts, 1966), p. 2.

7. To quote Luria: "According to these concepts, any animal or human activity, complex in its organization, is determined by a program that ensures, not only that the subject reacts to actual stimuli, but within certain limits foresees the future, foretells the probability that a particular event may happen, will be prepared if it does happen, and as a result, prepares a program of behavior." See *Human Brain and Psychological Processes* (New York: Harper & Row, 1966), p. 531.

8. The notion that perception is largely a passive process, and that stimuli impinge on the brain or senses freely, prevails widely but conflicts with a large, solid literature on perception that shows that in fact the brain *selects* what stimuli it will attend to, and usually *seeks out* the input it desires, which is then

elaborately processed. Reading and watching television often are described as passive activities, but actually involve intense mental, and some motor, operations. (To see at all, the eyes must constantly quiver rapidly!) The Selected Readings list includes several works on perception.

9. Teachers "driving" a conventional class and initiating most activity have little chance to observe what students do on their own. In good "open," Montessori, or similar settings, teachers can readily become observers because they have time and can be more detached. Students feel relaxed, absorbed in their work rather than on guard against criticism or a bad mark.

10

Our perceptions do not come simply from the objects around us, but from our past experience as functioning, purposive organisms. We take a large number of clues, none of which is reliable, add them together, and make what we can of them. All that this gives us is an estimate of our surroundings. It is never exactly right. It is never the same for different individuals.

—EARL C. KELLEY[1]

Prosters: Storing and Selecting Programs

Much that I present in this book represents synthesis—one is well advised to "stand on the shoulders of giants" whenever possible in dealing with the awesome human brain. The concept of *proster*, however, may be original, at least in simplifying and visualizing a complex brain function.

As we observe human behavior in program terms, it quickly becomes evident that we must deal with a huge number of programs, any of which may have many variations. And they cover an enormous range of complexity, from the relatively simple one of nodding the head slightly to signify approval, to the thousands of gross steps required to play a Chopin étude on the piano. These gross movements in turn utilize smaller, finer programs that bend fingers and wrists to the exact degree, for example, to press the keys as desired.

Language alone requires a tremendous number of programs. One must develop not only the complex muscular sequences for uttering each word, but also many variations for giving it the loudness, tone, and emotional color wanted.[2] To write the word, separate programs are needed for cursive writing, printing, and typewriting. Lettering the word with a brush or felt marker calls for still more variations.

As we deal with the real, and therefore complex, world, we find we need a collection of programs for almost any action. For instance we constantly deal with doors, which we variously operate by pushing, pulling, pressing down a latch, turning a knob, pressing a bar, pushing in a button, pulling on a handle, or sliding to one side or up. If we look at a handyman's shop, the array of tools suggests the many ways of dealing with wood and metal. An inspection of a kitchen reveals hundreds of tools, utensils, devices, machines, and materials for the production of meals.

I have suggested that we select a program by first detecting and recognizing the pattern, and categorizing down. This object, say, is identified as a door; a sign "push" or the construction tells which way it opens; the knob is identified as the type that one twists. We perceive all this so easily that we ordinarily pay no attention to the process. Also, in the cerebellum, the little brain (Figure 4, right, p. 42), we have built muscular coordination programs that are now used so that we know approximately how hard to push or pull a door, how much to twist a knob. (Observe a child of three trying to do this and the fact that much learning is required becomes apparent.)

As we enter a dark room in our own home, an arm goes out to reach the unseen light switch, the fingers find the lever or button, and apply just the needed pressure—all "automatically." In a strange house, however, that is not so easy. Attention is required to look for or feel for the switch—our grasp of the patterns of switch locations in houses gives us a good idea of where to hunt for it. But since we have to explore various possibilities and do not know just what kind of switch we are seeking (lever, button, twist, pull-chain), an observer might call us clumsy or dull-witted, since it took fifteen seconds rather than one to turn on the lights. A visitor from an Arabian desert, say, ignorant of our wiring customs, might have much more trouble—illustrating again the often overlooked fact that one's stock of patterns and programs reflects experience much more than something called intelligence.

It seems apparent that the brain must have some kind of organizational device that enables humans to rapidly categorize down patterns as they are detected, so they can be identified quickly. The principle of matching is well understood. In simplest terms, one receives an input from outside the brain—for example, visual input that comes from a door. Inside the brain, stored, is a pattern, *door*. If the current input and the stored pattern pretty well match, recognition occurs. Looking into the night sky, one may see any one of several patterns that match up with stored patterns for *moon*. Hearing some sound waves that compose a certain pattern, we recognize it as the word *scarecrow*, since it fairly well fits our stored pattern for scarecrow. The matches do not have to be precise—the other principle of *probability* applies. This permits us to recognize scarecrow whether spoken by a child in a thin, high voice, or woman or man in other pitches, and in spite of various pronunciations.

But to operate effectively, the brain cannot afford to search sequentially through tens of thousands of stored patterns to find the match. It seems likely that they are grouped in categories in hierarchies, or layers, much as mail is addressed (reading bottom up and in the wrong direction):

> The country (USA).
> The state (Connecticut).
> The city or town (Bethel).
> The street (Maple Avenue).
> The house number (628).
> The person in that house (Mr. or Mrs.)

This method, we know, quite efficiently makes a match between the letter and one out of more than 200 million inhabitants. If the address (the input) is a little wrong, delivery may still be made, but if error is larger no match will result.

Some speculation and experimental studies suggest that the brain does not usually need as many as six steps to categorize down. (That investigation is beyond the scope of this book.) Nor is the brain limited to one linear chain of categorizing down, such as that above—it can employ many such chains simultaneously as we have noted. This greatly speeds recognition.

Common experience tells us that we are able to make matches rapidly—though the time required is measurable and more than we may ordinarily assume. But the process must go further: after pattern detection and recognition, a program to deal with the situation must be selected, from huge numbers of programs stored.

To help visualize a theoretical apparatus for this, I have suggested the idea of proster, and from it the name Proster Theory. (Proster is a neologism, from a compression of the words *program structure*. It is pronounced "pross-ter.")

A proster should be viewed primarily as a simplified, diagrammatic concept of brain organization for the handling of patterns and programs, and as only one aspect of Proster Theory. The brain acts *as if* it were organized this way. But the proster concept is not taken out of thin air.

When the actual, physical structure of neurons in the cortex is studied, they are seen to be arranged in columns and layers, with some major connections of columns that seem compatible with the broad proster concept.[3] More importantly for educators, the proster device itself suggests some important and useful principles of human behavior and learning.

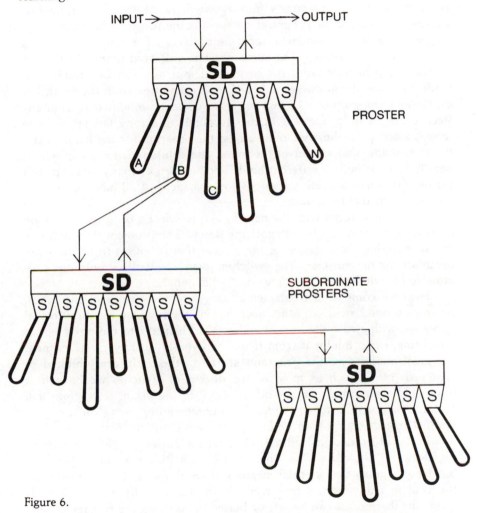

Figure 6.

A proster may be defined as *a collection of stored programs, related to a particular pattern, which can be used as alternatives.* A proster for locomotion, for example, would provide programs for walking, running, climbing or descending stairs, skipping, hopping, etc. All relate to the pattern of advancing by repeated steps of some kind. All the programs have the common purpose of getting to some other place on foot, and *only one of the programs can be used at any one time.* As an analogy for proster we can visualize the ubiquitous jukebox. It may offer a hundred choices of records stored in the machine for the common purpose of aural entertainment, but only one record can be played at any one time.

A proster can be represented in simple form by a diagram such as Figure 6. The input comes into a switching device, SD. Individual switches, S, control the programs composing the proster, shown as loops (suggesting a loop of magnetic tape, figuratively). For simplicity, only a few programs are shown, but some prosters will hold many. In the top proster the programs are gross or general, but any can be modified or made more specific in the second level, and even more so in the third. For example, a going-up-stairs gross program could be modified to climbing steep stairs, as on a boat, or further to climbing a rung ladder. Even to raise a glass to our lips, we must adjust the program for the hand to suit the size, shape, and weight of the glass; and drinking from a cup with a handle calls for quite a different hold. The neocortex's many layers permit further extremely delicate variations to be made, but all have to be individually learned as programs.

When one is faced with the need to act, to select a program, the brain finds a suitable proster by categorizing down. The problem then becomes one of *selecting the program in the proster that promises to be most appropriate for the purpose.* The switching device will allow only one program to be switched on at a time—but which one?

Here we come to a fundamental aspect of the nature of the brain. Neurons connect richly to other neurons, via the tiny gap junctions called *synapses*, with two quite opposite effects: to help excite the next neuron into firing, or to inhibit it from firing. Obviously, at any given moment the great majority of the programs stored in the brain are inhibited or switched "off," much as most of the dozens of switches we have in a household are normally in the off position. *In the brain, a program will be implemented only when the total of excitatory impulses ("on" or "go") applied exceeds the total of inhibitory impulses ("off" or "wait.")*

This is illustrated in Figure 7. Here we see *biases* entering the switching device at the sides. The engineering term bias may be unfamiliar, but we can grasp the essential meaning if we think of the thermostat on the wall in many homes that controls the furnace. By moving a little lever, the thermostat can be set, or biased, to turn on the furnace at 68°, or it can be biased so that the heat will not come on until the room gets down to 65°. In Figure 6 biases are shown as side influences that determine how readily any particular program in the proster will turn on and be used. The plus and minus signs shown next to each program suggest here, in very simplified fashion, the total of go and wait influences on each one. In this instance, Program C will be the one selected.

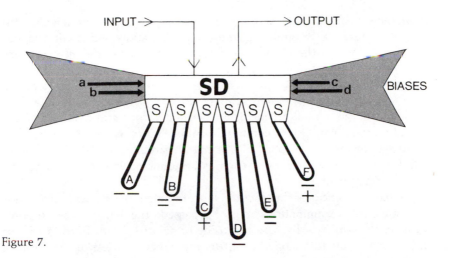

Figure 7.

The biasing affecting a proster is seen as very complex, reflecting not only current incoming biasing but also *the sum of what is stored in the brain, relating to this proster, from experience, plans, aims, fears, and older brain influences.* Human decisions usually involve a *balancing* of pro and con factors. A student may feel it would be wise to study for tomorrow's classes, but be reluctant to miss a favorite television show. An adult may consider purchasing a pair of shoes, and review the need for them and the inviting price, but then weigh other uses for the money, a lack of time to try on the shoes properly, the advantages of waiting until other shopping has been done, and some previous difficulties with this kind of footwear. A job offer may call for a decision much more complex, with many factors on one side and a list of negatives and uncertainties on the other. These go/wait decisions rest on fairly evident biasing, the sum of pro and of con reasons, many of which may be "feelings." The biasing that affects choices from a proster is similar, but vastly more complex, with *much of the biasing being well below conscious level.* Since we make thousands of program choices a day, most of them must be made quickly and without conscious attention. (What may be seen as awkwardness or stupidity in a person can be more accurately slow decision making—which in turn is likely to reflect lack of confidence.)

While the proster concept leaves many unanswered questions about brain functioning, it does seem to advance understanding to a degree—it perhaps gives a glimpse of what goes on, and of basic organization. For the educator, especially, some quite sharp conclusions emerge:

1.   Again it is clear that a program not in the proster cannot be used. The needed program may never have been built. *Or it may be stored, but "at another address" in the brain, in another proster.*

This seems clearly a key factor in instruction. It is not enough that the learner acquires a program; it must also be addressed so it remains available for use in the proper context. For example, a student may learn to work percentage problems in mathematics class, but never think of applying the program to figuring a sales tax or the cost of a bank loan. In civics, one can learn the organization of the city government, but have no idea how to go about getting some needed information on a governmental matter. Youngsters commonly make heavy use of the telephone for social conversations, but fail—as many parents can testify—to make calls for many other purposes, such as announcing lateness or canceling dental appointments.

When conventional instruction is dominated by student awareness that impending examinations must be passed, the normal uses of programs *in the real world* get pushed aside or subordinated. Both instructor and student may focus on the test-taking procedure. Asked to write a paragraph, for example, students may make sure that it has a topic sentence at the start; in real life they will worry about the meaning they want to convey. (In most professional writing, topic sentences more often than not can't be found.) In many cases the instructional setting provides strong biasing, especially when substantially new learning is being attempted. If it differs sharply from real-life settings, the program learned may not be transferred, because the biases don't transfer. We see this principle demonstrated when a language student can't converse with a foreigner, or the person who has prepared a speech at home has to deliver it to an actual audience.

2.   So long as the biases remain unchanged, the selection function in the proster will repeat, and exactly the same program will be selected.

While many instructors believe that varied approaches bring more learning success, nothing is more common in practice than to find reiteration and "review" which seem to express the conviction that the student who did not "get it" the third or fifth time around will somehow gain insight the seventh or tenth time! The proster diagram shows why this is not likely to happen. *To change behavior, the biases must be changed*, not the behavior directly.

While there is no way to greatly alter those biases already solidly stored in the brain from experience, there is the potential of altering those that reflect hopes, expectations, or threats and fears.

Most readily changed is the *setting* (the small world that a learner inhabits, such as the school-home combination) or the *situation* (the specific circumstances or ambiance immediately surrounding the individual). The student, or teacher, who day after day enters the same room, with the same furnishings, people, and routines, is subjected to unchanged biases that produce unchanged behavior.[4] Once the influence of biasing on program selection is understood, the often baffling resistance of learners becomes less of a mystery. We can see, too, why our own habits can be so difficult to change.

The proster diagram, I believe, can help to remind anyone concerned with instruction that:

3. All current learning is heavily influenced by previous learning (pattern recognition and programs acquired) and by a vast array of stored biases.

"Now, class," a teacher may say, "we are going to take up a new subject, logarithms" (or mechanical drawing, subatomic particles, baking, Shakespeare's plays, or computer terminal operation). But the students are not passive empty vessels into which new knowledge can be poured. Rather, each learns by aggressively *processing* the new input. And each learner will do that, inescapably, in relation to what that learner *brings* to the new effort.[5]

To illustrate, of three children getting instruction in first-grade reading, one may have had thousands of highly pleasurable hours of experiences with books, thanks to literate and dedicated parents; the second only a few hundred hours of any such exposure; and the third virtually no experience in being read to or handling books, but a good deal of being told stories and being sung to. The relevant prosters and biases of these three differ enormously, yet they will likely be offered substantially uniform instruction—with the one considered "brightest" probably getting the most attention, and the one in greatest need getting the least. Similarly, of three army recruits being taught to fire a rifle, one may have been brought up with firearms, the second may never have handled a gun and rarely seen one, and the third may be terrified of weapons as the result of an early, traumatic experience. They may be given identical instruction.

Though *diagnosis* is a word popular among educators, a candid observer may regard it with some suspicion. Teachers generally lack the time and resources that the procedure implies as a medical analogy, but in any case some grasp of the intricacies of brain functioning makes clear the difficulty of "seeing inside someone's head." To offer uniform instruction, and *then* try to diagnose why good learning did not result, seems to me to compound absurdities. The effort to "patch" appears doomed to failure, all the more so when it becomes a sort of ritual cover-up and the diagnosis, even if made by a specialist, gets put into the record but not acted upon—an elaborate and expensive way of blaming the victim for the institution's shortcomings.[6]

The proster concept suggests that:

1. The brain uses the categorizing-down process extensively, greatly speeded by simultaneous processing along many paths.

2.   The brain uses the principle of "the match" by which incoming pattern information matches, more or less exactly, the pattern stored in the brain, or else it is not recognized.

3.   The brain seems to be organized as if programs are grouped in prosters of alternative programs for a common purpose. Only one of these programs can be used at one time.

4.   Prosters are arranged in hierarchical layers, so that gross programs may be further and further refined or modified to meet slightly differing needs. (The neocortex itself is layered.)

5.   Neurons influence other neurons either by exciting them (go) or inhibiting them (wait.) The total of such influences determines whether a neuron does or does not fire.[7]

6.   Similarly, which program in a proster will be selected depends on the total go/wait influences on that program as determined by biases affecting that proster.

7.   Biasing involves all that is stored in the brain, relevant to a program decision, from experience, from plans, aims, fears, and older brain influences, and from the current, situational input.

8.   If the biases remain unchanged, the program selection will remain unchanged.

9.   To effect a change of behavior, or "open a new door" to learning, we must try to change biases, not behavior directly.

10.   How programs are addressed will determine where they are stored in prosters, and whether they will be utilized in real-world situations.

11.   Present learning depends heavily on previous learning and biases stored in the brain of each individual. Giving individuals uniform instruction without regard to what they bring to the learning effort virtually guarantees a high incidence of failure.[8]

NOTES

1. *Education for What Is Real* (New York: Harper and Brothers, 1947), p. 34.
2. Stephen D. Krashen points out that the brain must also put the ideas and words in proper order: "What is essentially involved in language production is the programming of an idea, itself containing no intrinsic temporal order, into a sequence of linguistic units, which are also intrinsically unordered." See *The Human Brain* (Englewood Cliffs, N.J.: Prentice-Hall, 1977), p. 117.
3. The reader who wishes to move further into study of the complexities of the brain's incredibly intricate structure may find my earlier book, *How The Brain Works* (New York: Basic Books, 1975), a useful next step, before plunging into more technical treatments. See also Selected Readings.
4. See Leslie A. Hart, "Necessary Ingredients for Retraining Teachers," *Bulletin*, National Association of Secondary School Principals, December 1973.

5. Jerome Kagan has stated this succinctly: "When we say that a new entity is learned, we mean that an element is connected with a second element that already has been learned. No act, idea, image or word is learned in isolation or ever becomes completely isolated. Every mind consists of nests of interconnected elements that are continually being reorganized with use. Practice of a skill has the inevitable consequence of making that skill more autonomous and more likely to operate as one unit, rather than a sequence of separate elements." (In Proster Theory terms, one program.) "Psychologists Advance Efforts to Probe the Mind," *The New York Times*, January 12, 1970, Education section, p. 72.

6. See a pilot study on reading, for example: A. Weinshank, *The Relationship Between Diagnosis and Remediation in Reading* (East Lansing, Mich.: The Institute for Research on Teaching, 1979.) It found the clinicians gave four times as many diagnostic as treatment statements, with only moderate relationship of problem to treatment, and used a core set of five treatments to blanket almost all cases. Other studies and observations have shown only a faint connection between diagnosis and subsequent effective treatment.

7. To be technically correct, it should be noted that individual neurons may spontaneously fire. What one or a few neurons do in the brain has no significance among the billions active.

8. In passing, we should also note that uniform instruction may also result in teaching students what they already know. Their subsequent success on an examination may then be taken as outcome of this unneeded, wasteful, and boring reinstruction. For example, a study recently conducted in six Long Island, New York, school districts by Educational Products Exchange Institute, funded by the National Institute of Education, tested fourth graders on the contents of a mathematics text before they used it. Sixty percent scored 80 or above.

11

When a person does an intrinsically disliked task because he fears not to do it, it is always necessary to *confine* him. This is what happens to animals in many psychological experiments.... Under such circumstances the creature is likely to seem more stupid than it really is, and to learn much less efficiently than it would in its natural habitat, where it is positively motivated.

Exactly the same is often true of children in school.... Parents, teachers, and everyone else concerned are so used to the idea that children will not go to school unless they are made to go, will not stay there unless they must, will not behave "properly" unless compelled to, and will not attend to lessons if there is a chance to do anything else, that they take it all for granted.... But human nature is only that way under certain conditions, and particularly under conditions of negative motivation.

—JAMES C. MURSELL[1]

The Triune Brain: Emotions, Downshifting

Learning involves emotions. Biasing, the triune brain concept, and some human history throw light on emotions that appear to be of great potential value in education.

In Chapter 5 we looked briefly at MacLean's scheme of the human brain as composed of three brains of very different ages (plus the cerebellum). The triune brain concept, in my view, ranks as a key, valuable aid to understanding both how we obtained our present brain and how it functions in life and learning.

MacLean has also suggested that we can, to help us visualize relationships, think of the three brains as bringing in from the "outside" world information displayed on internal television screens.[2] The very old reptilian brain produces murky pictures in which only gross outlines and shapes are discernible. (I am now using MacLean's analogy, but my language.) The old mammalian brain brings in a picture with much improved resolution, and therefore a good deal more detail; but it cannot begin to compare with the picture offered by the new mammalian brain, or neocortex, which is like a modern large-screen, full-color, well-tuned receiver obtaining vastly more detailed pictures.

In pattern terms, we might say that the reptilian picture could distinguish only large shapes, and do that crudely: this might be a house, that a tree, this a person. The old mammalian brain could go further to show that the house has windows and a sloping roof, and that the person seems to be male. On the neocortex screen, in contrast, each brick of the house, every detail of architecture, and even the number over the door would be sharp, and the person, a famous singer, would be fully recognizable with even strands of hair or weave of clothing being visible.

The quality of brain—which to a large extent means the number of neurons—*determines the degree to which patterns can be detected and discriminated.*[3]

Similarly, the quality of brain *determines the scope of program building.* Consider the turtle and its maximum store of programs—a few dozen. The far superior brain of a dog can handle hundreds. As any owner knows, a dog can communicate quite effectively by barks of several kinds, growls, yips, yelps, whines, whimpers, howls, tail wagging, position of ears, expression of eyes, body position and tension, jumping, stretching, capering, running about, begging, bringing a ball or a leash, and in many other ways. Its communication prosters offer a choice of many stored programs, each of which can be modified by many subprogram variations. Chimpanzees, with much larger brains, appear able to "talk" by learning and using standard sign language (a clever animal may even invent some signs of its own), by manipulating plastic shapes, or pushing an array of computer buttons. Scores of "words" can be mastered and used in appropriate ways.

But our human capacity for pattern detection and discrimination, proster organization, and program building and storage goes well beyond that of any other creature. (While some sea mammals have impressively large brains and learning ability, their physical limitations for program execution put them far below humans in that regard at least.)

In another basic aspect the ethologists have thrown much light on our human nature—ways in which we differ importantly from other animals because of the size and characteristics of our brain. In Chapter 9 we noted that programs can be transmitted with the genes, or instead acquired after birth. Clearly we accumulate the bulk of our human programs the second way, and this leads to the great diversity of human behavior and the need to recognize and deal with individuality. If you have a dog as a pet, I can tell you many of its behaviors just by knowing that it is a dog—how it wags its tail, how and what it eats, just how it scratches itself, leaves scent markers (if male), greets other dogs and strangers coming to the house. It is much harder to say what humans do—we do not even have a standard way of raising our young! Cultures vary greatly. We see that a bird can build a nest—an intricate program—though it has never seen one built before. Bees, which have only a little after-birth learning ability, carry on an elaborate communal life dependent on rigid programs genetically transmitted. In MacLean's laboratory near Washington, D.C., I have watched lizards use challenge-and-response programs probably in use for over 50 million years!

Have humans genetically transmitted programs? Unquestionably yes, although in our cases most of them appear to be much more generalized—more tendencies and patterns of behavior rather than sharp sequences such as those birds use for nest building, or spiders to build webs. The term *schemata* is often used for that reason. On the other hand, a neonate that does not have a program ready for sucking is in deep trouble; and it has been well proved that newborn humans have an immediate (therefore built in) interest in human faces, or anything with similar pattern, and will seek out faces quite aggressively.[4] The presence of many schemata is strongly indicated.

In order to evolve, a species must first of all survive. The oldest programs in an animal's brain will be those closest to the necessities for survival: knowing what food to eat and how to obtain it; how to recognize another member of the species, mate, and reproduce; identifying and somehow avoiding and escaping predatory enemies; choosing and returning to a home; and others on this level. These can branch out and multiply as the brain expands and can handle more patterns, prosters, and programs, to such an extent that a human home, for example, can be not a nest or burrow but a large structure holding five or ten thousand collected articles, from furniture and cutlery to medicines and books!

In the emotional area, a simple animal may make a decision between flee (fear) and fight (hate), with no choice in between. At the human end, these emotions have elaborated to many degrees: mild apprehension, nagging worry, dread, fright, all the way to outright terror. Hate can range from vague distaste through active antagonism to assault or even rage to kill.

Here we are once again really dealing with pattern recognition and discrimination. In ordinary speech one commonly discusses emotion as though it were unconnected with rational thought, and somehow a polar opposite. But it has long been recognized that in practice emotion cannot be separated from cognitive thinking.[5] One feels fear *because* a situation has been recognized as calling for fear. To be angry at an insult, we must first recognize that we have been insulted. To mourn a lost friend, we must grasp the pattern of death and its consequences. Most of the emotion we feel follows pattern recognition that often can be very subtle, as when a new wife feels that her husband's family is gradually warming to her, or an employee gathers that changes in the business are reducing his influence and value. A student may "read" tiny signals from a teacher that convey developing hostility, and so feel growing alarm.[6]

As we look at the three-brain structure of humans, it becomes manifest that, in general, *the old, more primitive schemata and programs and the cruder emotions are in the oldest brain tissue, and that the highly subtle pattern-detecting capabilities are in the newest, the neocortex.*

The old mammalian brain in between acts something like a broker. It can be influenced from the newer brain above, and from the older one below, and it can "take sides" either way. In humans, it is a brain much concerned with emotion.

Emotion as a word may lead us to think of love, sorrow, poetic ideas, and the arts, but understanding its less ethereal aspects leads to consideration of blood pressure, oxygen use, and *homeostasis* or balancing of body systems. The oldest function of emotional shifts, it is now clear, was to change the biasing of these systems.

Imagine a wild rabbit quietly feeding in an open patch of grass. Its internal systems are biased at a low setting. But now the rabbit catches sight of—possibly—a fox in a nearby group of bushes. Cognitively, the rabbit's highest level of brain decides "that could be a predator in there," and in effect sounds a general alarm. This is done, in all mammals, primarily by means of chemical messengers, moving through the bloodstream. The brain signals glands to release the appropriate alarm hormones into the blood, and these lead to the resetting of a group of biases. The rabbit's heartbeat increases, as does the breathing rate; muscles tense for action; digestion stops. The new biases ready the animal for action.

Now the fox charges. The biases, influenced by further hormonal signals (the term hormone derives from the Greek for "urge on"), push over to extreme settings. What happens in the next few seconds will determine whether the rabbit survives or dies, so a supreme effort must be made—energy will be used at a rate that can be sustained only for a few minutes. The rabbit bounds off in an all-out effort to escape.

The same resetting of biases, of course, occurs in the fox. As its brain interprets the pattern to mean "that could be my next meal," its glands pour out the messengers to prepare the entire body for the extreme effort of attack.

As humans, we have largely escaped this kind of drama, a daily event for less complicated creatures. Although as pedestrian one may leap for the safety of the sidewalk when surprised by an approaching car, or as skier desperately swerve to avoid a rock while coming down a slope, we live such relatively safe lives that this violent resetting of biases seldom becomes necessary. We commonly turn to active sports, travel, gambling, business risks, new ventures, and "taking a chance" quite voluntarily, to put more excitement into our lives. On any weekend, hundreds of stadiums fill with roaring spectators, obtaining at second hand the thrill of victory and the agony of defeat, as one broadcaster puts it. On a still milder level, people engage in card and board games, nonhazardous activities such as tennis, bowling, or horseshoe pitching, where competing tends to move the biasing to a higher—but comfortable—level. Or we may challenge ourselves with puzzles, self-imposed tasks such as jogging five miles, or choose a game of golf which has been deliberately contrived to be full of trials and obstacles.

We must note here the difference between voluntarily accepted and chosen *risks*, and externally imposed *hazards*. Being mugged on the street, or sent into armed combat in a police action or war, brings one back to the rabbit and the fox. In children, we can observe readily the gleefully *selected risk*—climb this tree, wade this puddle, walk this wall, jump off this high place—that involves physical challenge, and equivalent more cognitive challenges (that of course involve physical activities) such as putting together a model, learning to operate a typewriter, or building a tree house. *What risks a person will want to take, to what degree, clearly is a highly individual matter, with children as well as adults.* That there exists a deep human need to select and take risks seems hardly arguable; but when in instructional situations students are directed and coerced to take risks not of their choosing, the need is little met. Risk becomes threat.

The triune brain concept makes sense of these familiar observations. Our oldest, reptilian brain still holds its place in our heads. It was, and to large extent remains, a *survival* brain, attuned to crude rabbit/fox emergencies, and possessing perhaps a few dozen schemata or ancient, deep-laid programs. The middle of the three brains, the old mammalian brain, has much concern with the elaboration of emotions, with more subtle and complex adjusting of biases. The new neocortex has the job of interpreting situations, detecting patterns to varying degrees of discrimination. By and large, *the newest brain makes the "cognitive" decision as to what circumstances are being dealt with and what needs to be done, and the old mammalian brain (limbic system) resets the biases appropriately.* In extreme situations, the reptilian brain takes over, as in great rage, abject fear, or panic flight. Most adults lead such sheltered lives that we rarely experience this depth of emotion, though children may.

Emotions are physically expressed, and readily detectable. If spouses meet for dinner at a restaurant, one may quickly become aware that something is bothering the other, though nothing specific has been said. Joining a social group, one can realize a slight hostility exists—perhaps

some remark has just been made, or an interruption has been inadvertent-
ly caused. Parents will often sense emotion in a child returning to the
home. As we have noted, students usually show great sensitivity to
teacher emotions.

When we remind ourselves that humans have long been highly social
animals used to living in close quarters all the way back to caves, small
tents, and earliest buildings, we can see the value of this. To get along in
such circumstances, *it is essential to give and receive signals*. A cat approached by a dog may raise its fur, assume a tall stance that facilitates a
sudden swipe of claws, and put mouth and ears in warning position. The
signals given can hardly be missed. Human signals most often are subtle,
so much so that we may have difficulty describing them in words. Extremely slight changes in posture, in muscle tension, in breathing, in eye
movement and pupil size can be detected. (As in all human matters, individuals differ. We neither emit signals in the same fashion nor interpret
them uniformly.) While probably the old mammalian brain still has
charge of emitting the signal, only the new, great neocortex has the
resources to detect fine pattern changes and interpret their message.

All of this points to one major characteristic of being human that
often is not seen, or is lost in layers of confusion: *we are creatures that
have a deeply built-in drive to frequently reset body biases*—to exercise
rebiasing rather than lead a placid, cow-like existence. If our work and
daily routine does not provide enough shifting of bias, we actively seek
out risk, competition, art, music, theatre, and other activities that cause
shifts. Sad, thrilling, romantic, and horrifying theatrical entertainments
all draw audiences (but again, with strong individual preferences.)

What we may call *volatility of biases* is associated with youth.
Children can move from anger to laughter in seconds. People strike us as
old, whatever their actual years, if their biases seem fixed in a narrow
range, while a person of 90 who displays much volatility strikes us as
remarkably youthful even if immobilized in a wheel chair. Even though
the volatility of children decreases rapidly and steadily from 8 months to
18 years, the high volatility of youth relates importantly to instruction.
*The teacher or school or system that attempts to suppress or routinize
emotion in students, or take a group rather than an individual approach,
is flying in the face of deep human needs.* Many who teach suspect this
intuitively; not all know what to do about it, especially within the rigid
class-and-grade structure.

But the triune brain has even larger implications for instruction. We
must consider the effect of *threat*.

A student brings into the classroom not only personal but *species
history*—millions of years of evolution, very much present in the nature
of the brain. The reptilian brain, by virtue of being relatively small and
capable of only crude decisions, can make its decisions quickly. Our line

exists because over great periods of time such brains made decisions well enough and fast enough to survive when life or death hung on the next second or two of activity, as with our rabbit. The much larger old mammalian brain introduced a compromise: a brain far more complex and therefore slower to make decisions, but on the other hand much better able to detect and interpret situations (patterns) and to store and execute many more programs. But the huge neocortex that developed became impossibly too big and intricate, I submit, to make quick action decisions. So there arose another compromise: the newest brain was superb for pattern discrimination and the storage of a vast collection of programs, and was therefore a brain that enabled humans to adapt to and innovate living conditions as no creature on earth ever had before—but it had to rely on the older brain structures, especially the limbic system, when speedy survival decisions were needed.

In complexity we can compare the reptilian brain to a pocket dictionary, the old mammalian brain to a 20-volume encyclopedia, and the new mammalian brain to the New York Public Library. Finding desired information in the dictionary can take seconds, consulting the encyclopedia may require minutes, and the library can call for hours or days. For many survival needs the size and slowness of the cerebrum was intolerable.

Thus we have the phenomenon, readily observable in ourselves and others, including students, that I have called "downshifting." When the individual detects *threat* in an immediate situation, *full use of the great new cerebral brain is suspended, and faster-acting, simpler brain resources take larger roles.*

In at least a rough way, the degree of downshifting will reflect the degree of threat—always, of course, in individual terms. A severe threat to one person may be of little consequence to another.

One of the most familiar examples of violent downshifting occurs in automobile collisions, an experience few of us escape. One is driving along in comfort; suddenly an impact brings the crunch of metal and screech of brakes. Let us say no one has been hurt. But a half hour later the participants realize how much of the event has been "washed out." What was the color and make of the other vehicle? How many people were in it? Who was driving? What other cars were around? What was the sequence of events? Detail may be very hard to recall—witnesses to violent happenings notoriously differ widely on what happened, what people did or looked like, and what was said.

What occurred under the threat of violence, I suggest, was a quick downshift. Passengers in the hit car probably "ducked," using a program from the reptilian brain to pull in the head to the chest, throw up the arms to protect the face, and raise the knees to defend the vulnerable belly area. The old mammalian brain ordered hormones into the bloodstream causing, a few minutes later, a knot in the pit of the stomach and trembling legs. The limbic system took charge, but since this brain has no interest in makes and models of cars and rules of traffic, and lacks the pattern discrimination ability of the neocortex, it cannot provide the detail the police officer or an insurance company may ask for.

The basis of threat, as that term is used in Proster Theory, is physical: the ancient fear of predators who could quickly kill, or of death from natural forces such as landslide, earthquake, volcano eruption, flood, storm, or of any kind of captivity that could mean impending death. For many tens of millions of years of our evolutionary line, inability to move freely has implied just that, and confinement threatens right down to the reptilian level. The confinement of the school, of the classroom, of having to stay in a small area or in a specific seat stands as no exception.

Other forms of important threat to humans include separation from parents in childhood, especially the mother, and then, as some independence is gained, from the home group. For perspective here we must go back to the long ages of hunting and gathering in small bands; to lose contact with the band would usually mean great anxiety, suffering, and probably unpleasant death. Status within the band, we can feel reasonably sure, became an elaboration of being in or being out, and observation shows loss of status within what the individual regards as a home group to be a serious, sometimes devastating threat. (A home group is one the individual perceives in that light, not merely a group into which he or she is thrust, as for example the classroom, a military company, or an enforced work team.) Finally, since humans characteristically acquire possessions which may have both practical usefulness as well as status value, the threat of loss of possessions can be substantial in some circumstances.

If we now remind ourselves that virtually all academic and vocational learning heavily involves the neocortex, it becomes plain that *absence of threat is utterly essential to effective instruction*. Under threat, the cerebrum downshifts—in effect, to greater or lesser extent, it simply ceases to operate. To experienced teachers, this shutting down of the newest brain is an old story and a familiar frustration. The threatened child (threatened in the Proster Theory sense) "freezes," seems unable to think, stabs wildly at possible answers, breaks into tears, vomits, or acts up, perhaps to the point of violence.

Since language exists almost wholly in the new brain, downshifting leaves us speechless, quite literally. An unexpected insult, accident, piece of bad news, or other cause of sudden biasing produces even in adults temporary inability to talk, and quite possibly even to grasp what others are saying. Stage fright is similar. Another manifestation of a sudden downshift is "being rooted to the spot," often reported by people exposed to an explosion, train wreck, or similar disaster. In war, trained soldiers often fail to fire their weapons or use the tactics long rehearsed. Programs developed in the neocortex simply become unavailable because of the downshift, and the individual does nothing, unless the reptilian brain takes charge and the person flees wildly or holes up in some hiding place or shelter.

While rote learning can be accomplished under a good deal of threat, although the threat may impede learning, pattern discrimination and the more subtle choices of programs from proster suffer severe inhibition. So does the use of oral or written language and any form of symbol manipulation. The valuable learning that is built through any kind of play, of course, comes to a full halt; threat forestalls play—play implies absence of threat! The inescapable point emerges: *cerebral learning and threat conflict directly and completely.*

In the conventional classroom, threat to the student stands ever present through the basic setting of captivity; the power of the instructor to punish, demean, embarrass, reject, or cause loss of status; and the "fishbowl" effect of being forced to perform in constant danger of ridicule or public failure. The same factors may apply, though often to less degree, in training settings. Even in graduate-level work in colleges the threat of incurring a powerful person's displeasure, or failing to get over the next hurdle on the way to a degree that represents much desire, time, and money can have an almost paralyzing effect.

Threat pervades most educational settings, as a holdover from times not long past when teachers were invariably portrayed with a cane, switch, or other implement of torture in hand. A majority of public school teachers still favor corporal punishment as an ultimate resource of management, or last bastion of teacher power.[7] Grading, the issuing of marks and report cards, is widely abused, by common knowledge, for punitive or threat purposes.

Threat, we should note, means not so much what is happening as what reasonably can be expected to occur in the very near future. It is the sword hanging by a thread over one's head. Threat is not the same as pressure—one may rush to catch a train or plane with worry and fear about missing it, but without threat. Threat rather is what some power, usually a person or group, can do and may very well do to harm us.

Threat also gives us a profoundly revealing clue to the muddled area of learning disabilities. It is only necessary to read a score of full case histories of victims of this vague condition to observe a glaring, common factor: these students have long been subjected to acute, continued threat by a parent (often the father) or other dominating adults in their lives. One must wonder why this explanation, so obvious once examined, has been so little observed.[8]

The concept of downshifting appears to fit with both what is now known about the triune nature of the human brain, and what can continually be seen happening in instructional settings, as well as in our own daily living. In education and training we are concerned primarily with the superbly subtle and powerful newest brain. If we shut it down by threat, we must expect learning failure. One's neocortex functions fully only when one feels secure.

NOTES

1. *Psychology for Modern Education* (New York: W. W. Norton, 1952), p. 95.
2. In using this analogy, we must remember that there is no separate viewer in the brain, sitting in a comfortable rocker and watching the changing scene on the tube! Yet the input does come in, is displayed in appropriate parts of the brain, and is then interpreted, narrowly and broadly, by other parts of the apparatus. In addition, the "executive" frontal parts of the brain can evaluate the "picture" as it relates to plans and aims, and deeper parts of the brain can consider it in relation to past, even ancient, experiences. Philosophers have long worried and contended over whether *mind* and *brain* are a duality. In my view, this is an unnecessary and unproductive argument. We know brain is there, and a good deal about it. Mind is a vague, slippery term—a convenience when we can't be or don't want to be precise.
3. Research physicist Harris Walker has estimated the brain's processing capacity at about one trillion bits per second, or ten times that of a $12 million computer. See *Psychology Today*, June 1981, p. 108.
4. There is a considerable literature on the whole subject of schemata now. For a basic discussion of human face recognition by infants, see Robert L. Fantz, "The Origin of Form Perception," *Scientific American*, May 1961.
5. See the discussion of the point in D. O. Hebb, *Organization of Behavior* (New York: John Wiley and Sons, 1949), especially p. 147.
6. Emotions may arise, of course, from genetically transmitted sources, and become apparent with maturation. At around six months of age, the infant becomes distrustful of strangers—perhaps only partly due to limited ability previously to detect the pattern *strangers*. Young children have little fear of snakes as a rule; the fear grows with increasing age, even if no experience appears responsible. The horror and panic often shown may be strongly genetic.
7. The reluctance of school people in general to give up their traditional right to beat students is familiar. Classroom teachers particularly have always lived in fear of rebellion by the group or by older students. As youngsters have come to have larger physiques than teachers in many cases, and have largely lost the old privilege of dropping out of school without sanctions against them, real or potential attacks upon teachers have become an increasing problem. Threat affects both teachers and students.
8. See Leslie A. Hart, "Misconceptions about Learning Disabilities," *National Elementary Principal*, September-October 1976, pp. 54-57.

12

The human way of life is essentially social. To get the things needed to keep alive we cooperate with other people. This requires special programs of the brain and the whole pattern of human lives is organized around social activities. The sequence of human development, early helplessness, long childhood, late adolescence, and long adult life, is designed to allow the brain to develop and to acquire and use a set of programs for the skills of a social life.

—J.Z. YOUNG[1]

Brain Development: Until Adulthood

Anyone familiar with children knows the general scheme of physical development. The neonate has a huge head, a long trunk, short arms and legs. Within the first year, weight may triple. Next comes the chubby stage; then around age four or five growth stretches the body, which may remain thin for a number of years. Early in the second decade of life very rapid growth begins and the youngster "shoots up," and girls also show manifest sexual development. Around 15, boys are apt to be gangly and awkward, at least in appearance. At 17, a girl may have filled out and shows maturity; the boy usually takes longer. At 20 or so growth slows almost to a stop.

What has happened during this process *in the brain*? It is not hard to find people who have no idea about this phase of development, and who have given it hardly a thought. One does not ask a seven-year-old to reach something down from a high shelf—obviously she can't reach. But what are her brain capacities? A slender 12-year-old boy is not expected to lift a heavy barrel, but what is he capable of mentally? Parents often may expect too much or too little, and may be infuriated by the consequences. Those trained for education usually have given more attention to the idea of development. But unfortunately many ideas about mental development have been built into the school structure over centuries, and represent tradition and myths perhaps as often as sound studies. Only very recently has new knowledge of the human brain given the basis for much clearer, more factual understandings.

Piaget, of course, has helped greatly (after being ignored in America for a generation) to give educators some sense of youngsters' progression in intellectual growth, in terms of his famous "stages." His work was based on observation of human young, not laboratory animals, as they behaved in ordinary or gently contrived situations. It has considerable ethological content. But educators trying to apply Piaget tend to ignore the fact that he made no claim to having presented any theory of learning, nor explanation of how the brain functions in terms of its physical structure or evolutionary history. He did drive home the tremendously important point that children always develop their understanding of the world gradually. But in dealing with individual students this is hardly a handy guide for teachers. We know that each student moves through the stages of development on a private schedule, and is not necessarily consistently in one stage, nor in the same stage in all matters simultaneously.

Most limiting, in my view, is the emphasis Piaget put on intellectual growth, by which he seems to have meant pretty much our old friend, linear logic, which he returns to again and again as his main field of investigation. Piaget, I believe, should be read with the realization that he saw logical operations as the highest, and perhaps noblest, of mental goals—a concept one may at least question today.

Proster Theory conflicts with Piaget's conclusions—and then perhaps only on semantic grounds—on the ability of young children to extract abstract patterns. Pattern extraction, I have tried to show, is not a logical process. But Piaget's concentration on learners' development and the necessity for their active involvement have had great impact, and lead naturally to brain-based approaches. We can honor this great pioneer without trying to apply his findings in ways he never intended.

The essential picture we need may best be obtained by considering the neonate, and then the same person 20 years later. If a baby can triple weight in a year, why cannot it achieve adult weight in three or four, growing at the same rate? If a 1-pound puppy can become a 60 pound dog in a little over a year, why does it take a human such a large share of lifetime to reach adulthood? The physical growth does not seem to be the problem.

But the mental development is another matter. At or near the time of birth, we have about all the neurons we will ever have. Unlike most cells of the body, which die off rapidly and are replaced, neurons must serve us our entire lifetime. When they die, as many thousands do daily, we are left with fewer. But the supply we begin with numbers such fantastic quantities that we can sustain the loss: we start with (to use a moderate figure, as I have said) at least 30 billion neurons.

To hold this immense number, the head must be relatively large at birth; and even so, children must be born while still in a state of general helplessness far from "finished" if that head is to pass through the birth canal. It seems clear that the reason we develop so slowly physically is to allow time for those billions of neurons to become organized. The body waits on the brain.

Without getting into the complexities of neurons,[2] we can appreciate that development takes place in two quite different ways. On one hand, neurons (there are a number of types) *grow* by becoming more complex, much as the branches of a newly planted tree gradually divide and spread. Many neurons growing in this fashion come to have thousands of connections with other neurons. (These are not actual joinings; the connections involve a tiny gap across which chemical transmitters can move. This is the *synapse*, a mechanism that retains a good many secrets still, though much has been learned by persistent and often brilliant investigation.) The maturing brain steadily increases the number and complexity of these interconnections which by adulthood total high into trillions—into numbers beyond meaning for most of us.

The neonate of course has linkages or pathways already formed, particularly in the oldest brain, or it would not be able to survive, and the general plan of the brain has been genetically laid down during gestation. But adding new connections, particularly in the gigantic cerebrum, or newest brain, must go on at a staggering rate. Much evidence indicates that input and experience strongly influence not only what connections are made, but even how fast such growth proceeds. It has long been known, of course, that children deprived of a normal range of input, as was clearly the case in certain orphanages and foundling homes in the past, show greatly retarded development.[3] We may question how much input can be forced on a child; it seems probable that an ordinary home where there is affection for and interest in the infant provides a good supply. If we observe the motions of a baby's arms and hands over the first few weeks, the progress from random movements and jerks to controlled and purposeful actions shows the development in the brain going forward rapidly. Not only muscular control is involved, for soon eye-hand coordination and interpretation is evident, relating to objects, people, and even situations.

It is common to think of the baby's progress as very slow—the puppy gets organized a great deal faster, and romps around long before the infant can sit up. If we could somehow see the neuronal connections being formed in vast numbers, however, we would credit the baby with far more rapid progress. In favorable circumstances, it will continue through all the years of childhood. Actual physical growth of neurons is involved throughout. Much as a tree sends out more and more branches and twigs, the neurons send out their processes. Increase in brain size and weight comes in part from this kind of development.

The second kind of physical brain development involves *myelination*. A nerve is a conducting channel for electrical (more accurately, electro-chemical) impulses that travel in one direction along it. Unlike a wire that conducts an electrical current from a battery in a smooth, continuous flow, the nerve can only conduct pulses of energy that may make a succession of leaps along the fiber. But like insulation on an electric wire, myelin helps keep the pulses confined, and makes them move much faster. In the brain this insulation is provided by special cells which wrap around the nerve conduit many times.

At birth, relatively few nerve pathways have this insulation, and the myelination process continues for roughly 20 years. In this sense an adult brain is one in which all the insulation has been formed.

Much reason exists to suppose that this brain growth and development follows a broad genetic program, just as body growth does, and that the two are at least grossly coordinated. Similarly there can be large variations in the way neuronal growth and connections, and myelination, occur in any one individual. It is easy here to see a probable relation to Piaget's stages or periods, and again to realize that *individual variations have great practical significance*. No child is average or typical nor should be expected to be; nor treated as though defective or remarkable because of variations in ten or a hundred respects from a purely imaginary norm. To be different is to be normal—only within the artificial, bureaucratic *structures* of training and education would clones be welcomed. The structures are abnormal, not the people. To send children to school on the basis of their birthdates, and then in large part treat them as alike is to ignore how real children develop. Even if we put them in chairs that are the right size for their average, more than half will be in chairs that are the wrong size for them! Mentally, we have every reason to believe, the variations range far more widely.

In Chapter 6 mention was made of the prefrontal lobes, behind the forehead, which are sometimes called "the brain's brain." *This portion of the brain includes tissue structures that are exclusively human*—their equivalent does not seem to occur in any other animal. The late, renowned Soviet researcher, Luria, observed: "It must also be noted that the prefrontal regions of the cortex do not mature until very late in ontogeny, and not until the child has reached the age of four to seven years do they become finally prepared for action."[4] For a child at this period, a range of three years bulks large indeed, and to throw students into first-grade work with only lip-service provision for individualization may be accounted an invitation of trouble. Luria further describes these parts of the new brain as: "a superstructure above all other parts of the cerebral cortex, so that they perform a far more universal function of general regulation of behavior"[5] than other parts of the neocortex. Elsewhere he adds: "It can thus be concluded that the frontal lobes of the brain are among the vital structures responsible for the orientation of an animal's behavior *not only to the present, but also to the future*" (Luria's emphasis).[6] The frontal lobes, then, and especially the exclusively human prefrontal portions, provide the ability to look ahead further, to make longer plans, and to stick with them in spite of distractions. In an infant, up to roughly a few months over age two, old brain structures dominate attention: the child *must* give heed to new sights or sounds, and parents' verbal instructions to the contrary will be ignored. No amount of reproof or punishment will have effect. As the newer brain areas develop their powers, these old survival programs or schema come under more control; and as the prefrontal areas are brought into use, the child has enormously greater capacity to set more distant goals and carry through a chain of activity. No amount of teacher coercion will substitute for natural development, nor is the child properly subject to criticism or being labeled immature, impulsive, or learning disabled.

Particularly critical for success in early classrooms is a child's ability and willingness to follow verbal instructions, since teachers rely heavily on this kind of group direction. Conflict and frustrations inevitably result, since the whole concept of the classroom is unrealistic and brain incompatible. It ignores what is happening in the brain.

The surface area of the frontal cortex, Luria shows,[7] expands rapidly to around 3½ years, then more slowly to around 7 years, and from that point gradually until age 18 or more. Anyone who has raised children to adulthood has had opportunity to see the effect of frontal and prefrontal growth and myelination: the factor of lower-brain distractibility lessens, the concept of future time (later, tomorrow, next month, when you are 12) comes to have practical meaning, longer-term plans can be made and often completed, and in general self-governing capacity grows.

Observation suggests strongly, however, that parents and teachers alike tend to err far more often on the side of underestimating or misinterpreting what a youngster can do. A myth exists that children of a certain age have a certain "span of attention"—one more expression of the persistent idea that alikeness prevails, not differences. In actuality, a four-year-old may spend hours during a day building an elaborate system of roads and bridges with blocks and toy cars, for example. The capacity of six-year-olds to carry on rope-jumping, or fort-building, or an expedition through meadow and woods, is readily observable. Often children will leave the activity briefly to return to it later—exactly what office workers do with coffee breaks, lunch, short social visits, trips to the washrooms or drinking fountain, or making phone calls. Span of attention will often be short and fragile for activities forced on the child by others, but many times longer and more persistent when self-selected. The term, which in my view is more a mischief maker than useful, should not be confused with length and complexity of plans, reflecting prefrontal and frontal lobe development.

The most simple of approaches seems to work well to give adults a sound estimate of what individual children can handle: *provide the opportunity, stay out of the way, and then observe what the child chooses to do.* At a playground, for example, where children may freely climb, jump, or swing, self-caused accidents prove rare. Children know their own capabilities and "what comes next" in individual development. When even trained adults such as physical education instructors begin giving orders, injuries may skyrocket. When I was a youth, bicycles were thought suitable only for children at least ten years old; today one sees five- and six-year-old boys and girls who not only manage two-wheelers well but can rear up and ride on the back wheel alone. Yet other, well-endowed children may not get the knack of balancing a bicycle until two or three years later.

Adult worry about financial damages may inhibit youngsters' achievement: fear of lawsuit or of equipment being hurt. Although young students can handle tools quite expertly with the briefest safety instruction and a little supervision, they are often denied them. I have seen junior high school students, supposedly the least reliable, use expensive photographic, television, laboratory, and computer equipment with faultless skill and care—provided they were carrying out activities they wanted to do, not those forced upon them. I have also seen severely retarded children do exquisite hand lettering, and arrange and serve a meal at a beautiful, elaborately set table and watched films of retarded, blind children doing daring, difficult tumbling!

The key element that limits individual performance when following verbal instruction and doing or using long-term planning is frontal lobe development. Otherwise, ability to perform acquired programs can often be startlingly beyond conventional suppositions. The range of difference is huge, and the rapidity of change of limits can be surprising. The idea that the adult in parental or instructional role "knows" the child must be distrusted—the adult judgment may be mistaken or influenced by what is seen as convenient, economical, or least risky. *Only when the child is asked, not by test or examination but by being given options and time, without threat, can the true current state of capabilities be assessed.*[8]

We cannot see inside the brain what neuron growth has taken place and how far myelination has gone[9] in any particular area; and normal variation can be so large as to make "average" guidelines more harmful than useful.

When we view the child as possessing at least 30 billion neurons that will be organized in individual fashion over some 20 years we take a practical view. If we respect the mighty cerebrum and grasp what development is going forward, we may find it easier to respect the child and comprehend behavior.

The key points about brain development have profound implications for educators who deal with students at any age before adulthood:

1.   The brain can be used only to the extent that it has become organized. This occurs over roughly a 20-year period. The time is required not for muscular and bone growth, which could be accomplished much faster, but because of the huge number of neurons involved.

2.   At birth or within a short time after, a person has almost all the neurons he or she will ever have. They are not replaced as they die off.

3.   Neurons literally grow, becoming larger and more complex, and at least some of this growth is influenced by input and experience.

4.   Myelination, or the insulation of nerve pathways, improves their functioning, and is a process that continues until adulthood. Individuals differ sharply in the specific progress of myelination.

5.   The prefrontal portions of the cerebrum have a profound influence on human behavior, making possible longer-term programs. Individuals differ widely in terms of how soon these areas come into full use, and these normal differences are not under parental or teacher control.

6.   Children's abilities may often be underestimated by those adults who may claim to "know" them. Ability is best determined by providing opportunity, standing aside, and observing. Threat must be absent.

7.   The class-and-grade or factory school system is unrelated to present understandings of brain development, and in practice ranges from severely to violently brain antagonistic.

NOTES

1. *Programs of the Brain* (Oxford: Oxford University Press, 1978), p. 25.
2. The reader who would like some further concept of the functions of neurons without getting too deep technically is referred to my book, *How The Brain Works* (New York: Basic Books, 1975.) For a technical discussion of structure and the electrochemical aspects, see Charles F. Stevens, "The Neuron," *Scientific American*, September 1979, and other articles in this special brain issue.
3. Lack of stimulation and normal cherishing can even result in reduced physical

growth. See Lytt I. Gardner, "Deprivation Dwarfism," *Scientific American*, July 1972.

4. A. R. Luria, *The Working Brain* (New York: Basic Books, 1975), p. 87.
5. Ibid., p. 89.
6. Ibid., p. 91.
7. Ibid., chart, p. 87.
8. Tests given children by neurologists, psychologists, school specialists, and others in their office can be extremely fallible, especially if a parent having difficulties with the child is present or nearby. The conditions of the test create threat—as indeed they do for the adult under similar circumstances. Often the professional is pressed for time and relies on one no-time-lost reading. It can happen, too, that the child gathers how he or she is expected to perform, and obliges. It is remarkable how adults who themselves are terrified by any examination by someone in a white coat still feel that a strange test by a strange person in a strange setting should not affect the child at all.
9. "Up to the age of ten or so, vast areas of the cortex are not yet myelinated; and up to the age twenty, large areas of the frontal lobes are not yet myelinated." See Peter Nathan, *The Nervous System* (Philadelphia: J. B. Lippincott, 1969), p. 296.

13

From the standpoint of the child, the great waste in the school comes from his inability to utilize the experiences he gets outside the school in any complete and free way within the school itself; while, on the other hand, he is unable to apply in daily life what he is learning at school. That is the isolation of the school—its isolation from life.

Nothing is more absurd than to suppose that there is no middle term between leaving a child to his own unguided fancies and likes or controlling his activities by a formal succession of dictated directions.

—JOHN DEWEY[1]

Settings: Brain-Antagonistic Traditions

One good test of a theory is its practicality. If on close examination it turns out to be little more than so many words—especially grandiose, sweeping words hard to pin down or "soft" terms that mean something different to each person—it may at best be entertaining, and at worst, boring and time wasting. But if on the contrary a theory touches base with reality; with concrete, easily observed materials, structures, functions, behaviors, and scientific findings; and if its language can easily be translated into specific, familiar examples that make the terms sharp, specific, and not difficult to agree on, it may well have immediate utility.

That lucid philosopher, Whitehead, has observed:

Success in practice depends on theorists who...by some good chance have hit on the relevant ideas. By a theorist I do not mean a man who is up in the clouds, but a man whose motive for thought is the desire to formulate correctly the rules according to which events occur. A successful theorist should be excessively interested in immediate events, otherwise he is not at all likely to formulate correctly anything about them.[2]

Good theory applying to education should promptly suggest a great and rich variety of approaches, methods, techniques, materials, devices, and practices that might be explored, tested, demonstrated, or experimented with. It is not at all necessary that the theory provide wholly new ideas in these areas; in fact it is more than likely many of the suggested applications will turn out to have elements of familiarity. What is new is the formulation of rules that permit us and help us to see the old in quite a new way, and to move from tentative, personal intuitions that we can scarcely express to sharply etched insights that we can not only state but agree on and put into use.

If indeed we reach back over the centuries and check the concepts and intuitions of such people as Confucius, Socrates, Aristotle, Seneca, Quintilian, St. Augustine, St. Thomas Aquinas, Luther, Erasmus, Comenius, Montaigne, Locke, Hecker, Rousseau, Pestalozzi, Herbart, Froebel, Parker, and Dewey, we find ideas and injunctions recurring again and again that fit neatly with some of the main tenets of Proster Theory. But of course they were not formulated into coherent theory, nor could they be brain based before modern knowledge of the brain was available.

Educators in general lack familiarity with the whole idea of useful theory and its application (the basis of our astounding present-day technology in most fields) because useful theory has rarely been generated. In a 1964 Yearbook on educational theory, Winfred Hill noted "an extremely incomplete background for dealing with the problems of teaching" and N. L. Gage observed: "As is well known, after more than a half-century of effort, no such unification of learning theory has materialized." Knowledge was "inadequate to tell us what we should do about teaching."[3]

Educational literature in general pays little attention to basic theory, even to the point of discussing it much; but the views quoted must be judged typical rather than exceptional. Among teachers and principals, and other working educators, one finds overwhelmingly (as I noted earlier in Chapter 3) the feeling that theory means the dreary lectures on long outdated psychologies they had to suffer through to get their credits. Having sampled mainly muddled, fragmentary, and antique educational theory, they understandably do not realize keenly the potentials of sound, modern, useful theory.

It may then be proper to point out that useful theory does not mean a new, more fashionable or "in" collection of "what do I do Monday" cookbook-style recipes: do exactly this, and the outcome will be pleasing. Rather, useful theory clarifies how and why events occur, and suggests directions in which to move and areas in which to explore, invent, and develop techniques—as well as those to avoid. In my view a helpful image is that of a long corridor with many doors, some long open and in use, and others long locked. Useful theory leads us to close some of the familiar doors that have led only to failure or poor results, and to begin using new doors that open onto fresh territories, resources, and opportunities.

On the other side of those newly opened doors educators will find innumerable choices, unlimited room to be creative. But they will not find a storehouse of mint-fresh texts waiting to be used, procedures ready to implement, or machines needing only to be switched on. Between good theory and its daily application lies a large region of development (in some cases, "engineering") in which a huge amount of work and effort is called for. Theory is, after all, theoretical; it must be translated into the practical.

How large and exciting can we reasonably expect results to be when useful theory is applied, and how quickly can they be looked for? Are we speaking of a generation or two, or of a few years?

Two principles have importance here. The first question must be the size of the potentials, to the best of our knowledge. Here what we can call *instance of success* becomes a key. What the rare genius or very exceptional person accomplishes does not tell us too much, but when we find repeated examples of unusual achievement by individuals who seem to fall within more ordinary boundaries, we do not need great numbers to convince us of potentials. Instead of looking at grade levels and norms as guides, studying those who exceed usual attainment can be instructive.

In both special and common settings there seem to be amply sufficient instances of success to demonstrate that learning can be far better and faster than usual. Certainly many thousands of children learn to read before they enter school. Omar K. Moore and his associates established beyond doubt that children three and four years old of well below genius level could learn to read and write on typewriters, quite impressively, acquiring their skills easily and with apparent enjoyment. Later Moore showed that kindergarten and first-grade students in a school could consistently achieve reading abilities of sixth-grade and higher levels.[4] In almost any school system, one can find instances of students whose learning in such fields as mathematics, science, or music runs years ahead of the norm, although some do not evidence any exceptional IQ or special background. Instances of success appear to show clearly that the potential for much superior learning exists and is not limited to a small number of unusual, "genius" individuals.

The second principle helps to show why large and abrupt gains may be possible. It can be called the factoring principle: the recognition that *learning depends not only on what helps, but also on elimination or reduction of those factors that hurt.* Working educators commonly find it hard to think in these terms—a reading teacher, for example, may simply refuse to consider that some of the instruction being given helps prevent the students from improving their skills. When people give instruction, as when they offer advice, the intent normally is to be helpful, and the negative possibilities may get little attention. Traditionally medical doctors are warned, "above all, do no harm," yet the side effects of medicines, unnecessary operations, and too hastily recommended procedures continue to create serious problems for patients. Educators are seldom even cautioned. Rather the assumption is made that education is good, better, or best; and possibly harmful effects tend to be ignored, while those who venture to mention them may be ostracized.[5]

A brain-compatible approach, however, suggests that *present schools and conventional formal instruction of many kinds plainly are brain-antagonistic, and contain seriously negative components.* If the plus and minus influences were to be factored out, and then the positives strengthened and negatives reduced or eliminated, the push-pull shift in learning outcomes could be dramatic. Despite the investment of hundreds of millions of dollars in research, this effort to factor for negative as well as positive influences has seldom been made. Much research seeks to find correlations, which do not necessarily involve causal relations at all, or even show what is cause and what effect. Here again we see attempts to deal with complex, interactive systems with simple-minded linear logic. One large advantage of a comprehensive theory of learning is that it can suggest how to factor.[6]

In application of theory, as we have noted, what is stopped may be as important, or even more important, than what is introduced. Since humans live by familiar patterns and accumulated programs, stopping may be difficult to bring about within large organizations with intricate social structures, and especially within bureaucracies such as public school systems. This helps explain why, despite all the emphasis on change over the past dozen or fifteen years, in fact the schools have changed hardly at all, and why so many efforts boldly and enthusiastically begun have tended to fade out over a period of time as old patterns and programs reassert their strength of persistence.

It can be helpful to approach the problems of theory application on three fairly distinct levels: *settings, situations,* and *activities.* The following chapters will consider these three focuses.

The setting implies the entire ambiance of the instructional institution, whether it be a public school, an undergraduate college, or specialized training center. A key question to ask, and one particularly valuable for staff orientation, is "Why is the student here?" From a brain-compatible learning viewpoint, it makes a great difference whether the student is present under some compulsion—sent to school—or attends by free choice. It may seem evident that the student who must go to school under compulsory education laws later goes freely to college, but considering the student's view quickly shows that to be an illusion. The elementary school student usually has no concept of the law, and sees attendance as directed by the parents—and (at a guess) perhaps half of college students act under the same family coercion. The youth at any army school may have been sent under orders, or may have applied for the school as a lesser evil. Employees of businesses taking courses in computer uses, or seminars on sales, credit, accounting, supervision and the like, may have been sent, either overtly or through fear of the consequences of refusal. At the other extreme, training institutions may receive (and the unscrupulous actively invite) students whose expectations approach a fantasy level and who soon drop out when faced with the mundane aspects. Even in these instances attendance may be a way of avoiding criticism, adult competition, or simply, as in the familiar example of the perennial student, work and adult responsibilities.

Brain-compatible learning essentially occurs in a free setting. The core of natural learning is the desire to better understand how the world (experienced by the individual learner) operates. From earliest infancy there is a clearly visible built-in drive to make sense of what seems of value, as we have discussed. But making sense does not mean only an intellectual understanding; I have emphasized that the motor aspect must be involved if one is to act upon the world. The "learning by doing" relationship so closely associated with John Dewey (though embraced by many in education long before and since) should not prevent us from seeing that most natural learning is for doing: it enlarges the individual's control over a physical and social world. Learning is the acquisition of programs; programs have goals. A child learns to walk, to talk, to operate light switches and faucets, to ride a wheeled vehicle, to throw and catch a ball, to use tools, to enlarge the repertory of what can be done.

As we inspect settings and ask the question "Why is the student here?" a satisfactory answer from a brain-compatible view must be on the order of "to acquire the programs to do this and that." That is not the kind of answer we often get when we look at conventional schooling. Rather, even the avowed objectives tend to slide semantically away from "do" into vaguer terminology. The student will:

Get the fundamentals of an education.
Learn basic skills (probably not sharply named or defined).
Be processed through the curriculum.
Be prepared for further, higher education.
Be enabled to pass various examinations.

In short, the academic student supposedly will acquire skills and knowledge that form a latent pool, to be useful in some distant, unspecified future.

A historical look at the typical school setting throws some light on structure. A century ago, when our class-and-grade system was taking firm shape in a dominantly agricultural country, the school was seen as quite literally providing "book learning." Books and other materials in the home were few. At school the student could be exposed to more of such input, as well as hearing a little about the then "outside" world. A traveled teacher might be able to tell first hand of cities with buildings that towered five and six stories, of ships that crossed the Atlantic with many passengers in only a few weeks, of museums with fossils of creatures that lived millions of years ago. These were wonders to rivet attention. But on the whole children went to school little and only when their families could forgo their then indispensible free labor, helping about the home, in the garden, in the fields, with cottage industries and in small shops. The basic school hours of 9:00 A.M. to 3:00 P.M. still reflect, slightly modified, the arrangement that permitted children to do their chores before and after, and walk to and from school. The summer vacation, of course, recalls the originally much longer period during which farm work demanded the children full time. Schools now send their charges home to houses where no adult is present—more women work than do not, and many families have only one parent—with disregard for the great changes time has brought.[7]

The students of those days, in their hours and months out of school, were drenched in exposure to reality. They helped grow and process food, fed and birthed animals, helped maintain machines and build structures, made many necessaries, wove and sewed clothing, assisted manufacturing and business, knew the community and its people intimately. Their input was varied and often oppressively "real." The school could well afford, on balance, to bring them into a once- or twice-removed, symbolic world. Even so, the basic skills they sometimes acquired were intended for immediate use: arithmetic for ciphering in shops or to keep farm accounts, reading primarily for religious purposes, writing to keep records or occasionally send letters, since travel was very limited for most. Even music, which got much attention, was utilized in church and community events.

But today students are starved for exposure to reality. They have few chores, and these usually are trivial, rather than obviously essential to the family's survival as was the case a century ago. They do not see food being grown, or necessities being made: milk comes not from cows but from the supermarket. When my friends and I walked to school, we stopped to observe each stage of the building of a new house; today's students most likely whiz by in bus or car. The toys we designed and made have been replaced by those that are bought. Many children today have no real idea of what their parents do for a living; terms such as auditor, keypuncher, harness-maker (electronic), long lines installer, change-order checker, renting agent, margin clerk, patent attorney, facsimile

operator, interior decorator, actuary, router, manufacturer's represen-
tative, systems engineer, dot etcher, flow scheduler, analytical chemist,
and the like may have no meaning to youngsters, and even such as
secretary, fitter, cashier, inspector, and executive may relate to little
within the hearer's experience. Many children never see their parents'
places of work, or see only the exterior.

They are not likely to learn much of this nature in school, except as
they may select specific vocational courses at the secondary level. In most
communities academic paths get priority and most of the attention, and
college entrance stands as the assumed goal. Efforts to stress career education have produced little deep change thus far, and where there is no
special funding, the program may have faded away. After 12 years of
nonrealistic schooling, students usually emerge with few and limited
useful skills; superficial and often garbled understanding of the fields they
have studied; and virtually no substantial knowledge of their communities
and how they work, politics, the law, business, taxation, consumer
economics, other countries, other languages, recent world history, older
and younger people, marriage and the rearing of children, or even the
requirements of the fields that interest them. Frequently they have
developed no firm interests, and know so little about occupations that
they have no grounds for choice.

Worse, they have had forced on them the notion that the *credential* is
what counts, that passing an examination is a license to cease further
learning, that the objective of learning is not its application but getting
over the next hurdle toward additional credentials.

In at least four areas the schools, and to large degree colleges, appear
to have allowed their foundation to erode by ignoring the huge changes
going on in society:

1.   As students have lost the contact with reality most students used
to have amply, *the schools have failed to bring reality inside their walls to
offset the loss.*

2.   For centuries, schools aimed *to control what their students learned.*
Indoctrination and "teaching the book" were the undisputed objectives, and neither parents nor educators wanted students to explore or to
question the traditional wisdom. Rote instruction was generally used. But
as religious restrictions lost their force; as society became more fluid and
the middle class began to outnumber the poor for the first time in history;
and as new technology such as radio, television, recording, film, high-
speed printing, and others created a flood of information and spread new
knowledge, the idea of control through the schools became another "relic
of former times," as Foshay put it. *Yet commonly schools act as if control
were still possible and desirable, and an objective!*

3.   Similarly, schools have preserved the long valid notion that learning is primarily a youth activity, to be largely terminated as one became

an adult. Such a posture was practicable to perhaps 1940, when change began to occur so rapidly as to make the concept ridiculous. Quite recently, universities have begun to put more emphasis on lifetime learning through continuing education offerings—perhaps more for financial reasons than others. But the schools, where fundamental ideas of education are apt to be laid down, still cling to the idea of curriculum, static right-answer knowledge, grade norms, and teachers whose certificates qualify them to instruct without ever updating or retraining.

4. Despite the availability of new understandings of the brain and the potentials of brain-compatible education, most institutions still use instruction that was designed as suitable for "teaching the book," or for an educational factory. Even the first step, that of recognizing the brain as the organ of learning, has not yet been widely taken. (In 1982, however, a surge of interest in the brain was evident in the conference programs of most major educational associations, as well as in their publications. This fresh orientation of these influential organizations could well prove significant.)

These observations are made to sensibly suggest that not much can be expected from planting flower seeds in concrete. We cannot go far in applying new insights and theory as a new layer on an outdated, obsolete structure.

But we can begin, at once, to put the new brain-compatible concepts and techniques into use, wherever seeds can find soil. If this will hardly of itself free education from the consequences of failures to enter and keep pace with the modern world, it may nonetheless open doors to some sweeping reforms, painfully needed.

NOTES

1. *The Child and the Curriculum* (Chicago: University of Chicago Press, Phoenix Books, 1902), pp. 75, 130.
2. Alfred North Whitehead, *The Aims of Education* (New York: New American Library-Mentor, 1929), p. 102.
3. *Theories of Learning and Instruction*, 63d Yearbook of the National Society for the Study of Education (Chicago: University of Chicago Press, 1964), p. 53; and (Gage), p. 272, 274.
4. Moore's work is described in part in Maya Pines, *Revolution in Learning* (New York: Harper and Row, 1966), Chapter 5, and many articles and reports have been published on what he and associates have demonstrated in reading particularly. Moore is currently professor of sociology at the University of Pittsburgh, and continues work directly with children in inner-city areas. Perhaps because of his innovative (and brain-compatible) techniques, his striking successes have been largely ignored in educational literature. I have met with him, examined independent reports and other evidence, and found no reason to doubt that remarkable results were achieved. See also Omar K. Moore, "The

Responsive Environments Laboratory," in Beatrice and Ronald Gross, *Radical School Reform* (New York: Simon and Schuster, 1969), p. 205.

5. Despite the enormous volume of criticism that regularly appears in educational periodicals, and in the form of speeches or conference reports, rarely is the suggestion made that bad or wrong teaching may actively impede learning. Some research studies do report negative correlations but there is almost no tradition of examining negative factors further.

6. See John I. Goodlad, "Can Our Schools Get Better?" in *Phi Delta Kappan*, January 1979, p. 343: "How many researchers are moving from those studies of single variables in the learning process that have yielded no significant findings to those much more complex inquiries required for understanding school and classroom environments so that we might understand, also, how to improve them?"

7. From 1950 to 1977 the percentage of married women in the labor force rose from not quite 25 percent to 47 percent. About 48 percent of women 16 or over had or were seeking jobs. Of the female labor force, over 61 percent are married women. (*United Business Service*, September 4, 1979, p. 353.) The trend appears to continue for women with school-age children to seek employment, and probably a majority now work regularly.

14

Given the durability of American views of school practice, it is no surprise to find that, with few exceptions, school programs have altered little since the 1890's. Considering the prodigious changes in American society since 1900, it is remarkable, and not merely the result of chance, that only minor rearrangements have been seen.

—THEODORE R. SIZER[1]

Learning: Steps toward Brain Compatibility

How much learning public schools bring about is currently a subject of heated debate, but their influence on public and professional thinking about learning seems pervasive.

The schools, and their nonpublic equivalents (more often similar than sharply different) supposedly represent the foundation of education. From this base stem a welter of ideas that relate schools and learning, schools and education, and teaching and learning. Included are beliefs about when children should go to school; what represents basic and normal learning; conditions necessary for learning; desirable organization; the proper roles of students, teachers, and parents; the functions of the school in the community and its claim to tax monies; and the authority it can, does, and should wield.

Anyone who has closely observed schools over many years from a suitable vantage point, as I have for a quarter-century, will I believe readily agree that "chaos" is not an unfair word to describe this vast scene. Schools seem to have great difficulty stating what they are seeking to do, why they are doing it, and what the results are. Examination of why schools are as they are usually finds the reasons, if determinable, far in the past. But so large is the establishment, so huge the amount of money used, so numerous the jobs, that this outdated juggernaut colors most efforts to comprehend human learning. The influence of the school extends upward: much that is done at college level, in vocational schools, and in training programs plainly reflects conventional school practice and the often centuries-old and now plainly defective concepts of human behavior, nature, and learning that schools embody.

In considering settings suitable for learning (the purpose of this chapter) it is not easy to break away from these misconceptions. We have all been brought up with them, and may seldom have looked at them critically. While this book is focused on aspects of learning rather than criticism of schools, contrasting what could be in education with what is seems inescapable, if clarity is to be achieved.

Remarkably little attention has been given to the design of *complete, contemporary* school systems. As we consider settings in terms of brain compatibility, I will suggest four key facets: expectation, ambiance, mastery, and reality. If they will not provide an integrated picture, they will give us at least useful starting points.

1. *Expectation* plunges us at once into an unfamiliar area. Schools and colleges provide standards widely taken for granted, as for instance grade levels are used for various purposes year after year without even inquiry into their origins or current adequacy. Expectation has a number of dimensions, all largely unexplored:

- How fast can individual students learn, given the opportunity?
- How far up can learning be carried, relative to age and experience?
- How completely can gross failure be eliminated?
- How well can learning be retained?

On these and related questions, research has been scant and findings few. Many of the most prominent books on learning do not get into these matters in depth, if at all. We may at least suspect that the school has influence here too—*learning has been studied mostly in relation to the typical school classroom*; but instances of highly successful, notable classroom learning remain very difficult to find. Though each September more than two million classrooms go into session, reports of solid learning successes seldom appear, and the few that do seldom survive critical examination. Where we find individual students who have achieved far above the usual, the conventional classroom rarely figures in the achievement, since the student soon goes far beyond its level.

If learning is indeed a prime objective of schooling, as is so often proclaimed, one might expect that great attention would be paid to learning potentials. But I fear it does not take much study of schools to see that by no means can it be assumed that maximum learning is universally desired. While parents may welcome outstanding performance in certain fields, especially athletics or some form of social approval, it is no secret that many do not jump for joy at having their offspring come home with new and surprising ideas and information, expertise that puts parental abilities to shame, or observations that call into question firmly held concepts in religious, patriotic, or economic matters. Interest is likely to focus on credentials and the good record that is assumed to enhance employability. Higher-income parents may see the school as wholly preparatory for college and perhaps advanced degrees. Only a slim minority can be expected to value learning per se, and even some of these may see winning valuable scholarships as a goal.

If we think of two private teachers, one about to teach 20 beginners to swim and the other 12 to play the piano, we can anticipate their concerns. They do not want failures; they can almost hear voices saying, "I sent my child to _____ and he didn't learn a thing!" Any gross failure is a black eye, to be avoided through great effort and attention. At the other extreme, the rapid learner is cherished and encouraged, for such successes tend to attract more pupils. In the graded school, however, the teacher aims reverse. The lagging pupil can be sloughed off with a label: not motivated, uncooperative, immature, family problems, learning disability, previous failure, language handicaps, disturbed—whatever the term, it transfers responsibility from instructor and school to the student. The students who do middling well become the blessed, because they more or less fit the syllabus and the standards. At the top end, the bright or gifted students may be nuisances and perhaps threats, apt to become bored, difficult or withdrawn, or heavy consumers of teacher time and effort if the attempt is made to meet their needs so far as is possible within classroom limitations.

Teachers of graded classrooms seldom fail to realize that if they allow students to "run ahead," trouble will ensue with the teachers who receive them in the next grade, the following year. Somehow, the more able students must be prevented from saying "We had that!" when the next term begins. The lockstep grade system prescribes what learning students are to achieve. The structure also applies to teachers. Within the bureaucratic social system, those whose methods differ and whose students learn sharply better may expect not admiration and emulation but more likely some degree of ostracism. The instructor who produces visibly superior learning becomes a threat to those who don't, and quite possibly a boat-rocker and "disruptive element," in the eyes of an administration concerned with harmony, smooth running, and no problems. Testimony to this pressure for teacher conformity abounds.[2]

In plain and evident truth, accelerated learning can tear apart the conventional school. The economic penalties are apparent, too. If students can complete the present curriculum better in three years less, what will that do to staffing? If reading achievement becomes far better, who will employ the remedial teachers? If the "learning disabled" prove quite able to learn, what will those specialists be needed for? Since students learning with success at their own speed seldom create discipline problems (almost always a sign of impeded learning), why will the schools need all those assistant principals? At present, very few teachers or administrators ever are discharged for incompetence, since the failure of students to learn has historically been easily accommodated overall. But suppose the demands for competency continue to rise and achievement of student learning must be demonstrated—what of job security then? Some suppression of learning, deliberately and systematically, is essential to preserve the present graded classroom system. But we must wonder at the cost to society, and to the individuals held back or diverted by "enrichment."

A setting designed for learning must be so organized that fullest student achievement is welcomed, not feared. That does not imply going through the present curriculum faster, since there exists the widest agreement that present studies are far too narrow, producing graduates with pathetically inadequate skills and grasp of the world they must enter as responsible citizens. Alternative structures already are available, and more can be created, in which brain-compatible learning can be encouraged without constraint.[3]

2.   The *ambiance* of such schools (and higher-level centers for learning) must be strikingly different from what we are used to from school experience. As Proster Theory suggests, the learning sought has to occur almost entirely in the new brain, the great cerebrum that only humans possess. The cerebrum works fully only as threat is absent. The settings for brain-compatible education must be as free from threat as possible, not simply by good intention but by inherent design.

Here again escaping the version of school we have been brought up with is not easy. Though we no longer portray teachers holding an implement for physical punishment, they clearly possess substantial power over students in almost all classrooms, and it is freely used—often perforce on hasty judgment—behind closed doors and with no other adults present to observe, protest, or report. Not only can the power be used as of the moment, but it can have long-term, even life-long, effect on the victim when it puts an entry on the record, or a label on the child. Principals wield similar power, though as a rule theirs must be used more in the open.

Because of its history, the power to punish, to hurt, to demean is built into the system at every turn. Threat is pervasive, expressed in compulsory attendance, operation by the clock, the incessant giving of tests and examinations, constant use of marks and grades, awarding or withholding of approvals and permissions, on up to administrative transfer, suspension, and expulsion. Many considerate and good-hearted people work in schools who may soften the threat; but every child knows the adults still possess the power and can use it at any time. Overall persists the ancient threat of captivity.

School is not a safe place for youngsters; and when pressures are added by parents hungry for credentials, even the suicide rate can soar. It can be argued that youngsters need trials and not to be coddled if they are to survive later in a hard and uncaring world. But the trials of school and like institutions are more those of suffering under a rigid bureaucracy, than the complex, interactive, changing problems of the real world, and to the degree that they cause downshifting and inability to learn, they must *lessen* capacity to cope. I have seen quite a few candidates for high degrees as shaken, as terrified, as downshifted as primary children—their lack of self-confidence pathetic. The fear of examinations does not end early. Yet outside the academic world, and that of the lower end of civil service, examinations have only a minor importance. Those for accounting, law, and some other professions, we may note in passing, have a considerable quality of reality—the problems presented are those likely to be encountered in practice, unlike the quick, academic tests that heavily involve giving remembered right answers, or merely checking a multiple-choice question.

Creating a brain-compatible ambiance calls for deliberately identifying and stripping away sources of threat. Some are holdovers from the last century and before, when schools were avowedly punitive, disciplining institutions where students were to be taught to sit still, obey, and suffer patiently. That many students see faculty members as probably an enemy, eager to criticize, mark down, demean, restrict or "fail" them rather than help remains true today—the adversary role has been widely documented.[4] In visiting many schools, I have been struck by the different attitudes of students in genuinely open settings. A visitor is perceived as a friendly helper who can be asked a question, or for assistance, or even be pulled down to the floor to advise on work in progress. In conventional classroom schools, a strange adult is likely to be viewed with suspicion and avoided.

Equally dispensable are remnants of the factory concept, demanding that all students be present, at inflexible hours. One can find administrators who appear to suffer shock at the idea that it is hardly necessary or desirable today to still view students as future mill-hands, and that the ability to manage one's own time can hardly be acquired by responding to factory whistles. (Ironically, in literal terms, the whistle has all but disappeared, while the school buzzers or gongs continue in use!) Even more shocking to some (and parents) can be the idea that a certain amount of free, unassigned time, of contemplation, of reverie, even of just resting, can add to productivity. The coffee break, the "take ten" breather, the relaxed lunch period, have all been accepted widely by profit-pressed business and industry, but far less in education. One might suppose that learning was thought to be a function of the clock, or of how long buttocks remain in contact with a hard chair.

Captivity can be sharply reduced if the value of doing so is seen. Once the factory and classroom molds are broken, practical arrangements present little difficulty, and many models already exist of schools and higher institutions that allow students much freedom of movement and schedule. Nor is it difficult to allow students some room to select, rather than have forced on them, the instructors and planning counselors they relate to best. (That arrangement can be equally appreciated on the instructor's side.)

3. The *mastery* approach appears so simple in concept that one must wonder why it still has the capacity to startle some conventional educators.[5] Presently, we commonly require a fixed period of instruction, such as a semester, at the end of which time each student is given a grade. If passing is 65 percent, credit is given and the 35 percent not-passed portion is forgotten about. For a factory approach, this long seemed a convenient arrangement, even if one built on low standards. The mastery approach turns this upside down: *it makes 100 percent attainment of the key elements the goal, but leaves the time to achieve it flexible.* I have often illustrated the principle by asking, "Would you like to fly with an airline pilot who got 65 percent in landings?"

When mastery is demanded in basic areas of learning, the setting changes from one which emphasizes scraping over hurdles to get credentials, to one in which solid learning takes priority, is expected, demanded, and achieved. The sordid business of cramming for examinations, remembering answers for a brief period, and leaving the gaps in learning still open because a "pass" has been registered, can be ended. Mastery permits observed individual performance, or demonstrated abilities, to take the place of contrived tests. The "right answer," often quick, arbitrary and superficial, gives place to the cycle we have examined: detect the pattern, select a stored program, implement it successfully.

Mastery simultaneously helps create an atmosphere of high standards and achievement for the setting and reduces the threat of examinations, which put undue value on a single, artificial performance at one time under one set of conditions.

We have noted the difference between *threat*, inflicted upon the individual, and *risk*, selected by the individual in response to the built-in urge, peculiarly human in degree, to take chances, to dare, to seek excitement and new events and their stimulation. When students are always told what to do, the tendency is strong for those who give the orders to set objectives too low for many students. But in settings where students have more room to choose their own, they can often be startling in their originality and level.[6] If a student does overshoot, the results are not necessarily wholly negative—there can be a new appreciation of complexity, a new awareness of the problems involved. On one occasion while in school my son over-reacted to a librarian's objection to his taking out a book on submarines she thought too difficult for him. (In fact he was able to read a good deal of it, and to understand the diagrams.) I have always wondered why she did not see it as simpler to let him take the book and return it, whatever the outcome—what was to be lost? Where the setting offers mastery with a good deal of freedom of choice, students will in at least many cases take on surprising risks, and often make good on them. But the setting must allow the time and continuity the projects require. Conversely, students held to short efforts that can be completed within a factory-school time frame are being effectively prevented and discouraged from building experience in undertakings that demand more planning, dedication, and perseverence—qualities normally regarded as of high value.

Even at kindergarten level, complaints and labels based on short attention span often turn out to mean that some teacher feels "this child won't stick long with what *I* want him to do." In the course of schooling, the student may again and again be told, in effect or in so many words, to read a shorter book because the report must be in Monday; to write 250 words because the teacher has no time to read long essays; to forgo an experiment that would take more than a year because "the course will be over before that." Mastery is not only not a goal, but an idea often perceived as a nuisance that interferes with neat bureaucratic scheduling and the dominance of the clock.

4.   The facet of *reality* brings us back again to the place of the book in education. The book, of course, ranks among our greatest technological inventions. It has provided the basis for our information age, and a good many years are likely to pass before computer retrieval displaces the library shelf. But the book inherently is an abstract of reality. A brain-compatible approach introduces a considerable shift from defining an educated person as one "who knows a lot" (possesses much information, or can recite the sacred text, or is familiar with the language of the law) to seeing the educated person as one who knows what to do—who can detect the patterns involved, and select appropriate programs that can be implemented. While some may still argue that we need a sprinkling of scholars in the old sense, producing them is hardly the main or even a major task of our schools and undergraduate colleges or training institutions.

Yet in academic instruction teachers often cling to the book (the text) as though to a life raft. The book does not get translated into doing, or the doing consists mainly of exercises, still remote from acting on the real world. Unfortunately, the book is finite and convenient. The instructor can plan to cover the book by going over it with the class at the rate of 10 or 20 pages a week. Examinations can be based on regurgitating, on a similar schedule. And emphasis on "the" book may severely hold down the use of other books—especially "real" (nontext) books.

As I have noted, reality typically is complex, messy, random, and illogical. It may also be awkward, offensive, controversial, hard to partition off, and subject to many factors producing rapid and sometimes unpredictable change. The well-ordered classroom and rude reality clash head-on, and ordinarily the classroom wins. The same walls that confine the students as prisoners serve to exclude the inconvenient and often embarrassing real world.

The poverty of instruction that stems from this limiting use of the book becomes compounded manyfold by another invention, the "course." I am far from a pioneer in pointing out that courses are an academic convenience, not to be found in reality. When the setting is built on courses, the door is opened for translating x hours in y course into n number of point credits, and solemnly maintaining that a certain total of points constitutes an education, or qualification for some credential! Perhaps we should ask another version of the airline question: "Would you like to fly with a pilot who got his certificate points in other courses, without *any* study of landings?"

The fragmentation introduced by courses appears hard to deny. It becomes still more serious when those giving courses make too little effort to coordinate their efforts, and when the administration or school board accepts traditional and long-outdated notions of what constitute basics. A brain-compatible approach goes in the opposite direction—*the emphasis on patterns tends to unify; and to promote natural transfer of learning.* Such pattern-concepts (they can be called "grand ideas") as *continuum, feedback circuit, negative/positive, distribution curve, system, energy cycle, life cycle, push/pull or loaded switch, change process* and many more apply in a wide variety of applications.

The discussion of settings obviously involves matters of educational philosophy not to be treated in one chapter of a book on another subject. My intent is only to suggest that a brain-compatible approach, because of the nature of the brain, guides us, in designing settings, to become critical and intolerant of the now decrepit settings we still struggle to use, with frustrating degree of failure, and to move in these directions:

1.   A setting in which expectations of student learning possible and attainable are left open-ended, and in which high attainment does not create difficulties for the faculty.

2.   An ambiance that dominantly is nonthreatening, nonpunitive, and that reduces all aspects of captivity to the minimum achievable.

3.   An emphasis on mastery rather than passing, on domination of learning over the clock, scheduling, and processing.

4.   A far greater emphasis on reality than on "the book," and on avoiding the fragmentation caused by "courses," and on using unifying "grand ideas."

These proposals are hardly new, except as they may be seen in relation to what we now know of the brain. Nor are they "dream stuff"—while institutions embodying them may be rare, they exist, in whole and parts, amply enough to attest practicality and viability.

NOTES

1. *Places for Learning, Places for Joy* (Cambridge: Harvard University Press, 1973), p. 28.
2. A considerable body of literature that might be called teacher "confessions" has appeared in recent years, among the most insightful being those of James Herndon, *The Way It Spozed to Be* and particularly, in relation to staff relationships, *How to Survive in Your Native Land* (New York: Simon and Schuster, 1971). For a penetrating discussion from an expert outsider's viewpoint, see Seymour B. Sarason, *The Culture of the School and the Problem of Change* (Boston: Allyn and Bacon, 1971). On teachers' anxiety about colleagues' opinions, see James P. Comer, *School Power* (New York: Free Press, 1980), especially p. 115. This book gives a case history of efforts to improve schools and how and why "teachers close the doors and try to survive." There can be little doubt that the pressures on teachers usually are intense, complex, often amorphous, and contradictory. Teachers bear the brunt of the system's crazy unsuitability. In my opinion they do too little to protest it, having given scant thought to alternatives.
3. The furious interest in experimental approaches and structures that began in the 1960s and continued into the 1970s scarcely affected the great majority of classrooms, it has become clear, but did provide a considerable body of thinking and experience that has not yet been digested and summarized. There seems no question that many viable alternative plans exist, often in bits and pieces not organized into a system—in large part, I suggest, because of the lack of a comprehensive theory of learning until now. The literature is vast and highly variable in quality. Some starting points might include: Harriet Talmage, ed. *Systems of Individualized Education* (Berkeley: McCutchan, 1975); Allan A. Glatthorn, "Creating Learning Environments" in *The Teaching of English*, 76th Yearbook of the National Society for the Study of Education (Chicago: University of Chicago Press, 1977); Mario D. Fantini, ed. *Alternative Education* (Garden City, N. Y.: Anchor Books, 1976); and Harvey B. Scribner and Leonard B. Stevens, *Make Your School Work* (New York: Simon and Schuster, 1975). Also see the April 1981 issue of *Phi Delta Kappan*. These give a sense of the great range of alternatives. My study of school organization and its effects, *The Classroom Disaster* (New York: Teachers College Press, Columbia University, 1969) remains one of the few discussions of the kind, and

contains a description of a plan subsequently elaborated into a blueprint for a complete system known as IROSS. Few such full-system blueprints seem to exist.

4. Much evidence suggests teachers and other people working in schools are deceived, or deceive themselves, on how their students regard their efforts. For example, *The Fleischmann Report*, a massive study of New York State elementary and secondary schools, found that "Students generally felt that teachers did not help them to do their best, did not understand their problems, did not help them improve their skills and were not concerned with their future. More than simply not enjoying school, many students indicated that their school experience was actually painful.... Teachers appeared largely unaware of the negative feelings of their students." (New York: The Viking Press, 1973), pp. 46–47. Other studies also show wide differences between teacher and student views of what is happening.

5. The term *mastery* is associated by some with the work of Benjamin S. Bloom, who has pursued this approach. In using it here I am not necessarily referring to those specific applications, but to a principle I advanced in *The Classroom Disaster* (see note 3). Others have expressed similar ideas, notably John Carroll, at least as far back as 1963.

6. On the other hand, it should be noted that under present conditions students given choice at secondary levels may seek the easiest courses so they can pile up good grades for college entrance. This was a more serious problem when the struggle to get into college was more intense, but it may still influence many students who have been pressured into chasing credentials.

15

For more than 50 years now, studies have been documenting the effectiveness of nontraditional school programs in the United States. This research should cause us to question 95 percent of current educational practice.

—WAYNE JENNINGS AND JOE NATHAN[1]

The Classroom: Education's Curse

In considering *situation*, as I am using that term, we move to a shorter perspective and look at the immediate day-to-day surroundings of the student. Once more, our viewpoint is brain-based theory of human learning.

Here again the past dominates, and that monstrous invention, the *classroom*, colors all thinking in schools and far up the educational ladder. As once people referred to horseless carriages, we speak of nonclassroom schemes. Or we use such phrases as open classroom, at least a partial contradiction. As yet we do not even have convenient words to describe arrangements free from the blight of classrooms!

We can define the graded, conventional classroom as an arrangement for learning—or we might better say, for teaching—that calls for one teacher and a group of students, normally 15 or more, who are required to maintain a fixed relationship for a period of months. In the graded version, as opposed to the rare nongraded, the students are considered to be at a more or less uniform level of attainment. This may be on the basis of

139

chronological age—utterly fictitious, since age tells little about what a specific group of people know or can do, or what experience they have individually had and bring to the situation.[2] In any case, the teaching is geared to a level which denies the actual variations; the inmates of a classroom most often are there by assignment or as the consequence of forced, limited choice. In the terms of this definition, it matters little whether the classroom be elementary, secondary, or postsecondary.

The classroom today puts the teacher into an assignment virtually impossible to fulfill. There is simply no way to deal with the huge variations the students exhibit, other than to teach and let the chips fall where they may. If there were really a desire and aim of individualizing, the first step would be to abandon the standard classroom! It was designed and established for precisely the opposite purpose.

By the same token, the conventional classroom makes difficult or practically impossible flexibility of student grouping. To work with four or five students, the teacher must find some way to keep the others busy. To divide the class into three reading groups, as is often done, requires that two be ignored while one is given attention. It cannot prove too surprising that the instructor who feels obliged to manage or "drive" the entire class finds frequent relief in going to whole-class activities. In the true open or informal classroom and in Montessori schools, in contrast, a skilled teacher has no problem in concentrating attention on one or three or five students for many minutes at a time. The other students continue their activities. I am no all-out advocate of the open classroom (why have the classroom at all?), but ample observation shows clearly that it creates a great difference in the teacher's practical ability to have close contact and interchange with individual students on matters involving learning. In conventional classrooms, teachers seldom spend as much as 30 seconds in such discussions, and usually less than 10, and may dominate all talking to such a degree that weeks may pass before a student makes, in class sessions, a self-initiated remark of any consequence![3]

A number of studies agree that conventional classroom teachers behave in ways that they vigorously deny when presented with observations. Such is the pressure of the classroom's demands that a huge gap develops between the intentions of even good, experienced teachers and what they actually do.[4] Further, the pressure pushes most such teachers into behaving in quite uniform ways.[5]

The essential concept in the classroom teacher's role appears to be that of "driving" the class. We can suspect that some mix of several elements contributes to the overall posture and behavior of the teacher. Some are old, such as surviving bits of the notion that children are born evil and must be firmly disciplined for their own good (originally, to be "saved"); or the idea from the old, deadly dull days of rote schooling that students must be forced into learning, which would occur no other way. Other concerns are current and practical, such as the fear of many teachers that their charges might rebel or get seriously out of control (a nightmare of newer teachers) or that noise or exuberance might disturb the teachers of adjoining classrooms. There may be a niggling worry that a school board member, parent, or other potential critic might pop in and misconstrue or disapprove of what is going on. Prominent is a feeling that the assigned year's work must be covered at all costs so the teacher can't be blamed however well students learn or don't; and always there is anxiety about the unknown—what might happen if the teacher does not drive all the time. There are teachers who enjoy exercising their power; those who love to be "on stage," love to talk, or feel compulsion to work hard to earn their pay (far more appear to work than coast). Above all conviction abides, unshaken by outcomes, that *telling* is the largest, most fundamental aspect of instruction.

This kind of *aggressive teaching*, of course, puts the students into passive roles. The classroom is a place where one is told what to do, criticized or punished for not fully complying, and not allowed time or opportunity to do anything else. (Not a few teachers do reward students by permitting them to play games or read what is available, but this is regarded as a temporary cessation of instruction.)

Examinations, of course, bring more of the same driving of students. In addition, examinations can be observed in blatant use to intimidate or "motivate" students: "You better pay attention, Leroy and Tim, you're going to have a test on this Friday." Teachers displeased with a student's attitude or behavior may mark a test harshly, thus getting even with a show of objectivity. As many have observed, rather seldom are test results used diagnostically and followed up correctively. For administrators, standardized or official examinations may serve to show that the school cares about learning results, or is serious about outcomes—with again perhaps little or no real effort to seek to rectify failures.

Power is hard for anyone to resist. In classrooms, with no other adult observing (genuine supervision of teachers long ago virtually ceased in most schools)[6] teachers may easily come to use their power oppressively, even while convinced that they are concerned, kindly, and helpful. Classrooms provide little corrective feedback, and students who take home complaints may find parents receive them with disbelief, scant sympathy, or even approval: "Good, you need to be made to toe the line!"

Students learn early that in classrooms one suffers. That *is* school. The object then becomes survival, by whatever strategies will work. Since students regard the school as representing adult authority, their contempt or alienation may extend to learning in general and all authority.

When we evaluate this situation in brain-compatible referents, we are forced to regard it as about as brain-antagonistic as could be contrived.[7]

Teachers become the victims of this antagonistic situation along with students, although unlike the captive students they have (and in great numbers, take) the option of withdrawing. Beginning teachers in schools are often appalled, as many personal accounts show, at the realities of their working situation; and high ideals, aims, and spirits may rapidly evaporate. But the beginning teachers, often in their early twenties and with little experience as employees, have little expertise and less status to apply to changing the institution. Bucking the social system of the school may well bring resentments, criticism, and early loss of job. Like students, teachers are under much pressure to comply or face the agonizing choice of making a fresh start in some other field, casting aside several years of what was supposed to have been training for just this kind of work. In the open market, they may be aware, a bachelor's degree in Education is not an impressive credential.

It can hardly be surprising that a recent National Education Association survey found the great majority of teachers dissatisfied with their jobs.[8] The frustrations of instructors who want to produce learning results and to treat students as individuals, yet are thrust into situations where doing either is extremely difficult are all too apparent to anyone who has much contact with teachers. Curiously, in my experience, few relate their frustrations to the graded classroom. Most of them never think about the structure and its effect—the classroom is "invisible"[9] because it is taken for granted as the standard setting for instruction. (Those rare teachers who have become expert in open approaches tend to be more conscious of what they have escaped—but in a dominantly classroom school, they still feel its constraints.)

A person unfamiliar with educational research might assume that if anything whatever was known it would be what went on, minute by minute, in the classroom. Those more sophisticated will know that such observations have been avoided like plague. Some recent studies, however, have thrown some light on the question, though none as yet, to my knowledge, attack it directly. One done by Far West Laboratory for Educational Research and Development, and another by a group at CEMREL, Inc.[10] confirm other findings that great chunks of school time do not get used for instruction. Further, large variations from classroom to classroom were noted. Instruction might use fewer than three hours of the day, and seatwork took most of that time, ranging from 1.75 to 3.5 hours a day. For particular students, teacher-directed instruction could range from as little as 6 percent to 34 percent (CEMREL). In short, roughly half the day might be noninstructional, and at least half of that (up to 83 percent) in the elementary classes observed was of the homework-in-class variety. The Far West study found, similarly, that in reading and mathematics students in grade 2 and 5 "spend, on the average, at least 60 percent of their time in seatwork."

In passing, we should note that these and other "time-on-task" or "academically engaged time" studies have led to recommendations that teachers do more direct instruction, which seems to imply simply old-fashioned, aggressive, whole-class teaching. Thus many millions of dollars of research money in the hands of researchers who, lacking good theory, can't break away from simple-minded linear logic, encourages retrogression to the sweeping failures of the past. The research establishes what has long been in the literature: that conventional classrooms waste huge amounts of what should be learning time. It can hardly surprise us that if somewhat less time is wasted, learning results may show some improvement. But on examination, it turns out that the gains are small, to the point of having little bearing on present school problems; and worse, the learning that does result is heavily of the recall, right-answer kind, valuable not for real-world applications but for answering examinations or achievement tests—precisely the kind of learning that moves *away* from the excellence and understandings we urgently require. So myopic are many researchers, so eager to find some ray of hope for the conventional practices, that expensive research fails to reach the obvious conclusion: that if classrooms waste so much time, we should find better formats that don't.

Sober thought also tells us that any suggestion that some two million teachers be retrained to change what they do in classrooms must be called wishful. We have no means of reaching teachers isolated in classrooms, no inservice apparatus that might be effective, and no reason to believe teachers will alter their accustomed ways in unchanged settings, where all the biases support use of old programs. Only in new settings can we hope to bring about new teacher behaviors.

My own observations suggest that when classroom instruction is measured on a stopwatch basis, excluding the time that goes to disciplinary remarks or action, class management, giving out and collecting, housekeeping, tests and examinations, clerical matters, internal and outside interruptions, and so on, the net time shrinks typicallly to under 90 minutes a day, and often far less.[11] If this teaching is looked at in brain terms of input and program building, the amount of useful instruction falls incredibly low, often scraping zero. Time given to individual attention, so cherished by the public, by my calculations comes out to be about six hours *per year* per student.

These findings, I am painfully well aware, tend to infuriate teachers and many administrators, who believe that they are all wrong for *their* classrooms or schools. One can understand and empathize with well-intentioned people trapped in graded classroom schools who abhor facing the quite obvious facts, and prefer fantasized versions of their activities that let them maintain some semblance of morale and mental health. But while findings vary in details due to methodology used, the broad conclusions on time waste stand firm and inescapable.

From a Proster Theory viewpoint, time-on-task and academically engaged time approaches seem primitive. They require that some observer watch students and guess what they are attending to or thinking about—a bit of mind-reading that never offers the observer feedback on how right the guessing may be. But in any case the main questions are begged: how much input was there from which patterns could be extracted? What program-building was going forward? How many students were learning wrong programs—"practicing mistakes"? Wasted time, pointless tasks, mean no input.

In the higher grades, it may be that the proportion of teacher-instructed time tends to rise in academic subjects; but here we find a marked increase in lecturing. Still, a 1970 study using video tapes showed teachers behaving with striking overall similarity of pattern, in grades 1, 4, and 11.[12] The teachers had varying experience, and their subjects were mathematics or social studies, but these factors did not seem to much affect behavior.

This same study, supported by recordings that could be looked at again and again to verify findings, brought out another characteristic of the classroom situation.

> Changes occurred frequently and rapidly. For instance, in the *most* active classroom, a change of one sort or another occurred on an average once every *five* seconds. In the least active classroom, there was change every eighteen seconds. This means that there were 371 activity episodes in the average lesson.[13]

If this butterfly changing translated as variety of random input, it might be welcomed. But of course most of it presents very little that could be considered input for pattern extraction purposes, and the frenetic pace produces a blur. Most of what the teachers presented was information to be remembered, the centuries-old rote approach, diluted and disguised by currently conventional techniques. Very little time was spent on having students do anything.

In September 1979, The National Assessment of Educational Progress reported that test results on arithmetic ability had once more slid still lower. Students of all ages tested proved *strongest in knowledge of facts, and weakest in applying what they knew*. Asked how far a car going 8 kilometers in 5 minutes would go in an hour, only 28 percent of 13-year-olds and 56 percent of 17-year-olds could provide the correct answer. Similar problems, which a competent student could solve mentally in 10 seconds, proved as hard. When we consider that the tenth graders had spent eight to ten years studying mathematics, we must marvel at the potency of classroom instruction in preventing learning!

In brief and in general, how can the classroom and its procedures be replaced? The answer is not hard, at least in terms of organizational objectives:

1.   Students should not be held in one room with one teacher, but should be free to circulate in many, working with a great variety of materials, and many helpers: fellow students, volunteers, visitors, aides, apprentice teachers, teachers, instructional specialists. All of these can be *providers of feedback* on a one-to-one basis, as well as *providers of input* on an individual, small-group, or large-group basis.

2.   Groupings should be formed *as required for the work in hand*, and continued only so long as that grouping is suitable. In college, a student may at various times work alone (as in a library), with one or two others (as in a laboratory), with a small group (as in a discussion, carrying out a project, planning an event, conducting a survey or study, or rehearsing a play), in a class-size group (as for learning a language by rote or listening to a presentation), or in a large group (as in a lecture hall, assembly, theatre, or concert hall.) Similar flexibility is quite possible in schools, from kindergarten on.

3.   *The use of language by students* should be facilitated by providing continual room for asking questions, genuine student-originated discussion, working jointly, making announcements and broadcasting, writing real reports (not dictated exercises), and private or public communications. Student contact with people outside the school should be frequent and varied.

4.   Much of the learning and application of so-called basic skills should be *in relation to real events* (not contrived) and a large proportion should involve the outside world. A good deal can stem from following local, state, regional, national, and international news, and real projects (having some observable outcome) of great variety, selected by individual students.

5.   Students' work *should not be interrupted* by changing periods, but rather should take precedence over the clock. Students should not be required, especially after the primary-grade age levels, to be in a particular room at a particular time, or at times even to be in school, if their work can better be done elsewhere. Schools should, as feasible, reject the role of custodians.

6.   Students coming to school hungry, because of family conditions or emergency, should be fed. (At present they are more likely to be criticized or punished.) Those needing rest or sleep should be permitted to rest or sleep. Just as adults regularly take breaks or relax for periods, children should be allowed, at individual option, to do nothing for

reasonable periods. (Since they become bored quickly doing nothing, this is not likely to be a problem, except where this behavior indicates another serious problem.)

7.   Students should be exposed to, but should largely self-select, *perhaps ten times as much input as ordinarily characterizes the conventional graded classroom.* Much of the increase occurs automatically when the school walls are not permitted to shut out the real world; but more derives from escaping the classroom routine with its long waits and many no-input intervals and from bringing the real world into the school, via visitors, speakers, radio, television, film performers, craftspeople, and so on, as well as having the students go outside the school—not in awkward class-size bodies that defeat the purpose in most cases and generate much strain for teachers, but in groups of appropriate size, far easier to transport and supervise.

8.   Teachers should be stripped of power to give marks and grades, and to make evaluative entries in permanent records. The power by its existence makes every person who has it an active or potential judge and punisher; and for students puts a premium on conciliating teachers and "apple polishing," to use the politest term. In addition to the severe threat aspects, the power to grade prevents frank relationships between faculty and students, and encourages teachers to place the blame for learning failure wholly on the student.

9.   The progress of each individual student should be closely and continuously monitored, with corrective action taken as indicated. This is not done in the conventional graded school. Instead, teachers customarily take no responsibility for deficits in learning of children they receive, and simply pass them on at the end of a year. Principals today, especially in larger schools, rarely know how well individual students are achieving except as acute problems or occasional remarkable successes occur. Counsellors, with many pressures, seldom even attempt routine monitoring.

10.   Schools should be places where courtesy and respect for others is both demonstrated and learned. One of the most striking features of typical classrooms, to the outside observer, is the rudeness of address, the lack of civilities, the tone of voice conveying lack of respect for students or mistrust, and the frequent "hollering" that students often find the most objectionable teacher attribute. Students should have the option of avoiding such behavior, as they may have to some extent outside the school. Courteous teachers, inspection seems to make evident, have courteous students, and situations far more suited to learning accomplishment.

Experience tells me that when some of the concepts enumerated above are advocated, many readers or listeners at once form an image of wild confusion, with children running around in great excitement, jumping pointlessly from activity to activity, while anything that can be called discipline vanishes. In truth, some examples of the free-school movement involving schools set up by well-meaning but naive parents and romantic teachers have collapsed after a brief period for these reasons, among others. Let me suggest, if it be necessary, that nothing of the kind need occur.

First, we should realize that children who have been for years captives in traditional classrooms can hardly be expected to acquire wholly new programs just by virtue of being transferred en masse to less restrictive environments. New patterns must be understood, and new programs built.

Second, what is being suggested is not *no* structure, but a different and more suitable structure. *Students, like other people, like structure* — they want to know the rules of the game, and they need and want their "home base." In early enthusiasm for open schools, that word was at times taken literally, and students were dumped into great expanses without walls. The human species has spent too much time crowded into caves and tents and huts to feel comfortable for long in such areas. We like the security of some walls, some dividers, some markers of space such as rugs, furniture, arches, and the like; or outdoors, fences, hedges, or boundaries such as brooks or roads. Individual children, like adults, prefer a chair, locker, cupboard, space or something that is theirs. At home, each member of a household normally has a fixed place at table, a certain place to sleep, and closets and containers for personal effects. "Mine" is a powerful, old-brain word for humans; to suddenly ignore it in schools invites serious troubles.

The situational attributes suggested amply provide structure. The students' physical base can as well be six rooms as one, as departmentalized secondary schools partially demonstrate. The situations proposed do not leave students (after suitable orientation) wondering how to behave — they can see very clearly what is expected and what will not be tolerated. If we allow students to learn from many teachers and other adults, that does not prevent assigning students, with a good deal of choice and flexibility allowed, to guiding teachers who must accept a substantial responsibility for their students' achievement. But fundamentally, students must develop their own ability to manage themselves. When they are kept in four-walled rooms, required to have a hall pass to go anywhere else, and incessantly told what to do and not to do, they are being systematically prevented from developing judgment and taking responsibility. Only in fluid settings and situations can these be realistically asked for and expected.

Without necessarily realizing it, aggressive teachers and ritualistic taskmasters may come to think routinely in confrontation terms: teachers try to drive classes, to force behaviors; students seek to escape, evade, avoid. When opening up structure and the time frame is suggested, many such adults may see the student (the enemy) as winning. But once the student is treated with respect, given some room to self-direct and learn in an individual way at an individual pace, the confrontation disappears. One of the most arresting aspects of the genuine open plan is that it virtually ends the discipline problem. My observation, confirmed by a number of associates, is that any need for corrective or punitive discipline signals that learning is being actively prevented. (In individual cases, of course, personal clashes may occur, as they do in office or plant or hospital; and some problems may arise outside and be brought into school—family break up or fights, financial emergencies, sudden illness or death, or fear of street attack, for example. When months and years rather than days or weeks are allowed for mastery and fulfilling achievement, the wholly artificial and arbitrary pressures and threat stemming from the teacher's drive to cover the term's work roll away like heavy clouds. An ironic aspect of the conventional classroom is that the uninvolved observer can plainly see teachers working hard to make problems for themselves— clinging to unfruitful and at times disastrous programs as though to an oak in a hurricane. Continuing to act without regard to outcomes is, of course, the essence of ritual. Failure programs are retained, despite the punishment and pain that results, and the absence of reward.

The effort to force students to learn in strongly brain-antagonistic situations must and does bring about intense frustration for teachers. Some adjust, accepting failure as the norm and glorying in rare transient bits of success; others shrug and do their job in the easiest way, eyeing retirement; some break down mentally or physically; some grow mean, bitter, and shrill. Only a few look for alternatives.

But alternative situations such as I have broadly described are practical and viable, beyond question. In the better English open schools, and Montessori schools, millions of students have prospered. Thousands of schools in the United States have demonstrated a great variety of formats. Some have not endured when key leaders have left, or ritualists aided by budget squeezes have reversed progress; but others have. Few, of course, have had the benefit of the sharp, scientifically based theory of human learning now available. But to doubt that nonclassroom schools (and their images cast on education and training at higher levels) can function, can be real, can work is to argue with an impressive amount of consistent experience.

The classroom did not come from Mount Sinai. It came from militaristic, regimented Prussia, imported by Horace Mann.[14] Never has it worked to produce adequate student learning.

For a half century and more, we should again note, an American system of schools flourished, and produced citizens with basic skills with astonishing success considering the tiny resources allotted: the one-room country school. It had no classroom organization, no periods, no real grades. Students tutored students; groups formed and dissolved as needs indicated; the teacher had to view students as individuals and work with them on that basis. Reality was as close as the stove that had to be kept glowing, the winter path that no custodian was there to shovel. The books, though very few, were real books, not basals. If no standardized testing went on, the teacher hardly needed it—she could observe each student at work. If input was small because of resources and not every student made great gains, it can be said that few if any were prevented from learning.

The yellow school bus ended it all . . . in favor of schools with a thousand times the resources, that do prevent learning.

NOTES

1. "Startling/Disturbing Research on School Program Effectiveness," *Phi Delta Kappan*, March 1977. p. 568.
2. It is shocking to realize that a clear and definitive exposition of student differences was made by two prestigious educators, John I. Goodlad and Robert H. Anderson, as long ago as 1959, and published in a widely noted book, *The Nongraded Elementary School* (New York: Harcourt, Brace and Company). They pointed out then that: "Grade-mindedness has left so deep a mark on the teaching profession that its by-products are everywhere, and it often blinds teachers to the real facts of professional life" (p. 188). Two decades later it is hard to maintain that there has been substantial change. The welfare of children has been pushed aside, particularly by administrators and school boards, for the convenience of keeping a senseless status quo.
3. See Thomas L. Good and Jere E. Brophy, *Looking in Classrooms* (New York: Harper & Row, 1973), pp. 25, 27.
4. See John I. Goodlad, M. Frances Klein and associates, *Looking Behind the Classroom Door* (Belmont, Calif.: Charles A. Jones, 1974).
5. See Raymond S. Adams and Bruce J. Biddle, *Realities of Teaching* (New York: Holt, Rinehart and Winston, 1970).
6. See *Supervision of Teaching*, 1982 Yearbook of the Association for Supervision and Curriculum Development, Alexandria, Va. "In many school systems, formal feedback on teaching performance may come no more than once a year and then in a quite perfunctory way. One of the tragedies of American education is that teachers work in isolation. Their immediate superiors often have only a rather generalized perception of their teaching performance. . . . There is little contact among colleagues, classroom doors are seldom opened to each other, and teachers who are members of the same staff in the same school, even in the same grade or discipline, maintain a collusive and almost deliberate ignorance of the work of their peers." Robert J. Alfonso and Lee Goldsberry, p. 91.
7. Wayne Jennings, long principal of the famous and successful alternative open school in St. Paul, Minn., has observed with reference to conventional school structures: "It may be that current practice is the worst possible arrangement for the education of the young." See his article, with Joe Nathan, "Start-

150 HUMAN BRAIN AND HUMAN LEARNING

ling/Disturbing Research on School Program Effectiveness," *Phi Delta Kappan*, March 1977, p. 571. The article provides a devastating review of major studies and their findings, which have been persistently ignored.

8. Issued in July 1977, the study found morale at its lowest in years, despite higher salaries and improved working conditions. Only 38 percent felt sure they would choose a teaching career if they had the choice over again. More recent reports confirm the despair, including those from 1982 teacher unions' conventions.

9. See Leslie A. Hart, "A Classroom Is A Classroom Is A Classroom—and Invisible," *Toronto Education Quarterly*, Autumn 1971.

10. Beginning Teacher Evaluation Study, Report V-1 (San Francisco: The Far West Laboratory for Educational Research and Development, June 1978). See particularly Chapter 4. The massive study contains reports of many classroom observations. CEMREL, Inc., is located in Chicago. See publication "Teacher Resource Allocation: Consequences for Pupils," March 1978.

11. See Leslie A. Hart, "The Case Against Organizing Schools into Classrooms," *The American School Board Journal*, June 1974, p. 34.

12. See note 5, above.

13. Ibid., p. 29.

14. Educational historian Michael B. Katz states: "The structure of American urban education has not changed since late in the nineteenth century; by 1880, the basic features of public education in most major cities were the same as they are today." See *Class, Bureaucracy, and School* (New York: Praeger, 1971), p. 105.

16

Teaching is a skill so complex that no single factor can fully explain or describe the qualities of an effective teacher. In fact, it may not be possible to distinguish between "good" and "bad," or "effective" and "ineffective," teaching. Some education researchers...admit that they "do not know how to define, prepare for, or measure teacher competence," despite the urgent need for skilled teachers and for understanding teacher effectiveness.

—ALLAN C. ORNSTEIN AND DANIEL U. LEVINE[1]

Teaching: Some Exercises in Futility

As we now consider activities, both those of students and of instructors, we must shift our focus again closer, and approach answers to the key question, what should be done and not done to produce effective learning by instructor effort.

We must remind ourselves (as frequently as possible!) of the dual process necessary: on one hand, to stop and discard practices and uses of time and effort that prove harmful, inhibitory, or wasteful, and on the other, to introduce or expand those that help; or in other terms, cease what is brain-antagonistic and build what is brain-compatible.

The great majority of instructors at all levels of education and training tend to operate on one or more of these bases:

- Following a well-established ritual adopted as the result of training to instruct; or in imitation of others, more experienced.

- Relying heavily on texts and associated teachers' manuals and method guides.
- Following closely the detailed instructions of a supervisor (particularly in specific training settings, and in industry or the military).
- Using a "bag of tricks" and fragmentary methods and techniques accumulated over the years.
- Implementing a sharply conceived plan built on more or less specific principles and using certain specific arrangements, machines, or procedures. (Examples would include individually prescribed instruction, computer-based methods, Montessori, some open classroom, etc.)

In short, rarely in reality do we find an instructor facing the problem, "How do I accomplish this body of desired learning?" and freely looking for the best solution. As we have noted, the new instructor entering an institution may have the least feeling of freedom to innovate, and becomes the most sensitive of the staff to the pressures of the social system and standards of expected behavior. In my own experience, which includes commercial training, I have observed how even there the decision on methods is influenced by the views, or supposed views, of executives who *might* be critical though two or three levels removed from the operation. While use of modern devices such as computer-guided instruction or video-tape techniques may seem safe, conventional ideas on learning, discipline, order, sequence, reinforcement, and examinations may prevent genuine innovation almost as thoroughly as in school and college bureaucracies. The instructor, director, or supplier of services usually is not able to get backing at a high enough echelon to feel free to follow best judgment or to experiment.

Robert Gagné has written that, "the essential task of the teacher is to arrange the conditions of the learner's environment so that the processes of learning will be activated, supported, enhanced, and maintained."[2] The same thought has been expressed by many others. But in practice classroom teachers seem rarely to feel either powerful or competent enough to carry out such a mission. Teachers are themselves driven by the concept of "material to be covered" within the semester or other time period. Thus management and material concerns crowd out most effort by even the most diligent and well-intentioned teacher to actually *arrange conditions for learning.* As anyone like myself who has labored in the harsh landscapes of educational reform can testify, instructors actively teaching seem almost obsessed with "what do I do Monday" worries, and rapidly become impatient with those who may attempt to interest them in theoretical or longer-term considerations. One can sympathize with their distress and anxiety, even while seeing that large problems are not going to be relieved by having some plans for keeping their charges occupied on Monday.

Some of this bind can be avoided, perhaps, by a close focus on activities from a brain-compatible view. To at least some degree any teacher can shift from brain-antagonistic practices to brain-compatible ones, even within the rigid classroom framework; and this may prove a practical first step toward challenging the framework itself and demanding better settings and situations. But a shift of this kind, I believe, can have effect only if the theoretical base is well grasped and the instructor knows what is being done, rather than using the primitive "let's try this" trial-and-error approach.

With Proster Theory as a touchstone, we can evaluate some of the major aggressive-teaching activities.

1. *Lecturing.* When, for centuries, the teacher had or knew the book and the students did not have it and had to learn its contents, lecturing made very good sense. It makes no sense today for young students and has feeble impact for most even through the secondary range. Age plays a large role simply because how much one can understand a lecture depends directly on how much learning and experience one can bring to the lecture. If I know a good deal about Bach, boating, or Barbados, hearing a lecture on one of those subjects might provide input to fill a gap of pattern understanding, or add to a verbal program I can later execute in a discussion. But should I know nothing about Caribbean islands, and be unable to relate much in the talk on Barbados to previous learning, I must depend on *rote memory of words* to be able to regurgitate anything on the country the next day. Listening passively to a lecture is a poor way to develop even rote memory. The speaker may attempt a logical presentation: location, size, topography, agriculture, economy, history, without in the slightest adding to my grasp. (There can be, of course, innumerable logical presentations.) A key point to note is that the lecturer controls only what is uttered, and *has no control whatever as to how the input is processed or utilized in the individual brains of the audience.* As we have seen, they don't work logically.

Lecturing has long been thought of as pouring knowledge into an empty vessel, or some such metaphor. We can see, however, that the importance of previous learning produces a surprising anomaly: the emptier the vessel, the less the lecture will fill it; the fuller it is, the more chance of something more entering! This explains a familiar classroom phenomenon: certain more advanced students appear to pay attention to and profit by a lecture, giving the teacher some encouraging bits of feedback. (They may, of course, be drawing on learning they had prior to the lecture.) The teacher then feels that if some learned, the others should have, too—and so proceeds to lecture all the more. The vicious cycle aggravates the failure for those who need instruction most.

When we define learning as the acquisition of useful programs, we illuminate to the fullest the hopelessness of lecturing. No program can be built by listening, but only by acting in some fashion. Parents, too, often seem oblivious to this fact, and endlessly tell their offspring to shut doors, turn off lights, wipe feet, hang up clothes, wash hands, brush teeth, not interrupt, and so on, without the slightest success. (Indeed, husbands and wives commonly lecture each other on favorite topics with no better outcomes, and probably more annoyance to the lecturee. We must suspect that the goal of such programs is not to produce learning, but simply is to *tell* the other party, to conduct a ritual that signifies superiority or vents frustration.) Possibly teachers' resorting to lecturing also represents effort to cope with frustration. For many teachers, talking is easy, especially when there is no adult audience to judge its quality, and gives the instructor the feeling that "if someone came into my room now they would see I am *trying* to teach these students, I am *trying* to cover the material."

But whether we use the terms lecturing, telling, explaining, or orienting, the activity must fail to bring about any substantial learning. Few teachers have the high skills and content to hold an audience, and even the most remarkably endowed can hardly succeed day after day. Most who will look during their lecturing will see bored, slumping, squirming audiences; if they will tape-record their remarks, complete with frequent admonitions, they will appreciate on review how little input is being provided. But there is another, just as serious negative: while teachers talk, students by and large cannot. It is the students who need to talk. To talk is to use and enlarge communication programs, to develop the essential skills of presenting and receiving aims, ideas, information, agreement.

2. *Telling combined with demonstration* at first glance seems a sounder way to instruct. But the same pitfalls exist. Those who readily follow the demonstration step-by-step are probably those who need it least; others may watch and listen with no idea what is going on, especially when, as is often the case, "something new" is being introduced. But the brain does not learn anything new, except by rote and under duress; *it persists in attaching any new learning to previous learning*, to enlarge and refine pattern recognition and to expand the store of programs. One does not generate programs by watching a demonstration, however expert it may be. Further, there is the basic problem we have examined in defining the process of learning as the extraction of patterns from confusion. The more clearly a teacher explains, the "neater" the demonstration, the less the student is able to extract the pattern for himself, as is essential to grasp it, and the more the desired learning does not occur.

To accept that this is the way the brain works, and that the conventional teacher talk of the classroom has negative results is assuredly not easy, even when the instructor constantly experiences failure. Yet there are thousands of open classrooms of various styles that demonstrate that teachers can reduce talking to the whole group to a few minutes a day, clearing the way for other activities.

3. *Seatwork* constitutes a large part of instructional time in most conventional classrooms. It is hardly a professional secret that seatwork helps keep students quiet and at least looking busy, while giving the teacher considerable respite. Much seatwork involves the use of workbooks or prepared sheets, which means that once again students are being told, in detail, what to do, in what sequence. And here again the student who can easily do the work is able to move through it rapidly, learning little if anything and suffering boredom, while one who has yet to grasp the work struggles painfully, actually practicing doing the work wrong, building programs that will produce further error and bafflement! The essential requirement of feedback is lacking—nothing happens when a wrong figure or fill-in or choice is entered. There is no equivalent of shooting the basketball at the hoop and seeing it miss. (A computer, of course, can provide immediate right/wrong results, which may be helpful to a degree; but this is an arbitrary answer from unseen authority, not one deriving from reality, and may not help the student see why the answer is right or wrong, or grasp the pattern involved.)

The principle is simple: *a learner can improve by practice or exercises only when the learner has some way of knowing what has been executed well, and gets feedback at once.* We build programs *by doing things right, even if clumsily, very gradually working toward mastery.* But much seatwork consists of many right/wrong alternatives in small units with no gradations. If we were to allow a student to shoot for baskets, closing the eyes as the ball left the hands, we would have the equivalent. Unable to follow the flight of the ball and gradually refine it, the student would find it extremely difficult to improve. It would not help much to be told later, "you got 13 in out of 60 attempts."

Seatwork conceived in brain-compatible terms is not impossible. (I have developed some techniques for the purpose, and adapting others seems clearly feasible.) But the bulk of seatwork done in classrooms with commercial or teacher-generated materials simply wastes time and often has negative effect, especially when students are unable to see how they are acquiring any programs useful to them. While seatwork is being done, some teachers may wander around the room, peeking at the work and offering some help or correction to individuals. Such attention potentially can be of value; but when a stopwatch is held on the contacts they usually prove to be only seconds in duration, and the total for the class a scant few minutes per day. Teachers may have the impression (perhaps partly wishful) that they are spending substantial time on individualization. But building programs is a *slow* process. While a quick bit of feedback helps, a huge quantity is needed for effective learning, not occasional dribbles.

4. *Recitation*, like lecturing, dates from teacher-has-the-book times, and like lecturing tends to aggravate the problems of the less successful learners. To call on a student who cannot give the desired (and largely

directed) response is to embarrass both student and teacher. To move the lesson ahead, the teacher needs the answer, and so goes to the student most likely to supply it, possibly allowing more time for a reply than is vouchsafed the poorer achiever.[3] The assumption is constantly made that since one or a few students can answer the whole group grasps the point—the most obvious of fictions. But in any case recitation normally provides no appreciable contribution to learning. Patterns are difficult to sort out from slow, painful questioning that often brings wrong, garbled, poorly expressed or inexact answers, and if any programs are built, it is likely they will be for answering questions of just this kind. Since the student responding cannot give an answer unless it already has been learned, recitation tends in large measure to be a highly inefficient, boring form of examination, with the input level extremely low.

5.   *Discussion* has some popularity with less rigid teachers in conventional classrooms, because on the surface it appears to give students a participatory role, and does permit more utterances by students than other activities. But observation suggests that groupings of 20 to 30 are far too large for genuine discussion, and that the stopwatch will show the teacher still talks more than all others together, while many students do not talk at all or give only minimal replies under pressure. For the verbally clever student, discussion provides a golden chance to manipulate the teacher by playing up to known teacher views. Like other people, teachers tend to regard those who agree with them or accept their values as admirable. Those students who deliberately "earn Brownie points" this way may indeed be learning programs: for dissembling and "faking out" adults in authority. But otherwise discussion ordinarily provides very low input, and the purely verbal exercises seldom reach the level of true communication—students talk because the teacher calls for talking. To be sure, some discussions do take off and may reveal student interests and views that otherwise might not come to light. That can help the teacher; but often the discussion gets into shaky ground and is choked off. Individual students talk hardly enough to matter.[4]

6.   *Testing*, whether standardized achievement, IQ, aptitude, diagnostic, or other along with quizzes, weekly tests, teacher-generated or institutional formal examinations and the like, seems to come into increasing use as learning failures come more to public view—a sort of reflex action. Absurdly, administrators and boards seem to feel that doing more testing will of itself prove the school effort is more rigorous! But giving tests simply takes time away from instruction and learning; and the more tests are emphasized, the more the teaching focuses on the learning of right answers to test questions, with deadly results for genuine learning. As I have suggested, diagnostic tests at best disclose areas of weakness in answering other tests. They may fail utterly to show why there is weakness, and still less lead to remediation. Most likely, more work will

be assigned in what are seen as the weak areas, and if the work creates more threat, repeats teaching that has already failed, or is negative in learning effect, the outcome is just the reverse of what is wanted!

The notion that students learn from giving wrong answers and being so informed (usually a good deal later) persists. It would seem evident that one cannot build useful programs via wrong answers. Even if one learned what not to do, that is hardly a substitute for learning what to do and how to do it. Examinations, whether of the pencil-and-paper, verbal, or chalkboard variety, produce virtually no learning, except perhaps for building programs for answering examinations.

7. *Rote* method, or what used to be called "learning by heart," is both highly effective and useful. Proster Theory, it may be, makes much clearer the *program* aspect of rote: we learn this way not by listening or silent effort, but by acting—usually declaiming with vigor the poem or table or formula we wish to retain, or playing over and over the piano piece to be performed, or running through the intricate steps of a football play. Rather than "by heart," we learn by muscle. If rhythm can be added, learning is speeded; melody in addition will help further. The alphabet, for example, can be picked up rapidly and permanently to the "Twinkle, Twinkle, Little Star" tune (that Mozart put to amusing use in the well-known theme and variations). A marching band represents complex rote learning, blending maneuvers and the playing of music on instruments. A huge amount of practice may be required—a reminder that we build programs slowly and only with far more repetition than we tend to realize.

Rote, of course, makes possible "parrot" learning in which comprehension is not necessary, and the word rote often is used pejoratively. But it can hardly be doubted that comprehension can help the rote learning process. A grasp of the pattern of the football play or of the band's formation certainly will speed learning. So will insight into the relations of numbers and the patterns they form aid mastery of multiplication tables. (While I have learned at times in strange cities to drive to destinations by a rote sequence of turns, I am always unhappy until I can see a map and get some idea of what I have been doing.) The combination of pattern recognition, words, rhythm or music, and vigorous muscular activity means that much cross-modal power of the brain will be used. The learning that results often is amazingly sure and durable; with a little brushing up, one may easily recite a long poem learned decades before. Most people have to say aloud or in suppressed speech "6 times 8 is 48" to recover that "fact"—demonstrating that we do not really recall a fact but rather implement a program that produces those words.[5]

In breaking away from old-style parrot learning, educators have tended to downplay rote. The irony is that most classroom progress is still measured by ability to give right answers, and the answers depend heavily on rote acquisition. Teachers drill their classes over and over to answer expected examination questions. The more pressures are put on teachers to have students attain minimum competence, or to teach the basics, the more rote methods come to be used, often with little realization that this is what is happening. Consequently the rote teaching is done weakly.[6]

This review of activities of the conventional classroom will, perhaps, profoundly discourage and upset some who conduct aggressive teaching in conventional ways. (As we have noted, teachers tend to be unrealistic about what they are actually doing, and to think that criticism for clinging to antique methods applies to other teachers, not them.) To suggest that lecturing, telling, explaining, recitation, seatwork, discussion, and testing are in sum almost totally ineffective and probably a negative factor in producing learning can be a shock throughout the establishment.

The most common response, I have found, is the protest, "But that does not agree with the obvious facts! Our students do learn." Certainly students learn to a degree across the years of schooling, but that is not quite the issue. What I am submitting is that they do not learn appreciably from the aggressive classroom instruction I have been describing. The great bulk of evidence shows a profound inability of instruction by these techniques to produce learning. If they did, we should have millions of reports of such success; we have almost none. It would seem simple enough for teachers to routinely test before a lesson or unit is given, and test after it. But it is easy to see why that is seldom done. If the teacher finds on the pretest that a third or half of the students know the material, what is to be done with them while the others are taught? If the posttest should show little learning resulted, who wants that information? Nobody stands to gain by proving that the rituals are only rituals.

Students learn to a degree *outside* this main body of instruction, by reading texts and other books, by getting help from parents and friends, and from the huge input they get from all media and experience out of school. It has long been apparent that how well students do in school, on the record, relates closely to family income and their out-of-school resources,[7] and that conversely those students who lack such alternative support tend to do very badly in school.

Such studies as those of the National Assessment and more recently competency testing by states or localities more and more reveal how shallow and limited actual student learning has been. But this is hardly surprising: the literature critical of the aggressive teaching methods we have reviewed fills libraries to overflowing. It is not radical to suggest that lecturing, for example, is ineffective. What I have tried to do is show that, in brain terms, it *must* be ineffective.

As I observed in Chapter 1, teachers have long been thwarted and puzzled by the failure of teaching to "get across" to students. But producing learning results has not been mandatory or even necessary to draw salary, get increases, or win promotions. Times may now be changing, as public and educational customers at all levels become more and more unwilling to accept and pay for empty rituals.

NOTES

1. "Teacher Behavior Research: Overview and Outlook," *Phi Delta Kappan,* April 1981, p. 592.
2. *The Psychology of Teaching Methods,* 75th Yearbook of the National Society for the Study of Education (Chicago: University of Chicago Press, 1976), p. 42.
3. Various studies suggest that when the "wait time" of the teacher is increased from about one second to two or three, student responses greatly increase. For example, see Mary Budd Rowe, "Give Students Time to Respond," *School Science and Mathematics,* March 1978, or in *Education Digest,* May 1978.
4. Perhaps because teachers may want students to talk, they tend to overestimate greatly the amount of time that they do—usually only a few seconds. I have often suggested to teachers that they tape some class sessions (the presence of the tape recorder is soon forgotten) to replay for themselves later. As yet, I have never known a teacher to take this simple step. It may be that teachers feel they have enough problems, without doing research of this nature to discover some more. I have, however, witnessed some impressive discussions that were student-led, with the teacher resolutely sitting apart and silent. Students had prepared for these sessions, which usually were held elsewhere than the regular classroom (in one instance, in the principal's office!). The biases of the classroom may inhibit talking freely. Groupings of not over 15, and preferably not over 12, work best for discussions.
5. This was strikingly brought home to me when I met a woman who had spent her early school years in France. She then moved to the United States, where she acquired excellent English and for 35 years rarely spoke French, except when doing arithmetic, which she could not do unless she whispered her numbers tables in French!
6. For a further discussion of rote use and downshifting under threat, see Leslie A. Hart, "The Three-Brain Concept and the Classroom," *Phi Delta Kappan,* March 1981, p. 504, and "Brain Language and New Concepts of Learning," *Educational* Leadership, March 1981, p. 443.
7. The factor has shown up consistently in a long series of studies over recent years, from *Education and Income* by Patricia Cayo Sexton (New York: Viking Press, 1961, 1964). *The Fleischmann Report* (New York: Viking Press, 1973) noted: "The most striking fact that emerged from our studies of school performance in New York State is the high correlation shown between school success and socio-economic origin of pupils. This is true at all levels of the performance scale" (p. 25).

17

There lies ahead of us the enormous task of translating what we know of language acquisition, language development, and the nature of learning into structures by which teaching and learning in school may be organized. Too often today the call for "structure" takes the form of demanding the preservation of, or a return to, lockstep procedures that grew up in ignorance of the nature of learning and reflecting a mistaken view of knowledge, and hence of curriculum. In this task teachers must take a lead, both as to theory and as to practice, if the structures devised are to be workable and grounded in experience. The further participation of linguists, psychologists, and sociologists will be essential.

—JAMES BRITTON[1]

What Works: Directions We Can Go

We have looked at activities in the graded classroom in terms of what the teacher does, because in those settings the teacher is aggressive, in charge (or in trouble), and drives the group and its doings, making or imposing most of the decisions. As we turn in contrast to brain-compatible settings, we need to look rather at what students do—students who are now permitted and encouraged to act as the aggressive learners they by nature are.

The role of teacher now changes to that of *facilitator*—the role Gagné described (see page 152) as "to arrange the conditions of the learner's environment so that the processes of learning will be activated, supported, enhanced, and maintained." We must note that *learner* here must mean *individual*. The aggressive teacher runs a group, but aggressive learners largely direct themselves, and 25 or 30 students may go in as many different directions. It may seem at first as though the teacher must abandon everything associated with the ancient role of teaching, but that, we will see on further consideration, is far from the case.

For analogy, think of the mother who regularly feeds a child or two at conventional meals. The mother selects the menu, perhaps seldom inviting the children's ideas, and serves the food largely on a "here it is, eat it" basis. Suppose now the mother is required to feed 30 children the same aggressive way. Among this number of youngsters the range of tastes and eating habits will be far greater, and much more resistance to the menu may be encountered. Although the mother may try to make each meal a balanced one for good nutrition, some eaters will unbalance it by refusing to consume some food offered, and they will be unable to get other food they may want because it is not served. But now the mother tries a new tack: a choice of foods is offered at every meal, in part based on the eaters' preferences. Resistance may be much reduced. The mother has given up the arbitrary "you must eat this, now, because I say so" dominance, but she is still performing the vital function of feeding the children, and by skillfully and attractively offering choices, the eaters' diets may well become better balanced.

Assume now that the mother's job is extended to feeding 150 children, who cannot practically all come at one time. A cafeteria or smorgasbord arrangement is made, and the children serve themselves as they come in. Since they have much choice and come when they are hungry the feeding goes well. The mother has opportunity, not being busy serving, to observe what individual children put on their trays, and to take some action to correct abuses. But here patience can be exercised. If a child goes on a binge for a particular food for a week or two, no real harm is done, and probably it will end of its own accord. But if it is seen that a child's diet is distinctly off balance over a longer period, correction can be attempted, tactfully and gently at first, perhaps more seriously if change does not follow. Again, we can hardly say that the mother's role has diminished; nor has it fundamentally changed. Rather, there has been a shift from reliance on raw authority to a far more professional approach of recognizing differences and responding to them in ways that sharply reduce conflict while achieving better outcomes.

Of course, the mother who would rather have and use power than achieve a fine outcome will not be happy with this kind of shift. Education has long attracted and been plagued with those who enjoy power over others. The same appetite for power appears everywhere in human affairs, but there is no easier and quicker way to obtain authority than to become a teacher. It comes with the job—in the classroom, the raw beginner has substantially the same powers as the seasoned, mature instructor. Doing trying, demanding work, teachers can readily come to feel that their power is an important compensation for their effort.

But the great majority of neophyte teachers, most observers agree, burn with eagerness to help children and produce learning. New secondary teachers hope they will inspire and help launch careers. It is only as they become disenchanted with a bureaucratic, brain-antagonistic system that most teachers, I believe, come to see power as needed for class control and their own protection against administrative, parental, or political criticism or complaint. From contacts with thousands of school people, I feel sure a great many would happily choose the nonconfrontation, smorgasbord approach if they could.

Obviously they cannot be expected to give up what is seen as a job benefit and protection at a mere suggestion. Many teachers have never actually seen a good open program or Montessori school in operation, where for hours on end teachers have no need to make a single disciplinary remark. Some do not believe this other world of instruction exists.

To make the transition from conventional aggressive, driving teaching to fully brain-compatible approaches, teachers and the administrators who will support them need some time, practical help quickly available, and protection against unfriendly criticism during the changeover. They need to be thoroughly clear on the theory being applied and the program goals.

The specific activities—what students do—feasible in a brain-compatible setting and situation have few limits and can hardly be set down in a definitive list. But if the principles are well grasped, activities can be assembled and made part of the smorgasbord in ways suited to local needs and resources.

We can consider some of the most important aims, and some means for achieving them:

1. *Input*, we have seen, serves as the raw material from which patterns are extracted from confusion; and that is the basic process of learning. Setting, situations, and activities must all, then, provide a huge amount of input—as a rule of thumb, I have suggested ten times as much as present low-input schools. Major factors that can help raise input include:

a. Increasing the number of hours during which input is provided (possibly lengthening the school day and week, if not necessarily the teacher's workweek), the school year,[2] and increasing the net use of each hour.

b. Giving students exposure to and interaction with many people rather than very few, including a team of teachers, other staff, apprentices, volunteers, visitors, older students, peers and other helpers.

c. Providing a great variety of machines, devices, equipment, and materials (usually possible at minor cost[3]), and ample opportunity to use them, including

typewriters
calculators
public address systems
duplicators
copiers
printing systems
water tables
plant tables
scales, balances
electrical, magnetic
   materials
cameras
projectors
movie equipment
closed circuit TV
lighting, lenses
rigid panels, lumber
clamps, stands
measuring devices
garden plots
nature study plots
musical instruments
   and materials
timing devices
newspapers

maps, roadmaps
tape recorders
television receivers
small computers
radio and shortwave receivers
art rooms and supplies
shops (wood, metal, etc.)
kitchens
heavy construction materials
drafting equipment
chemical supplies
pneumatic equipment
hydraulic equipment
video recorders
sewing room
field glasses
telescopes
microscopes, magnifiers
playground materials
retail store
live animals, fish, etc.
visiting animals
telephones (outside lines)
periodicals
timetables (air, rail, bus)

...and much more, as available from parents, local businesses and manufacturers, or other sources, as gifts, loans, or via funding.

    d.   Offering hundreds of presentations to students in such forms as

visitors' talks
exhibits
performances

films, filmstrips
demonstrations (real, not verbal)
multimedia events

organized, arranged, and perhaps presented by staff, students, parents, volunteers, local businesses and professional people, local or other governmental employees and officials, etc., in any combination.

    e.   Arranging many field trips of varying duration, most often with a small number of students making the trip at any one time and then reporting to other students.

    f.   Tying in closely with current news, news events, television programs and specials, local public issues and emergencies, openings, dedications, ceremonies, inaugurations, and the like.[4]

A school, in short, can be transformed by emphasis on high input from a dreary egg-crate of classrooms largely isolated from one another, and almost empty of anything real one might learn from, into an exciting center where there is constant encounter with the richness and variety of the real world. (We do not have to worry about overstimulation so long as the students select input rather than having it forced on them.)

2.   Students must talk and communicate to learn well. Few disagree that a good command of language, an ability to convey ideas and information in speech and writing, and to receive and understand communication is an essential body of skill to function well in almost any role in society. Yet conventional schools expend a huge amount of energy and time suppressing talk, and communication becomes corrupted into exercises to be marked for grades. Desirable brain-compatible activities, then, include talking about what one is doing (especially for youngest students); talking within small teams working on common tasks or projects; asking questions for guidance, information, or clarification; public talking such as in making announcements or addressing an audience; and communication by speech directly and via writing or some instrumental means. *Communication* means that an actual exchange occurs and "something happens." (Exercises are not communication.) If writing (memo, report, proposal, request, complaint) is used by both students and faculty as a means of effecting some action, its usefulness becomes apparent.

3.   *Feedback*[5] is necessary for learners to find out whether their pattern extraction and recognition is correct or improving, and whether programs have been appropriately selected and executed. As we have noted, the right/wrong responses of teachers, often delayed, provide poor quality feedback. What is wanted, and should influence selection of offered activities, is feedback from reality rather than from an authority, and graduated rather than being classified either right or wrong. Programs have to be acquired by progressively refining the initial crude and clumsy execution so that it becomes smoother and more exact after many trials. If the slow or halting or inaccurate early performance is called wrong, the feedback gives a false message. We build programs by having a *correct general idea* of what we are trying to do, and then gradually reducing error by getting and heeding feedback. To tell the learner who is on the right track that an effort made is wrong because performance is poor is to confuse and inhibit, as we see in early reading when the student is permitted no error and gets corrected on every wrong word. Inevitably the learner becomes a word-by-word reader, trying to use a dreadfully wrong overall program. In general, brain-compatible instruction requires that students *not* be permitted to pursue wrong programs at the outset, nor to practice making errors. Practice and drill should be assigned and encouraged only after the student is clearly on the correct track and has begun refining a desired program.[6]

Feedback stems from using real rather than contrived learning devices and materials. A child using a typewriter, for example, sees at once whether the intended keys have been struck, and the spacing is as planned; one connecting an electric circuit finds out quickly whether it works. In many instances, practical, useful learning can be achieved only through reality: nursing students may start building programs by using a dummy, but sooner or later real patients, responsive or resistant, must be experienced.

A key word may be suggested here: *design*. In the aggressive-teacher situation, students deal almost always with what other people, usually unseen, have designed, and they have much the same experience outside school. My experience with students suggests that most have utterly no idea of how books are written, news is transmitted, products are developed, or large works are constructed—all these seem to come out of thin air, mysteriously (an observer is reminded of Cargo Cults in Melanesia)[7] and presumably reflect the efforts and powers of people never encountered. This ignorance may well contribute to both a feeling of being powerless and to alienation from established society. Preschool age and primary-grade children quite normally like to design, if not prevented, structures built with blocks, games, sand and snow sculpture and engineering, forts, models built with construction toys or materials, etc. Conventional schools tend to crush design activities, providing neither time nor materials, and forcing other people's design on the students.

Yet design, in broadest sense, provides some of the most productive kinds of feedback. Students designing a special-purpose space, a cage for an animal, or scenery for a play quickly discover whether the design works, whether parts fit, whether it provides what is needed. At the same time, shortcomings in their sense of pattern must come to light, as grasp is increased of how complex even apparently simple projects turn out to be. Design, whether it involve words, drawings, plans, construction, decoration, invention, arrangements, mechanisms, or aesthetics, gives a student or small team opportunity to "play God," to experience the process of choosing among alternatives and making the compromises engineers call trade-offs. Inherently design entails problem solving, and builds those frontal-lobe super-programs by which previous knowledge can be transferred to fresh applications, and automatically, the use put to practical ends of communication and basic skills.

4. *Risk*, as we have noted, is what the individual voluntarily assumes to meet the built-in human need for challenge, excitement, variety, adventure. *Threat*, in contrast, is imposed. We have examined the downshifting of the great human cerebrum under threat that effectively inhibits cerebral learning except by rote. Obviously brain-compatible learning demands activities that offer students the degree of risk they choose (within reason), and the opportunity to carry them out in nonthreat or very low-threat circumstances. Captivity is the first aspect of threat that must be attacked, and emphasis on sitting in compulsory places for com-

pulsory periods, a flagrant denial of the movement so characteristic of youth, must be eliminated if the learning situation is not to generate friction and confrontation interminably. Even when a student must be kept in the antagonistic classroom situation, it is both feasible and easy to set up an area to which he or she may withdraw from the prevailing activity—in adult terms, take a break. But that seems an extreme minimum. If the school is seen as a safe place, adequately supervised, there seems no reason why students should not move freely about it as their needs dictate. That this approach is practicable has long been demonstrated; in contrast rigid schools fight a constant battle, often lost, to control students' whereabouts and behavior. I have put forward, without claiming originality, the concept of *circus*, a group of rooms and spaces around which a unit of about 125 to 150 students may circulate for most of their earlier half of schooling, and which offers them a wide range of resources and facilities.[8] Such an arrangement calls for no great architectural changes in existing school buildings, and permits an enormous variety of activities to be readily accommodated. Older students may circulate still more freely.

Threat also can be sharply reduced by ceasing the practice, centuries old, of continually marking student activity—perhaps systematically recording all failures in a Doomsday Book—and by reducing all testing and written examinations to barest minimum. When activities multiply in number and variety to provide the smorgasbord choice, the group examination becomes less and less usable. Individual student progress can be far better followed and guided by reporting observations of accomplishments as they occur. The shift is made from what the student knows (often meaning "remembers for the moment") to what the student actually does in appropriate circumstances. The student writes a clear message; solves a real arithmetical problem; translates a foreign newspaper story; takes and processes some good photographs; seeks out and compiles some needed information; designs a rack for chemical equipment; chairs a meeting; reviews an unassigned book; keeps accounts for the store; plans and arranges a visit by the mayor; paints a portrait; plays a part in the orchestra. Whatever the achievement, *it is recorded only if it attains an acceptable level of mastery*—it is pointless to record failures except to lay blame on the student. I have suggested that, using computer resources, each student's progress can be rigorously followed, with lack of progress made a signal for corrective action and investigation.[9]

The school then becomes a place where ordinarily students succeed, not one where failure is endemic and to considerable degree expected. (Students enrolling in commercial or industrial schools to learn typing, keypunching, welding, or lifesaving, for examples, expect to succeed to at least practically acceptable levels, and in legitimate schools usually do. Some drop out, mostly on finding they do not like the work or lack physical aptitude, but few fail as large percentages do in conventional schools, even if granted fictitious passing grades.) The smorgasbord approach provides both much chance to find areas in which one can succeed through interest and aptitude, and room to enlarge success areas. We may note, too, that the student who is enjoying clear success in any learning area of importance is likely to have a self-image and confidence that encourages wider achievement—and such a student is little likely to present behavior problems. In contrast, the student in a conventional school who because of competitive marking and grading attains no clear success over the years, but has many spotlighted failures, easily may come to have a low self-image and to look upon the whole formal learning process with strong distaste. Quite correctly, the school is viewed as a punishing enemy.

These four main factors, *input, talk-communication, feedback, and threat/risk,* offer a means of looking at student activities from a factoring point of view—an idea that may be, I think, substantially new in education and potentially of pervasive importance. Using theory, we can analyze what helps, what hurts, what doesn't matter.

Curriculum today is still arrived at by a process ludicrously defective, because it embodies two flagrantly untrue propositions: that what is taught will be learned, and that what is to be learned can fit into a neatly packaged, exactly timed *course,* even for basic learning. Curriculum making becomes a process of decisions as to what courses shall be taught at particular times. The courses are further broken down to syllabus, or topics to be covered, and these in turn to units, sequences, and lessons to be aggressively taught. Instructors who have to execute these ill-conceived efforts break them down further, eagerly seeking "things to do" and procedures, all of which must square with the limitations of *course* and the oppressive demands of classroom management. What the individual instructors select will (as we have noted) vary greatly, reflecting many differences in personality, experience, training, and personal beliefs, prejudices, convenience, aptitudes, and intuition.[10] The end of this chain, students' activities (*what the students actually do*) becomes almost lost to sight (we have very few studies reporting what students do), haphazard, heavily ritualized, and out of control. Where the learning must take place there is only confusion.

Brain-compatible curriculum must start from the other end, from the realization that the entire structure exists only to provide student activities, and these must produce the learning desired. What learning is desired? Not passing courses, not accumulation of Carnegie points, not certified attendance for a certain number of days, not obtaining paper credentials—these are hardly learning. But we can state what learning is desired in a broad way that is acceptable to virtually all citizens: *the child should become familiar with and able to operate successfully in the real, complex world in which he or she now operates to limited degree and will soon operate to adult degree.*

This is, historically, a new concept. Even a century ago many and perhaps most people felt that youngsters should be exposed only to carefully selected slivers of the real world, and that their learning should be tightly controlled and limited. If such a plan was feasible then, obviously it is not today.

If we observe the infant and preschool-age child, we see plainly the vigorous natural-learning attack on the world, which at first is limited largely to crib and mother's arms, but rapidly expands. Today's five-year-old has had experience in many ways beyond that of the fifty-year-old of past centuries—exposure to mass media, to a variety of locales, to perhaps several thousands of miles of travel in family cars alone. Input has climbed enormously, and with it opportunity to grasp real-world patterns and to build programs useful in that world. It seem clearly desirable that this process should continue in school, and not run into curriculum in the antique, restrictive sense. *The brain-compatible school must be one in which the process of world-discovery accelerates and broadens*—courses may be a useful narrowing and focusing of interest to come later. To move from broad input to narrow is natural and makes sense in terms of results; to try to start with a few narrow approaches and then broaden slightly with a few more optional courses is plainly inadequate, in concept and in outcomes.

One reason is that the most important, insightful, and transferable pattern understandings transcend courses. Such concepts (the "grand ideas" earlier mentioned) as energy cycles, systems, negative/positive, innovation/obsolescence, new generation, probability, causation, critical mass, and feedback, apply in almost any field. To illustrate, the negative/positive concept has critical usefulness in mathematics, photography, molding, chemistry, accounting, politics, electronics, and—as in factoring—in education. Only as these multiuse patterns are detected, recognized, and employed to select programs do learners establish the base for easy, rapid acquisition of narrower learning through courses.

Using the four main factors we have examined, I believe, any person concerned with instruction can better evaluate proposed activities and with considerable accuracy select those that will produce learning effectively and discard those that will not, or that will have negative effect.

Some other factors deserve at least mention here:

* Young children especially must *manipulate* what they deal with. Manipulation remains helpful, if less essential, at later ages.
* Learning must always be dominantly *addressed to immediate and later uses*, not to testing or examinations, and not to a future use beyond the ken of the learner. ("You will need algebra to get into college.")

• The freedom of the human brain to function in *natural* (as opposed to logical) ways should not be infringed, and its output as a result should be accepted and honored.[11]

• *Rote learning* should be achieved by vigorous, fast-paced, preferably multimodal means, only as individually necessary to achieve mastery.

If now we summarize our focus on the activities of the *students*—the activities that directly affect what will be learned—we emerge with these points:

1. The smorgasbord principle permits broad recognition of and allowance for individual differences, and accommodates a wide range of learning styles.[12] Student conflict with the institution can be greatly reduced without the school giving up control of main, consequential objectives. Giving students many choices in interests and short-term strategies for learning and exploration allows individual choice making to become visible, rather than only the degree or manner of compliance or resistance, in response to inflexible demands. Students acquire ability to take responsibilities through experience in taking responsibilities.

2. Appropriate settings and situations and selection of activities largely by student initiatives can increase input up to tenfold, while student exposure to a rich variety of people and the real world is greatly enhanced.

3. The employment of spoken and written language for actual communication purposes (in contrast to exercises) can be stepped up 500 to 1,000 percent.

4. Feedback from reality, rather than from authority, can be greatly enhanced by making available activities with this built-in characteristic.

5. Design functions can readily be introduced into activities to increase reality feedback, foster a sense of control of the student's world, add to problem-solving experience in a real context, and strengthen skills in transfer of patterns and programs to fresh applications.

6. As threat is reduced and the setting becomes safe for the student, emphasis can increase on mastery rather than partial learning, and on actual accomplishment, with the opportunity to stress quality and excellence rather than pen-and-paper test answers.

7. Student activity and attainment can be readily and meaningfully followed to monitor and assure progress, with success expected and obtained.

8. Curriculum can shift from meaning what teachers do to broadly planned provisions for what students will do.

9. Grand ideas or concepts that transcend courses can readily be incorporated in student activities.

10. Particularly for younger children, manipulation activities can be provided for and encouraged.

11. Natural thinking (intuitive, heuristic, frontal, lobe directed) can be encouraged and accepted.

12. Rote learning methods can be vigorously used where appropriate for the purpose.

13. What the student does can be largely oriented to the real, outside world rather than to school artificialities, recognizing that the student already inhabits this real world and will take on increasing responsibilities within it.

While this even in summary is a long list, it is not, I submit, a "laundry list." The elements in it intertwine and interrelate, and become mutually supportive. They stem from a common source: a brain-compatible approach.

I have put much emphasis on real world. It may be proper to conclude with a look at the real world of education and the prospects for implementing new brain-based approaches.

NOTES

1. *The Teaching of English*, 76th Yearbook of National Society for the Study of Education (Chicago: University of Chicago Press, 1977), p. 37.

2. Most Japanese schools provide 240 or more days per school year against our 180, and students are engaged in learning perhaps 85 percent of the time compared with 25 percent or less in our schools. See "Japan: The Learning Society," *Educational Leadership*, March 1982, p. 412.

3. Two points should be noted here briefly. First, almost everywhere but in education managers think in terms of equipment/labor trade-offs, introducing equipment when it will more than offset labor costs. Schools and other similar institutions tend to remain a century or more behind and as a result fearfully expensive, to the point that much desirable is not done because of labor costs. Second, school people seem to believe that everything needed must be bought from special school suppliers. But actually much useful material and equipment can be obtained at no cost, or by modest expenditures, as good open-style teachers often demonstrate. Expensive equipment in schools is frequently found, unused or needing maintenance, in closets and store rooms.

4. A quick survey of my neighborhood children after a recent space shuttle flight revealed that three had followed at least the landing in school but most had not. One might find it hard to think of an event that afforded more high-interest "handles" for science, mathematics, geography, and language arts.

5. As observed previously, I am using the term loosely. Also required here is "feedforward," as those familiar with this concept will realize. One feeds forward intention, aim, or plan, and gets feedback that tells how well it is working. This permits revised, better feedforward. Steering a car down a winding road provides a good example.

6. Rising interest in computers puts emphasis on the "debugging" process. After a new program is written, it must be tested for bugs, or faults, which normally show up. Their elimination, at times a difficult and tedious task, is viewed as an essential step that may increase understandings and skills. In times past, when students did more writing in school, many teachers insisted on the debugging of essays in somewhat the same way. Today, this valuable process in learning more likely gets scant attention—the effort is marked right or wrong, errors are circled in red but not followed up, or an overall grade or mark is given.

7. Having no idea of how industrial nations produce manufactured goods, the cultists assume it is the result of magic. They may erect sticks that look like a radio antenna in the hope that this will bring the radio receiver. The problem is only to find the right magic, an idea that prevailed in Europe for centuries during the heyday of alchemy and associated metaphysics. To today's students, auto parts may be seen as coming from the auto parts store, with the magical aid of money.

8. See Chapter 16, Leslie A. Hart, *The Classroom Disaster* (New York: Teachers College Press, Columbia University, 1969.)

9. See Chapter 20, *The Classroom Disaster*. This idea has since been developed further: to create a separate office and function, that of the Evaluator, who follows in detail the progress of each student throughout the years of attendance and is the prime reporter to both parents and administration.

10. One consequence of classroom organization is that teachers duplicate rather than pool effort, a huge and constant waste of effort and salaries.

11. See Chapter 16, Leslie A. Hart, *How The Brain Works* (New York: Basic Books, 1975) for discussion of natural thinking.

12. The learning-styles approach, which considers individual environmental, sociological, and psychological elements, has grown into a considerable movement, closely related to brain-based considerations. See "A Learning Styles Primer," by Rita Dunn (a pioneer) in *Principal*, May 1981.

18

There are two very significant signs of our being at the end of one era, even if we cannot yet discern the character of the next. First, principles previously unquestioned or questioned only by "radicals" begin to come in for more serious, popular questioning...second, the less tenable long-established principles come to be, the more intense the ceremonial rain dances by those who fear the personal consequences of new ones.

—JOHN I. GOODLAD[1]

Prospects of Change: Can Schools Survive?

In preceding chapters we have considered:

- The brain, its roles, history, and triune structure.
- Programs, prosters, patterns, and the new scientifically based theory of human learning that focuses on them.
- Methodology and arrangements at three levels:
  a. settings, usually the institution.
  b. situations, or students' day-to-day surroundings and experiences.
  c. activities, or what individual students actually do.

Even the reader who has questioned or taken exception to one or another assertion that I have made will, I think, agree with the overall thrust of this exploration: that current educational effort tends to be choked with antique structures and cobwebbed ideas and rituals. Nor can it be seriously argued, in the light of many recent studies of learning achievement and general public dissatisfaction, that schools and other educational institutions function with acceptable success. While some educators feel the storm of public criticism may include excesses and inaccurate charges, it would not be easy to find one of prominence who does not feel that major changes are needed.

A dozen years ago, any suggestion that schools as we know them could not survive much longer brought sharp and angry reactions. Today that notion, if far from universally accepted, hardly raises eyebrows. Educators at many levels, frustrated, wearied with battle, gloomy and discouraged, circle their retirement date in red and count the days. For younger staff people, there is a new fear of events: any news is likely to be bad news, and confidence in the future gives way to grim holding on.

Can schools change? Do the new concepts of learning now available offer practical hope? These seem pertinent questions to address in this final chapter.

Our educational system, based on and dominated by the public schools, consists of an enormous bulk of payroll, plant, and peripheral interests. Employees are numbered in millions, students in the tens of millions, expenditures run into hundreds of billions of dollars each year. Countless suppliers of all kinds have a huge stake, and influence. The greatest portion of this whole rests firmly in the hands of bureaucracies, usually multilevel, in conflict with one another, and highly resistant to change. Unions, associations, and interest groups fiercely defend against moves they see as threatening, often in knee-jerk fashion. Public influence is sapped by the prevalence of myths, a lack of information, diverse interests and attitudes toward children and education, and the difficulties of penetrating the bureaucratic citadels.

To even contemplate trying to move such a mass in a particular direction can be dismaying. Yet I remain among those who after many years of painfully slow visible progress feel that a variety of influences—including some historical accidents—may be opening the way for change more than seems apparent. The most consequential may be these:

1. *Falling enrollment.* The prolonged drop in the birth rate has abruptly ended the "bigger and better" euphoria that schools and colleges long enjoyed. The old security that served as a major attraction and comfort fell victim to a steep decline from a peak in 1965 to a new low ten years later. Birth rates can be tricky, and fluctuations can be expected; but the impact of the pill, increased working by women outside the home, and diminished enthusiasm for the cost and problems of raising large families, all point toward continuing low enrollment for years to come.[2]

For institutions, growth tends to hide and ease problems, while shrinkage not only intensifies them but adds all the pain and strain of cutting back and determining what and who shall remain. Had the schools had adequate, unified national leadership (in my view there has been little) the occasion might well have been reason to review needs and emerge with a substantially improved, leaner, and more effective system. Nothing of the kind happened. Schools retrenched, often in the crudest, blindest way, as boards of education tried to cope with dismayingly unfamiliar conditions. Under the dubious banner of back to basics (as though basics were sound and successful, not the site of the worst failures), confused and quarrelling local leaders tended to retain all the hoariest, costliest, and least productive forms of effort.

2. *Inflation.* As enrollments tumbled, general inflation also hit schools and colleges hard, sending costs soaring. The combination of rising expense for fewer students brought a chill response from taxpayers, who had already been showing an increasing tendency to resist higher budgets. Even in communities where only a few years before citizens had boasted of how lavishly they spent on schools, budgets already trimmed were defeated. In a few dramatic instances, schools shut down for periods as funds ran out. In a great many more, individual schools have been closed, perhaps permanently; and the process continues.

The coincidence of these two factors seems to have significance, not always noted, for facilitating change. So long as members of school staffs usually felt impregnably secure in their employment, they and their unions could look at proposals for change as less than compelling. But teachers and others who see closings, dismissals, and forced retirements all around acquire new worries to add to those about reduced prestige, personal safety, and depressing conditions of work. Much as one may deplore these hardships, they clearly make resistance to change harder for boards, administrators, staffs, and unions.

3. *The demand for learning.* Whether by coincidence again or in part because of the two influences mentioned above, *for the first time in recent American educational history the amount and quality of learning achieved by students has become a major issue.* Though it sounds absurd to state bluntly that interest in learning is new, historically that seems to be precisely accurate. The schools have emphasized order, socialization, moral considerations, manners, and compliance; but learning has been made a responsibility of the student, or the student's background, even when failure to learn was massive and pervasive in the student body, and even middle-class as well as poor and minority children were victims. While some schools boasted of scholarships won and college admissions obtained, on the whole schools have long evaded or avoided giving "the bottom line," the learning outcomes obtained across the board. When some years ago a few big city systems began to publish reading scores, the move was regarded as radical in the extreme.[3]

But public demand to know outcomes has risen steadily over recent years, fueled from a variety of sources. Employers found candidates unqualified and unready, colleges complained of freshmen grossly ill prepared, the armed forces had to reject great numbers of potential recruits as hopelessly lacking in elementary skills even though many were high school graduates—on paper. A long series of studies and reports, led by those of the National Assessment[4] kept winning publicity as they brought dismal confirmation of poor learning, grade inflation (lowered standards), alarming gaps in knowledge, and stunted skills. "Educational malpractice" emerged as a new term—as yet the courts have protected the schools, but hardly in a way to bring comfort to educators.[5] Steadily falling college entrance test scores, and glaring shortcomings in the study of science, mathematics, and foreign languages, induced public worries about our ability to compete as a nation, accentuated as imports took larger shares of markets we had long regarded as ours. As the disturbing findings came in, they inspired more studies.

If in general the schools appeared to pay little heed other than by some window-dressing, some important, and unprecedented, movement nevertheless occurred. The old myths and attitudes that had long protected the schools from pointed criticism on learning achieved began to crumble, and educators found themselves confronted with legislation in most states that now *ordered* the schools to produce a minimal amount of learning. The laws may be considered essentially foolish—one cannot legislate learning. But the message was not: student achievement was now demanded, as the schools' responsibility.

If I may venture an observation, many boards of education and administrators still regard this demand as one more crotchet to emerge from state capitols, another technicality to be endured. But others, especially at higher levels, appear to believe that this extraordinary change in the rules of the game has a broad public base and has come to stay. It seems clear that pressures on schools to produce real, substantial, useful learning will increase; it is not at all clear that school people know how to bring that about. My own informal sampling, down to the building principal level, suggests a much expanded willingness to consider alternatives and—cautiously—undertake leadership. A new question is repeatedly asked: what can we *do*?

We have come full circle. When Horace Mann took up his new office a century and a third ago, he looked at the schools of his day and found them wanting. Sensibly, he wasted no time on tinkering but set out actively to find a replacement system. In Prussia he found a model to adapt. The American class-and-grade system that resulted was a smashing success in meeting the political and funding needs of a common-school system; it was equally a disaster for producing reliable learning, a consideration given scant attention at the time, and has been a curse to us ever since. *Today our clear need is to look actively for a replacement system that will bring about learning.* If momentarily there seems to be more moaning than looking, it hardly appears impossible that looking may be the next step—a very large step away from lifting the drawbridge and defending the castle.

Throughout the sixties and into the seventies, a spirit of looking found much sustenance, in part, oddly enough, due to the earlier success of the Russian space experts in launching Sputnik and so proving they were far ahead in that technology. Both private and public funds flowed into experiments and new formats and arrangements. At almost any conference—and there was then money for many conferences—innovation was a prime topic. The criticisms of the dominant system that compose a portion of this book were then aired in detail and with vehemence, verbally and in a succession of books, some of them virulent, that found wide readership. The Johnson administration attacked the problem of student failure on a huge scale, lavishing funds on "compensatory" programs to unheard of extent. For a time it seemed probable that sweeping change would indeed come, fueled by the emotions of civil rights drives, lubricated with easy money, and guided by many of the most creative, enterprising people within education.

Not much happened. The old system survived, unchanged.

A study of that period is far beyond the scope of this book. Much more literature on it would be welcome to explain why a period of ferment brought only fragments of permanent change at best. Some conclusions seem evident,[6] although complex, crisscross forces produced a welter treacherous to analyze:

• Many of the experiments were not carried into practice. They were protocols on paper, resisted in the classroom by teachers who often resented them and continued doing what they had always done, though sometimes using new labels and terms in mock compliance.

• The great majority of efforts were fragmentary rather than systemic, concerned with students at a limited age range or level. Others dealt only with certain topics, subjects, or areas of accomplishment.

• Implementation was often grossly inadequate, with little attention given to the needs and views of teachers and others at the working level. The "new math," for example, was thrust on ill-prepared teachers; open techniques were jumped into hastily, with little provision for training and support.

• The problem of evaluation was frequently left for later; or methods designed for the old system were applied to new efforts, leading to endless wrangles about outcomes.[7]

• "Change agents" who supposedly could introduce the new techniques and arrangements came into hot demand, but moved frequently to take advantage of better job offers, leaving vacuums behind.

• School staffs, little involved in and mistrustful of change pushed on them, bided their time and when possible reverted to old, comfortable ways. Even where new approaches took some root, boards of education and administrators who felt their own expertise and control diminished made no effort to build on the success, and allowed it to slough off as the enthusiasts for it moved or retired.[8]

• Money was flooded in. Educators had long used lack of funds as an all-purpose excuse for not solving problems and shortcomings. Generous funding wiped out the excuse, but at the same time the money itself created new bureaucracies, and attracted people eager to share the bonanza while it lasted, but often little interested in building programs that could endure on regular funding. When the foundations, disenchanted by scant results, turned off their money, projects tended to slide into oblivion even when they had merit and promise.

But the overwhelming reason why this era of change produced so little in proportion to the rhetoric and effort now stands clear—the more so if this book has served its aim. The efforts went in all directions because there existed no unifying theory. One enthusiasm, one experiment, was as good as another. Foundations and government funded almost anything that might work, even where admittedly the proposals had conflicting rationales. Some of the largest programs, especially in compensatory education, were based on logical plans innocent of substantial learning theory. As one collapsed, another was put in its place. Project Head Start, for example, was intended to prepare certain children to fit the schools they would attend, not to prepare the schools to fit the children. Hailed in revolutionary terms, it was actually a massive effort to bolster the failing status quo.[9] Because the cheerful, hopeful, well-intended blunderings into unmapped regions were largely unrelated to each other, they failed to add up. Cumulative effect requires theory; there was no theory. Good intuitions of the sort sensitive educators have had for centuries were mixed in with novelties, hot fashions of the moment, conventional curriculums and materials, new "teacherproof" programs from academic ivory towers, and ancient traditions and folklore. Open approaches for classrooms, corridors, or schools, some more or less inspired by British experience, ranged from expert to inept, from well considered to crackpot, with open nonetheless taken as a meaningful descriptor by researchers who solemnly wrote up comparisons with graded classrooms. The same foolish use of vague labels was made with team teaching, ungraded classrooms, flexible plans, and other formats.

To imply that this era of change produced nothing of value would be most incorrect. Obviously, a great deal was learned about what *not* to do, and the difficulties of bringing about change in any kind of organization came to light to provide lessons to naive enthusiasts. But amid the failures and wash-outs there was much that worked. Perhaps most important were the thousands of demonstrations that arrangements other than the conventional graded classrooms were *viable*. They could be set up, usually in existing buildings; they could be staffed with teachers and others with conventional backgrounds, after training; they could continue for years to serve not only hand-picked but also a quite broad flow of students. Once established, costs fell within normal range, and might even be lower. For a number of years I have checked informally on the effects on disciplinary and attendance problems, which seem almost always, in the viable instances, to lessen strikingly. Equally, teachers who have a year of experience in such situations strongly prefer not to return to conventional classrooms.[10] Despite retrenchment and the often mindless back to basics cry, thousands of exceptions to the conventional classroom continue to function, even if they total only a few percent of the whole.[11] Unfortunately, to my knowledge no adequate studies of any large sample of these departures from the conventional have been made and reported. Survivors of the era of change tend to maintain low profiles, and often must divert effort to defending against the troglodyte elements in their systems. But some smaller studies, quietly reported, tend to be positive, even impressive.

We have, in short, a rich body of ore to turn to, once there arises the desire to prospect. And whereas the graded classroom is overaged, exhausted, and feeble as a device, these newer forms usually stand at the threshold of their development. Seldom are they integrated into a system, or vigorously supported with resources.

4. *The availability of coherent theory.* In Proster Theory and such other brain-based theories of human learning as may be put forward, we have at last the crucial element that can accelerate successful change, in my view.

Not having ever experienced great advances, people in education generally neither expect them or look for them. In operating schools and much other instruction, they continue to use approaches and techniques that date back 20, 40, 80 years . . . up to centuries, in large part because *they have no programs, no procedures, for obtaining major improvements and advances within the parameters of ordinary, sanctioned behavior.* Only individuals who feel very secure, or are daring by nature, ordinarily venture beyond the bounds willingly. But today new pressures may well be changing that generality, pushing people into action because the status quo has become intolerable and threatening and the availability of radically new theory beckons them to consider breakthrough possibilities never before contemplated.

In 1966, on the eve of the drive for change, cognitive psychologist Donald Snygg stated the issue plainly:

Knowledge of what has happened in one situation cannot, without a theory of why it happened, enable us to predict what will happen in any other situation if it is different in the slightest degree.... Without a scientific theory of learning, teachers and administrators have to meet new problems with inappropriate routines that were devised long ago to meet other problems or to base their decisions on folk beliefs about learning which, although thoroughly disproved in the laboratories, still pass for common sense.[12]

Educational philosopher Harry S. Broudy is among those who have stressed the same thought, noting the fundamental impact of "the lack of any body of accepted theory or expertise in terms of which one can tell in advance something about the viability of a project or experiment." But Broudy has gone further to observe:

> Between the theoreticians and operatives there must be an interposition of practitioners enlightened by theory from mere rule following. The almost farcical attempts to evade the task of providing this professional layer are the prime cause of most of the ills from which the schools of America suffer.[13]

This emphasis on the need for people who (1) have theory and (2) know how to use it, I believe, gets to the core of practical advancement of education.

Brain-based theory, even in its early stages, gives us what has never been available before: the ability to design settings and methods likely to work much better to produce student learning. The broad objective of brain compatibility can be factored: the theory strongly suggests what elements will impede learning, facilitate it, or be neutral. True experiments become feasible, not aimed at trying to determine the influence of one variable in a complex situation (a kind of effort that has wasted hundreds of millions of dollars on valueless research), but at designing and conducting actual instruction for a period and reading the outcomes against what theory predicted for the factors used in combination.

In medical research, awareness is keen of the great differences between *in vitro* or test tube studies, and *in vivo* or actual living bodies, where outcomes can be unexpected and highly variable with individuals. In the end, only *in vivo* success has broad, practical human value. In education, the *in vivo* efforts, without good theoretical design, have been of necessity blind, "try it and see" investigations, and as Snygg points out, of little use for prediction if even a single element is changed.

Working from theory to factors, from factors to design of complex situations, permits experiments that can rapidly refine both basic theory and the engineering necessary to apply it. At the same time, the outcomes of trials can be analyzed in theory and factor terms, producing far more understanding of why they occurred as they did. This technique, used virtually everywhere except in education, yields steadily cumulative results.

It would be pleasant to report that the institutions which train teachers, administrators, and specialists now offer leadership and courses to meet the needs Broudy identifies, but such programs remain exceptional. However, since teachers colleges and departments of education also feel the shaking-up effects of lower enrollments and the demand for learning achievement, they may well respond in due course.[14] That interest in the brain approach has steadily risen seems hardly disputable, and a sprinkling of largely self-directed graduate students and holders of doctorates have taken brain-oriented paths. A 1979 yearbook of the Association for Supervision and Curriculum Development, a respected official organization, offered these blunt views:

> As practiced, schooling is a poor facilitator of learning. Its persistent view of learning as product interferes with significant learnings connected to such complex processes as inquiry and appreciation. What often passes for education is noise that interrupts the natural flow of learning. Schooling too often fragments learning into subject areas, substitutes control for the natural desire to learn, co-opts naturally active children for hours in assembly line classroom structures, and ignores both individual and cultural differences. . . . The formal educational system often destroys opportunities for learning from elders, from each other, and from the new generation. . . . *Much is known about the learning process but little has been applied to education. . . . The American education system is not making use of brain research findings, findings which shatter the S-R learning myth*[15] (emphasis added).

If useful theory can be valuable to those directly engaged in instruction, it would seem just as valuable to those who undertake to train teachers and administrators. To be sure, colleges cannot offer programs on brain-compatible approaches until they have people to teach them. This is a hen-and-egg problem that can lessen in a few years. The institutions that take the lead may find it less onerous than those who trail.

5. *Other Influences.* Three trends that may operate to push or encourage major changes should be at least mentioned, although their effects must be speculative. The *civil rights movement* which has produced some large gains for minorities in many ways (reminding us how fast large-scale changes in society can occur, once they get going) seems currently to have encountered reversals, particularly in working-class employment and the educational achievement on which it often seems to depend. Blacks seem to have felt for a long time, as an article of faith, that if their children went to schools with whites, learning would follow—they have enormously exaggerated the ability of schools to bring about learning achievement for students, and ignored the tight link between family income and all levels of educational credential achievement.[16] It seems possible this unwelcome fact may now be coming more to light, to meld with other acute (and justified) dissatisfactions. In my experience, blacks, Hispanics, and others have been slow to see how classroom schools harm their children the most.

Women's rights, too, have made rapid progress, though the struggle has still far to go. As women commonly spend less time in the home, gain more exposure to the world of work, and speak with firmer voices, women's demands for more effective and desirable schools may well become stronger and less patient. In general, the schools appear to have ignored these changes, and even continue, often, to complain about lack of parental involvement, as though major social changes could be dealt with as naughty behavior. Some day, too, feminists may wake up to the low regard for women built into the classroom system.[17]

Competition is the third influence, and perhaps the most inscrutable. The near monopoly the public schools have long enjoyed has obviously been crumbling. Nonpublic schools appear to be gaining, with high-income-family children accounting for only a fraction. Should the trend accelerate even a little, perhaps aided by vouchers of some kind, the impact on public schools already shrinking would be shattering. In the immediate offing looms a new competitor: the host of electronic developments, including video cassettes, small and low-cost home computers and terminals, and disks which can make any of 100,000 pictures or pages instantly available on a television screen, or present motion which can be reversed and repeated. The potentials are staggering, and the cost already modest. Each such device—more are on the way—makes the conventional school look more primitive and feeble. For the conventional class-and-grade school, alternative schools, public or private, also offer direct competition that seems only to have begun. The greater flexibility of such schools and their willingness to consider new approaches could quite possibly lead to their explosive growth.

The notion of "the one best system," to use David Tyack's title,[18] has already begun to fray badly. The more alternative schools bring choices, the more the opportunity grows for brain-compatible schools to demonstrate much superior outcomes. We do not need many such successes, I believe, to have potent effect, if the successes are unquestionable. If even a scattering of schools in a variety of typical communities can show zero failure in the basic skills (including children from low-income and non-English-speaking homes, and the millions imaginatively labeled learning disabled[19] or otherwise improperly segregated), and can achieve much better results in quality and range of other learning and development of personal abilities, along with much improved disciplinary climate and even lower overall cost, a wedge will exist to crack resistance elsewhere. Comfortable, antique grade-level standards will become ridiculous, and insufferable.

Until now, exemplary schools have been hard to find, and usually able to claim only modest superiority, mostly as the consequence of having outstandingly able principals. No way is presently known to produce such leaders in any quantity—by definition they are exceptional! But brain-compatible schools, with a clear theoretical base, would not be so dependent on happy accidents of personnel selection. Vitally important as staff would remain, the various forms of brain-compatible settings should prove easily replicable and extensible.

Many designs for brain-compatible schools are possible. Positive factors can be emphasized and negative factors eliminated by various combinations. The engineering can take many forms. Certain patterns, however, are likely to be common to all successes:

a.   The classroom fixed grouping, for a fixed period, under a fixed instructor will largely vanish. Grouping would be temporary, for only as long as the grouping serves a common purpose—an hour, a day, a week.

b.   Sharply identified learning goals, by the hundreds, would be sought, over an extended time period, and in largely random order.

c.   In place of aggressive teaching, students will usually come to instructors (of all kinds) for assistance with perceived needs, and for continuing individual guidance.

d.   Students will be far more engaged with realities, much less with writing at a desk.

e.   Students will talk with, work with, and learn from a wide variety of individuals, only some of whom will be on staff.

f.   Mastery of learning goals will be required, not "65 percent to pass."

g.   The progress of each student will be known in detail and reviewed frequently, with failure not acceptable to the school.

h.   The school will become a learning center for all in it, including staff; not a punitive institution where confrontation is normal.

i.   Schools and colleges will be much more closely integrated with their communities and regions.

j.   Attendance will be largely descheduled, to reflect individual activities, aims, home circumstances, enthusiasms, explorations, and out-of-school learning opportunities, as student age and maturity permits.

Although the various forms of brain-compatible schools do not appear to demand, necessarily, substantially rebuilt or new buildings and plants, the problem of retraining staff at first looks formidable. I doubt it would prove so. Retraining can be difficult indeed when the people involved do not want to change, see little point to learning new ways, and master new programs, if at all, only under continuing compulsion. It can be quite another matter when the goals are most attractive, seem well conceived and attainable, and very quickly produce visible results as the new approaches are implemented, with strong, on-site support. The shift to brain-compatible instruction would, I think, be mostly on-the-job and real, rather than by lecture and meeting as in feeble, futile in-service programs.

In addition, it appears pertinent to point out that Proster Theory itself suggests strongly how effective retraining can be planned: by identifying the new programs sought and changing the biases so that old ones will not be called up from the proster.[20]

When television was all black-and-white and color waited on the threshold, I was peripherally involved, and recall the seemingly insoluable dilemma: color sets could not be made at reasonable cost except in great volume; people would not buy receivers unless there were a lot of color programs to make it worthwhile; broadcasters could not afford expensive color programs unless there preexisted a large audience able to view them in color. Somehow the problems, involving many parties and hundreds of millions of dollars, were resolved. Relatively, the difficulties of setting up a small number of pilot brain-compatible schools seem simple, and the time may be ripe. We live in days when changes come with a rush. Let us speculate on outcomes that seem possible:

- Student failure or serious lagging, even where endemic, might well be virtually eliminated so far as core learning is concerned.
- Most students would go far beyond present grade levels, achieving much solider learning.
- The discipline problem would largely vanish, as it already has in many nonclassroom schools.
- Teachers would find their burdens sharply reduced as confrontations gave way to enhanced individual learning, with teachers taking on much more professional (and gratifying) obligations and roles.
- Administration could become far more focused on education rather than often minor, time-consuming duties.
- The cost of schools could be substantially reduced by a variety of savings, even as the environment became enriched.
- Public and community would be directly and continuously involved, and supportive.
- Youth crime and drug abuses, at least in part attributable to school failure, boredom, and age grouping, might be reduced.
- Student and staff morale could show great improvement, as the tone of schools changed to successful, cooperative effort rather than conflict and decline.
- Students from poorer or certain minority homes would escape many current disadvantages.
- No limits would be placed on excellence of achievement by gifted and highly able students.
- Students would emerge from secondary school far better prepared for further education or work, with substantial grasp and experience of the real world.

The gains suggested, if achieved, should become apparent to large degree within two years or less, though refinements will of course take much longer. It is easy, to be sure, to scoff at large advances, so unfamiliar in education; it is less easy to pooh-pooh the acute problems that threaten collapse. We cannot afford minor gains, any more than a drowning person can afford to go under more slowly.

Beyond argument, learning is a brain function. We do have profound new comprehensions of the human brain. Surely we should welcome and explore the potentials of brain-compatible approaches.

NOTES

1. "Can Our Schools Get Better?," *Phi Delta Kappan*, January 1979, p. 345.
2. Sociologist Joan Huber of the University of Illinois predicted that the fertility rate would continue downward below zero population growth, and viewed the last "baby boom" as only an interruption of a 200 year declining trend. She noted estimates of child-rearing costs of up to $175,000, birth through college, and that children no longer represented later security for parents as in preindustrial societies. *The New York Times*, December 28, 1980. These views appear to be quite widely shared by other population specialists.
3. Innumerable individual teachers and others, of course, have taken personal interest in their students' learning achievement, and to some this has been a source of deep concern. On institution levels, however, it is difficult to find evidence of similar distress. Bottom-line reports remain a rarity, and at best tend to be rigid, statistically overwhelming, and obscure as well as very limited in scope. Instances of deliberate manipulation or falsification of scores are not unknown. Dismissal or demotion of employees primarily because of poor learning outcomes seldom occurs. The success of individual practitioners and administrators is not known, nor is direct reward often feasible.
4. The National Assessment of Educational Progress was set up by joint action of several parties in 1969, over widespread opposition of educators. It periodically samples student attainment by special examinations, and issues public reports. It is currently conducted by the Education Commission of the States, headquartered in Denver, Colorado.
5. See Arlene H. Patterson, "Professional Malpractice: Small Cloud, but Growing Bigger" in *Phi Delta Kappan*, November 1980, p. 193. Also, Mitchell Lazarus, *Goodbye to Excellence* (Boulder, Colo.: Westview Press, 1981), especially chapters 6 and 7. The book deals mainly with "minimum competency testing."
6. In 1972 the Ford Foundation issued a frank and valuable summary, "A Foundation Goes to School." The foundation was a leader in encouraging and supporting reform and experimental efforts, but later severely cut educational efforts, presumably because of the unrewarding outcomes.
7. For a number of years I have sought evaluations of results when I have visited or heard about innovative in-school programs, only to find they seldom are made. One difficulty is that standard forms of testing may be unsuitable.

Another, I believe, is that those in charge of the new programs avoid "making waves" and seek a low profile.

8. Seymour B. Sarason, in *The Culture of the School and the Problem of Change* (Boston: Allyn and Bacon, 1971), has brilliantly explored these difficulties, illuminating the emotional factors involved, but often not given sufficient attention. Some of his readable reports on encounters provide good examples of the effect of threat, as that term is used in Proster Theory. See also the valuable study by Philip J. Runkel et al., *Transforming the School's Capacity for Problem Solving*, (Eugene, Oregon: Center for Educational Policy and Management, College of Education, University of Oregon, 1979).

9. The value of Head Start continues to be debated, with latest reported findings on the positive side. Possibly, however, some improvement in achievement may be attributable to the better feeding and other incidental factors of the program rather than to the instructional aspects. In general Head Start enabled needy children to get more attention in many forms, no small benefit.

10. For a striking example, see James H. Lytle, "An Untimely (but Significant) Experiment in Teacher Motivation," *Phi Delta Kappan*, June 1980, p. 700. The article shows the sacrifices teachers were eager to make to continue in the famous Philadelphia Parkway Program.

11. The growth of alternative schools within larger systems, intended to give parents some choice, has been impressive. From a handful in 1970, these schools now number in the thousands. See Vernon H. Smith, "Alternative Education Is Here to Stay," *Phi Delta Kappan*, April 1981, and other articles in this issue. A still greater number of nonclassroom programs exist within conventional schools, some as alternatives parents or students may select.

12. Association for Supervision and Curriculum Development 1966 Yearbook, *Learning and Mental Health in the School* (Washington: National Education Association, 1966), p. 77.

13. *The Real World of the Public Schools* (New York: Harcourt Brace Jovanovich, 1972), p. 67.

14. As a considerable straw in the wind, see the October 1980 issue of *Phi Delta Kappan*, a special one concentrating on reform in teacher education.

15. Norman V. Overly, ed. *Lifetime Learning*, p. 107. ASCD headquarters are in Alexandria, Va.

16. The correlation with family income has long been common knowledge. Recent studies also show similar linkage for SAT college entrance scores.

17. Leslie A. Hart, "Classrooms Are Killing Learning," *Principal*, May 1981, especially p. 9. In the parent involvement area, Salt Lake City public schools have been in the lead in showing what can be done, even as more parents work.

18. David B. Tyack, *The One Best System* (Cambridge: Harvard University Press, 1974). This much noted revisionist history documents a number of observations made in this chapter. Tyack writes: "In most cities failure in school was a way of life for vast numbers of children" (p. 200).

19 This dubious condition, which has at best only a rambling definition, has become one of the many vested interests, as well as a convenient blame-the-victim way of dealing with poor learning outcomes.

20. See Leslie A. Hart, "Necessary Ingredients for Retraining Teachers," *Bulletin*, National Association of Secondary School Principals, December 1973, p. 9.

Glossary

These entries are offered to assist readers in quick review of terms used. Since the language is compressed, it is suggested that the more explicit main text be used for any quotations or references. Items that strongly express a Proster Theory viewpoint are marked by asterisk.

*ABORT.   A program that is interrupted or fails to achieve the intended goal is said to abort.

ACTIVITY.   In a schooling situation, what a learner, or teacher, actually does.

ADDRESS.   Where information stored can be reached for recall. In a file drawer, the label on the folder; in a computer, the coded location; in the brain, relevant uses. See MEMORY.

AGGRESSIVE TEACHING.   Instruction that a teacher decides to give unilaterally, without learner request or evidence of desire or interest.

AMBIANCE.   Atmosphere prevailing, in the immediate environment.

ANALOG.   An approximate representation, in contrast to DIGITAL. A clock with hands is an analog device.

BEHAVIORISM.   General term for the psychology dominant in the United States through most of the 20th century, heavily using such terms as *stimulus-response, reward, reinforcement, motivation, mediation,* etc.

*BIASES.   The upper and lower settings for HOMEOSTASIS; also all the factors affecting choice of PROGRAM in a PROSTER.

BRAIN.   The main, central mass of the nervous system housed in the skull, comprising 95 percent or more of the entire human NERVOUS SYSTEM. See TRIUNE BRAIN.

BRAIN BASED.   Utilizing scientific knowledge of the brain, especially the human brain.

*BRAIN-COMPATIBLE.   Fitting well with the nature or shape of the human brain as currently understood; in contrast to **BRAIN-ANTAGONISTIC**.

BRAIN STEM.   Those parts of the brain rising from the spinal cord, from and around which more complex portions developed during evolution.

*CATEGORIZING DOWN.   The process of making finer and finer classifications, as: vehicle, car, sedan, Plymouth, Horizon, 1982 liftback model, etc.

CEREBELLUM.   The "little brain" near the back of the neck, primarily concerned with coordinating muscular activity.

CEREBRUM.   The new mammalian brain, composed of two largely mirror-image HEMISPHERES, in humans about 5/6 of the entire brain. See TRIUNE BRAIN.

CLASSROOM.   An organizational device by which a group of students, often 20–35, are confined in one room with one teacher over long periods of sessions, frequently a school year. If graded, as is conventionally the case, the students are purported to be sufficiently alike to benefit by grouping in a grade, in spite of massive evidence to the contrary.

*CLUE.   An attribute used by the brain in pattern recognition. See PROBABILITY.

CONCEPT.   A general term for any consistent portion of an individual's progress in "making sense of the world"; a working hypothesis.

CONSCIOUS.   Brain activity of which a person in aware is said to be conscious, as opposed to SUBCONSCIOUS activity going on at many levels. Awareness may be compared to a spotlight which illuminates one area after another. The brain is *not* sharply divided into a conscious portion and an unconscious or subconscious portion.

CORPUS CALLOSUM.   Large bundle of nerve fibers forming a two-way bridge between the left and right cerebral HEMISPHERES.

CORTEX.   The "bark" or outside layers of brain lobes; the gray matter of the brain in which THINKING proceeds. The CEREBRAL CORTEX, around the two hemispheres, is a multilayered sheet in which each area has a dominant function, and represents the main power of the brain. It can be estimated to contain 25-billion NEURONS.

*DIGITAL.   Expressed in units or numbers, and in that sense precise rather than approximation or analog. The brain is very strongly analog, and typically handles digital material poorly and reluctantly. See ANALOG.

*DOWNSHIFTING.   A shift in control of an individual's activities from a higher (newer) brain to a lower (older) brain. See TRIUNE BRAIN. Particularly, inhibition of use of the new mammalian brain under THREAT, interfering with learning or use of what has been learned and stored there.

*EMOTION.   A shift in BIASES, changing the range of HOMEOSTASIS, to adjust to a different perceived situation, AMBIANCE, or THREAT.

ETHOLOGY.   The study of creatures in more or less their natural environments, rather than in laboratories, with emphasis on SPECIES WISDOM.

EVOLUTION.   Development and/or changes in genetic programs, resulting in changes in the structure and behavior of creatures, usually over periods of many thousands or millions of years. Evolution produces individual differences which may permit species to survive environmental changes.

*FEEDBACK.   The return of information or report to the brain on how well a PROGRAM is working to achieve its GOAL. In opening a door, for example, feedback may indicate that the pushing effort is greater than needed, or not enough.

FEEDFORWARD.   Information projected within a system as an estimate of what may be needed.

FORMAL OPERATIONS.   Broadly, effort to use LOGIC. Within Proster Theory, not regarded as the highest form of mental activity, nor as generally useful.

FRONTAL LOBES.   Portions of the CEREBRUM close to the forehead. (PREFRONTAL, most anterior.) Human frontal portions are exceptionally well developed and important in directing the brain as a whole and in longer-term planning. MYELINATION is completed very late.

*GOAL. The aim, objective, or purpose of a PROGRAM. In general, the program goal is clearly determined before the brain institutes the program. Achievement toward the goal is pleasurable as the program proceeds and contributes to confidence; ABORTION of a program short of goal produces alarm or other EMOTION and likely DOWNSHIFTING.

*GRAND IDEAS. CONCEPTS of importance which have value in several or many areas of application; unifying ideas. The fractionating effect of courses may inhibit formation of grand ideas.

HEMISPHERES. The left and right portions of the CEREBRUM, roughly mirror-images. The left in most people handles language, the right spacial, nonverbal matters; but the division of functions is highly individual and complex, and the CORPUS CALLOSUM provides pathways for massive exchanges. (Discussion of hemispheric functions in recent years has tended to be simplistic, overstated, inaccurate, and conjectural, to misleading degree.)

HOLISTIC. Taking a large, overall view, rather than attending to details or only certain aspects. Hence MACRO.

HOMEOSTASIS. The balancing of interacting body systems within limits set by current BIASING, to produce a relatively steady state suited to the current situation of the person.

HORMONE. A "chemical messenger" carried by the bloodstream to various organs and controls, in a slower and more diffuse way than messages via the nervous system. Some hormones may alter BIASES within a second or less, others may have effect over years, as for body growth.

HUMAN. A member of the species **HOMO SAPIENS**, the only surviving species. Other species of humans existed perhaps as recently as some tens of thousands of years ago. One definition of human involves: (1) standing erect, (2) living in social groups, (3) using language, (4) using tools.

INFORMATION. The content of any form of message, or PROGRAM, or stored program (without regard to right or wrong.)

*INPUT. The total INFORMATION offered to the brain in a given situation; the raw material from which individual brains extract PATTERNS, without regard to quality. An individual human brain *selects* what input it will receive, moment to moment, and determines how far it will process it. Settings can vary enormously in the level of input they offer, and instructors can provide more or less; but each individual learner controls how much and what input will be admitted to that brain and how it will be processed. To best facilitate learning, input should be *varied*, in part *repetitive*, presented *randomly*, and in great *volume*. High input does not automatically produce learning, but low or restricted input tends to prevent learning.

*KNOWLEDGE. See INFORMATION. Knowledge almost always takes the form of stored programs or pattern recognition. **KNOWLEDGE STRUCTURE**: A hierarchy of levels, from common knowledge to higher and higher specific, detailed, technical, broad and theoretical, professional levels.

*LEARNING. The acquisition of useful (in the view of the individual learner) PROGRAMS. **PROCESS OF LEARNING**. The extraction from confusion of meaningful PATTERNS, which can subsequently often be recognized by MATCH.

LIMBIC SYSTEM. A complex group of brain structures more or less below the cerebrum, largely concerned with what are commonly called emotional matters. The term may be equated with OLD MAMMALIAN BRAIN for most purposes. Portions are involved in **ROTE** learning.

LINEAR. Arranged in a line, or simple sequence; single path as opposed to MULTIPATH.

*LOGIC.   Broadly, unnatural, contrived style of reasoning. Logical is commonly used to imply orderly, neat, arranged in some scheme, in contrast with HOLISTIC, intuitive, RANDOM, recursive. Logic is often assumed to mean Greek-type, LINEAR progression from point A to point B to point C to compose a logical chain, or "sound thinking" as popularly understood and traditionally admired in spite of its general uselessness and tendency to lead to simple wrong answers. Many modern logics, complex and not linear, have highly useful special applications. See MULTICHANNEL, SYSTEM.

MACRO.   A large, HOLISTIC approach, as opposed to **MICRO** concentration on parts or details.

MANIPULATION.   Literally, handling physical objects or materials, in contrast to using words or representations. Manipulation can greatly aid learning in many situations, especially for younger learners.

MASTERY.   The concept of allowing as much time as necessary for an individual to learn thoroughly, in contrast to giving a score or grade for learning achieved in a fixed period of time, such as a semester. An implication is that every student is capable of learning, given time.

*MATCH.   A sufficiently good fit between incoming input and some stored pattern to permit probably correct recognition or identification. Many CLUES would be those expected, with absence of strong negative clues. For example, four legs, fur, tail, visible ears would match *dog*; horns or wrong size would be negative clues, preventing that match. See PROBABILITY.

*MEMORY.   A convenience term; the brain has no separate part or place for memory, which appears to be stored at many points in the brain. Within Proster Theory, memory is seen as one tense of PROGRAM: a program used in the past is seen as memory, the same program to be used in the future is seen as plan. To recall "how much is 6 times 7" the program for answering that question is located and actuated.

MIND.   A vague term, used as a convenience.

MODEL.   A hypothetical concept of how the parts of some entity or pattern are interrelated; its "shape."

MULTICHANNEL, MULTIPATH.   In contrast to LINEAR, moving along many pathways rather than one, usually simultaneously. The channels or pathways may be discrete, extending in many directions, or they can be parallel, or they can form a network. FEEDBACK and FEEDFORWARD may be involved. The brain is characteristically designed for multichannel processing. This gives the brain huge advantages over digital electronic computers, which thus far tend to be linear.

MULTIMODAL.   Utilizing more than one mode, such as sight, hearing, touch, motion, song or music, etc. Multimodal INPUT appears to greatly accelerate learning.

MYELINATION.   The process by which nerves are insulated by acquiring a coating, wrapped around by special cells. The pathway then carries messages faster and with less loss. Myelination continues to about age 20, with timing and sequence highly variable by individual. The apparent maturity of a child's behavior may relate to the progress of myelination.

NERVE.   General term for specialized fibers that carry electrochemical messages.

NERVOUS SYSTEM.   The extremely elaborate, complex system by which external or internal information is brought to the main part of the system, the BRAIN, where some may be analyzed and interpreted in the light of experience. The brain makes decisions on action and on regulating the many body systems, such as those for breathing, pumping blood, digestion, etc. All meaningful learning occurs in and is stored in the brain. The brain sends out instructions to muscles and organs, and controls all emotions as commonly called. (See EMOTION.) An autonomous system, not under the brain's control, was long thought to exist, but this concept has been dropped. (See literature on "bio-feedback.")

NEURON.   The specialized cell of the NERVOUS SYSTEM, which has 30 billion or more. There are a number of categories of neurons, with different shapes and functions. Essentially neurons are sophisticated switches, in a sense equivalent to diodes and transistors in electronic computers, but much more complex and subtle. A newborn child has at birth or shortly after a lifetime supply of neurons, which are not replaced as they die. The long human growth period is necessary to allow time for organization of neuronal structures.

NEUROSCIENCES.   Those that are concerned with physical, direct study of the brain, in contrast to psychiatry and psychologies which stay outside the skull.

NEW MAMMALIAN BRAIN.   In MacLean's scheme of the TRIUNE BRAIN, the CEREBRUM, in evolutionary terms the newest, and by far the largest, brain. Language and use of symbols are functions of this brain, to which the great bulk of formal education is addressed.

NOISE.   In communication theory, unintended signals that do not carry meaning, such as interference on radio or television.

OLD MAMMALIAN BRAIN.   In MacLean's scheme of the TRIUNE BRAIN, the middle brain in point of age and size; roughly the LIMBIC SYSTEM.

*PATTERN.   An entity, such as an object, action, procedure, situation, relationship or SYSTEM, which may be recognized by substantial consistency in the CLUES it presents to a brain, which is a pattern-detecting apparatus. The more powerful a brain, the more complex, finer, and subtle patterns it can detect. Except for certain SPECIES WISDOM patterns, each human must learn to recognize the patterns of all matters dealt with, storing the LEARNING in the brain. See process of LEARNING. Pattern recognition tells *what is being dealt with*, permitting selection of the most appropriate PROGRAM in brain storage to deal with it. The brain tolerates much variation in patterns (we recognize the letter *a* in many shapes, sizes, colors, etc.) because it operates on the basis of PROBABILITY, not on DIGITAL or LOGIC principles. Recognition of PATTERNS accounts largely for what is called insight, and facilitates transfer of learning to new situations or needs, which may be called creativity.

*PROBABILITY.   The principle by which the brain recognizes PATTERNS on the basis of receiving a number of CLUES which combine to suggest a probable conclusion. The assortment of clues may vary at any given time. This permits the brain to recognize as *chair* furniture of widely varying design, or to detect the word *water* spoken in many different ways, or to recognize a friend despite different clothing, hair style, change in weight, etc. The human brain *naturally* uses this principle.

*PROGRAM.   A sequence of steps or actions, intended to achieve some GOAL, which once built is stored in the brain and "run off" repeatedly whenever need to achieve the same goal is perceived by the person. A program may be short, for example giving a nod to indicate "yes," or long, as in playing a piece on the piano which requires thousands of steps, or raising a crop of wheat over many months. A long program usually involves a series of shorter subprograms, and many parallel variations that permit choice to meet conditions of use. Many such programs are needed, for instance to open different kinds of doors by pushing, pulling, turning, actuating, etc. Language requires many thousands of programs, to utter each word, type it, write it in longhand, print it, etc. Frequently used programs acquire an "automatic" quality: they can be used, once selected, without thinking, as when one puts on a shirt. Typically, a program is CONSCIOUSLY selected, then run off at a sub-conscious level. See LEARNING, PATTERN, PROSTER, ADORT. In general, humans operate by selecting and implementing programs one after another throughout waking hours.

PROSTER. A diagrammatic concept, based on the physical arrangement of cortical brain cells, which suggests how PROGRAMS may be stored in the brain as if they were grouped as alternatives for achieving some broad GOAL. For example, a locomotion proster provides alternatives such as walking, running, going up stairs or down, etc. An arithmetic proster provides programs for addition, subtraction, multiplying, etc. Successful selection of a program from a proster first requires recognition of the PATTERN to be dealt with. Only one program from a proster can be used at a time, and selection can only be from those already stored and available. BIASING of the switches in a proster leads to choice of what the brain considers the most appropriate program; unless the biases change, the same program will be selected again. The term proster derives from *program structure*. The concept seeks to clarify many aspects of human behavior and learning.

*RANDOM. In chance or jumbled order, as opposed to some logical approach or a conventional sequence. The sounds of letters of the alphabet can be taught in sequence A, B, C, D, or in random order such as M, O, W, R. Since life presents input in random order, the brain prefers random to alternatives.

*REAL. As found in life, in contrast to what has been prepared, ordered, analyzed, simplified, or fragmented in conventional formal education. Real objects, situations, etc., usually involve complexities and present more INPUT.

REINFORCEMENT. A key concept of BEHAVIORISM which holds that a behavior that is rewarded will more likely be repeated more often. Contrary evidence is now strong, and reward is difficult to define, especially for humans. Proster Theory emphasizes that a GOAL is always evident *before* the program is implemented, so the idea of reward appears unnecessary and artificial in real life.

REPTILIAN BRAIN. In MacLean's scheme of TRIUNE BRAIN, the oldest and smallest brain, concerned with operating many systems of the body essential to life, some crude "fight or flee" emotions, and probably with genetically transmitted schemata. See SPECIES WISDOM.

RETINA. The inner lining of the eye, on which light falls to begin the nervous system processes of vision.

RIGHT ANSWER. An official or approved answer to a question, examination item, or problem, etc., often viewed as the only acceptable answer. The assumption is made that one, simple, right answer does in fact exist.

*RISK. The need felt by humans, because of their evolution, to take chances and compete, in activities such as travel, skiing, games, gambling, and many others. Risk, in contrast to THREAT, is taken *voluntarily* by the individual, by intent, to a selected degree. Risk shifts BIASES to settings for more alertness, faster consumption of energy, etc.

RITUAL. A program, or group of programs, conducted as conventional behavior, without regard to how well stated GOALS are achieved. Example: a rain dance. How well, long, or elaborately the ritual is performed has no bearing on the outcome avowedly intended.

SCHEMA, SCHEMATA (pl.) A term used for PROGRAMS which are not learned after birth but are genetically transmitted. *Example*: a bird "knows" how to build a nest. In humans schemata may be vague, to be refined by the culture. Some, such as sucking at the breast and taking interest in human faces, have great importance for the neonate's survival. See SPECIES WISDOM.

*SETTING. For each individual those aspects, more than transient, of an environment that have direct, continuing effect or influence.

*SMORGASBORD. By analogy with elaborate buffet, the principle of offering learners a wide, appealing choice of INPUT or ACTIVITIES.

SPECIES WISDOM. PROGRAMS or SCHEMATA transmitted with the genes from parents to offspring. Recognition of certain PATTERNS is included. Contrasts with learning after birth. (Relates to instincts, a term rarely used scientifically today.) The importance of species wisdom in humans has been little investigated, but may be profound. Most is probably stored in the REPTILIAN or oldest brain. See TRIUNE BRAIN.

*STIMULUS. An old and perhaps obsolete behaviorist psychology term, very difficult to define. The brain chooses whether or not, and how much, it will respond to a stimulus, which makes the term questionable.

SYNAPSE. The connection between one NEURON and another; actually a tiny gap across which neurotransmitters act. Since a single neuron may connect with 10,000 or more others, synapses in a human brain run into vast numbers.

SYSTEM. An arrangement of components or subsystems in which there is interaction in various directions. Any living creature is a system; so is any social entity. Characteristically a system has no starting point and cannot be dealt with by LINEAR LOGIC. Systems are inherently complex; the human brain is by far the most intricate.

*TEACH. In practice, the term has two meanings, (1) to carry on a RITUAL called teaching which may have little, no, or negative effect on student learning; (2) to carry on BRAIN-COMPATIBLE activities which directly or indirectly (via SETTING and INPUT arranged) do in fact facilitate the LEARNING of one or more individuals.

*TEST. In schools, typically use of some instrument of evaluation which directs students to give RIGHT ANSWERS to selected questions. A test rarely evaluates what a student can do or does when undirected.

*THINKING. Switching processes in the brain to make SYSTEMS decisions. The brain does not use LOGICAL or LINEAR thinking except under duress to do so.

*THREAT. The imminent prospect of harm, in the view of the individual. The degree of harm perceived may range from minor to loss of life, and DOWN-SHIFTING produced will relate to the seriousness and imminence.

*TRIUNE BRAIN. A concept of brain architecture based on evolutionary knowledge, propounded notably by Paul D. MacLean of the National Institute of Mental Health. It views the human brain (excluding the CEREBELLUM) as composed of a very old REPTILIAN BRAIN, around and above which is a larger, more recent old mammalian brain (LIMBIC SYSTEM), around and above which in turn is the massive new mammalian brain (CEREBRUM, HEMISPHERES), the newest brain. This approach is highly useful for gaining more insight into behavior and learning, and why findings derived from work with small laboratory animals which lack the giant human cerebrum can be seriously misleading. See DOWNSHIFTING.

Selected Readings

This list is intended to assist the reader who may wish to explore further from the base offered in *Human Brain and Human Learning*. Literature relating present knowledge of the human brain to systematic efforts to bring about learning is, as of the moment, scant; but a rapidly growing amount now is available that bears on various aspects. The grouping that follows, and the comments, of course reflect the opinions of the author and effort to help primarily those readers who may not have a substantial scientific background or familiarity with the brain. Some excellent but quite technical works have been omitted.

Leslie A. Hart, *How the Brain Works* (New York: Basic Books, 1975). Presents Proster Theory in more detail.

Muriel Beadle, *A Child's Mind* (Garden City, N.Y.: Doubleday Anchor, 1971). An excellent, lucid discussion addressed to learning in the preschool years, but providing a wide, most valuable range of coverage showing the emergence of brain-based psychologies. Highly recommended to teachers.

Frank Smith, *Comprehension and Learning* (New York: Holt, Rinehart, and Winston, 1975). "A conceptual framework for teachers," brain-oriented, by a psycholinguist.

Carl Sagan, *The Dragons of Eden* (New York: Random House, 1977). This best seller, focusing on the evolution of human intelligence, presents a dazzling amount of authoritative information on the role and importance of brain. Useful and enjoyable as background.

Richard M. Restak, *The Brain: The Last Frontier* (Garden City, N.Y.: Doubleday, 1979). By a neurologist, this clearly written exploration gets into many areas, including psychobiology, and offers much of interest, with some perhaps premature speculations.

J. Z. Young, *Programs of the Brain* (New York: Oxford University Press, 1978). Holding closely to the brain, an eminent British scientist provides an exhaustive discussion in plain language. Also useful for reference.

Jeanne S. Chall and Allan F. Mirsky, eds., *Education and the Brain*, 77th Yearbook of the National Society for the Study of Education, Part II (Chicago: University of Chicago Press, 1978). The Wittrock and MacLean chapters are pertinent and important. Certain chapters are too technical, remote from education, or speculative.

Morton Hunt, *The Universe Within* (New York: Simon and Schuster, 1982). A highly readable, fascinating report on the relatively new field called cognitive science, including problem solving and creativity.

More Technical Approaches

C. U. M. Smith, *The Brain* (New York: G. P. Putnam's Sons, 1970). Outstanding treatment by a British biologist.

A. R. Luria, *The Working Brain* (New York: Basic Books, 1975). The late Soviet author was a recognized world authority in neuropsychology.

Karl H. Pribram, *Languages of the Brain* (Monterey, Calif.: Brooks/Cole, 1971). For advanced readers interested in neuronal coding. Exceptional technical illustrations. The author is a major authority and investigator.

Steven Rose, *The Conscious Brain* (New York: Alfred A. Knopf, 1973). A clearly written work by an English neurobiologist with emphasis on brain functions.

Special Emphasis or Treatment

Colin Blakemore, *Mechanics of the Mind* (New York: Cambridge University Press, 1977). Despite the title, human, highly readable and wonderfully illustrated.

Keith Oatley, *Brain Mechanisms and Mind* (New York: E. P. Dutton, 1972). Heavily illustrated, very readable.

R. L. Gregory, *Eye and Brain*, 2d ed. (New York: McGraw-Hill, 1973). How the brain sees brilliantly explained.

Lloyd Kaufman, *Perception* (New York: Oxford University Press, 1979). Clear, thorough discussion, including consideration of reading. Well illustrated.

H. Chandler Elliott, *The Shape of Intelligence* (New York: Scribner's, 1969). Beautiful, informative book on the brain's evolution.

Peter Denes and Elliot Pinson, *The Speech Chain* (Garden City, N.Y.: Anchor/Doubleday, 1973). A brief, readable, classic study that counters many common ideas about spoken language and reading instruction.

George A. Miller, *Language and Speech* (San Francisco: W. H. Freeman, 1981). Clear, but requires technical background.

Edmund Burke Huey, *The Psychology and Pedagogy of Reading* (Cambridge,

Mass.: The M. I. T. Press, 1908, 1968). Famous work by a pioneer in the brain approach, still valuable.

Robert M. W. Travers, *Man's Information System* (Scranton, Pa.: Chandler, 1970). Called "a primer for media specialists," it offers a sophisticated, brain-based discussion.

Sally P. Springer and Georg Deutsch, *Left Brain, Right Brain* (San Francisco: W. H. Freeman, 1981). Authoritative, thorough, scientific discussion of hemispheres and functions.

Human Background

Nigel Calder, *The Human Conspiracy* (New York: Viking, 1976). Newer findings on learning and mother-child relationship, very well presented.

John E. Pfeiffer, *The Emergence of Man* (New York: Harper & Row, 1969). Superb, very complete account of the rise of humans by a noted, brain-oriented anthropologist.

The Classroom

John I. Goodlad, Frances Klein, and associates, *Looking Behind the Classroom Door* (Worthington, O.: Charles A. Jones, 1974). Observations, detailed and broad, based on visits to 67 schools.

Philip W. Jackson, *Life in Classrooms* (New York: Holt, Rinehart and Winston, 1968). This famous, candid study remains accurate and shocking.

Thomas L. Good and Jere E. Brophy, *Looking in Classrooms* (New York: Harper & Row, 1973). An exhaustive discussion that illustrates the extreme complexity of classroom teaching.

Leslie A. Hart, *The Classroom Disaster* (New York: Teachers College Press, 1969). Still one of the few analyses of the effects of the classroom on teaching and learning. Part II contains a description of an alternative approach.

Harry S. Broudy, *The Real World of the Public Schools* (New York: Harcourt Brace Jovanovich, 1972). An incisive, broad view of school structure and practice with much regard to the need for good theory.

John I. Goodlad and Robert H. Anderson, *The Nongraded Elementary School* (New York: Harcourt, Brace, 1959). This classic study of individual differences and ranges within classrooms is still powerful and cogent.

Kenneth Dunn and Rita Dunn, *Teaching Students through Their Individual Learning Styles* (Englewood Cliffs, N.J.: Prentice-Hall, 1978). A practical approach to identifying and responding to individual differences that conventional classrooms tend to ignore or resist accepting. Prof. Rita Dunn heads the Learning Styles Network, based at St. John's University, Jamaica, N.Y. 11439.

Index

Key: n indicates note; Q indicates a direct quotation. Illustrations are shown (37).

Date Due